Escaping with his Life

From Dunkirk to D-Day and Beyond

Nicholas Young

Pen & Sword
MILITARY

First published in Great Britain in 2019 by
Pen & Sword Military
An imprint of
Pen & Sword Books Ltd
Yorkshire – Philadelphia

ISBN 978 1 52674 663 4

A CIP catalogue record for this book is
available from the British Library.

Printed and bound in the UK by TJ International Ltd, Padstow, Cornwall

Pen & Sword Books Limited incorporates the imprints of Atlas, Archaeology,
Aviation, Discovery, Family History, Fiction, History, Maritime, Military, Military
Classics, Politics, Select, Transport, True Crime, Air World, Frontline Publishing,
Leo Cooper, Remember When, Seaforth Publishing, The Praetorian Press,
Wharncliffe Local History, Wharncliffe Transport, Wharncliffe True Crime and
White Owl.

For a complete list of Pen & Sword titles please contact

PEN & SWORD BOOKS LIMITED
47 Church Street, Barnsley, South Yorkshire, S70 2AS, England
E-mail: enquiries@pen-and-sword.co.uk
Website: www.pen-and-sword.co.uk

Or
PEN AND SWORD BOOKS
1950 Lawrence Rd, Havertown, PA 19083, USA
E-mail: Uspen-and-sword@casematepublishers.com
Website: www.penandswordbooks.com

This book is dedicated to my three sons,
Edward, Alexander and Thomas, and my nieces, Catherine and
Natasha – and to the brave people in Italy who saved
my father's life

From Fontanellato to Corvaro

Along mountain pathways
In dark autumn nights
Their stealthy footsteps.
They speak foreign languages,
They wear hostile uniforms
But they find shelter and living.
Ordinary peasants – fearless
And courageous people
Hide them in houses and barns.
Any day a common meal,
Then on the track again
Towards a faraway horizon.
Years later, the return
Along those mountain pathways,
Feeling the scent of memory.

Lungo sentieri montani
In buie notti di autunno
Calano i loro passi furtivi.
Parlano lungue straniere
Indosso divise nemiche
Eppure accolti e sfamati.
Gente comune dei campi
Senza timore e per nulla
Li cela tra stalle e fienili.
Per giorni lo stesso desco
Dopo di nuovo in cammino
Veso una linea lontana.
A distanza di anni il ritorno
Lungo quei sentieri montani
Con il profumo della memoria.

Pierluigi Felli

Contents

Preface

My father, Leslie Young, hardly ever spoke about what he did in the war, what he saw, what he felt; never mentioned the escapes he had, the friends who died or the memories that haunted him; never talked about his two 'mentions in despatches'. Many of them, the 'old soldiers', were like that. Was this reticence caused by modesty, a determination to focus on the future, the deep desire to forget a nightmare? Who knows? Maybe all those things, or none of them. For that generation, it was just what you did. My father, like so many, was driven by the deepest sense of duty.

All my sister Vanessa and I can recall from my childhood is the occasional reference to Dunkirk, or to his time on the run in Italy – not much else. But even those infrequent reminiscences were sketchy, quite superficial – and certainly not an encouragement to ask further questions.

How I regret that now. Suddenly, one grey Sunday morning in 1986, my father was gone, and with him a mind that must have teemed with memories and stories that are now beyond recall or imagining.

And yet, not quite. Amongst his papers, tucked in a drawer, I found a small, tattered notebook, its dog-eared pages crammed with his instantly recognizable, almost completely illegible, pencil scrawl. Clearly, a diary of some sort. I put it to one side and got on with the legal stuff, and with looking after my mother. Only a couple of years later did I take it out and start to read.

What I found set me off on what has become almost a life's work, to trace the story of my father's war. Long days at Kew in the National Archives; trips around Europe and North Africa, retracing his footsteps, feeling him there beside me; talking to people who knew him, or fought with him, people who admired him, for qualities that I barely knew he possessed, that decent, quiet, kind man I called 'Dad'.

Now I have researched enough, and it's time to write. To write the story of his war, of how he escaped with his life from a dozen difficult and sometimes tragic situations, and of my own search for him in the fragments of memory and history that are left. And then to pass the story on to my own family and others – lest we forget.

Nick Young
Lord's Waste,
Bredfield,
Suffolk
December 2018

Acknowledgements

Thanks are due to a host of people, without whose support this book could never have been written.

First and foremost is my darling wife Helen, who came with me on all my journeys of discovery and whose constant encouragement, and willingness to allow me to shut myself away for long periods to write, made all the difference.

My boys allowed me to read them great chunks of the book as I went along and, since it was written primarily for them, I have taken their willingness to listen at least as some kind of approval!

Henry Wilson and several others at Pen & Sword have been brilliant throughout the process and have given me constant good advice and help, as has my editor, George Chamier.

My friend Mik Sparrow read and checked the text and found many errors that I had missed – any that remain are mine alone. I am not by profession an historian and if, despite years of careful research, I have misrepresented historical facts in any way, I hope I may be forgiven.

Numerous former colleagues and comrades of my father gave me their time and shared their memories, and to each of them, now mostly sadly deceased, and to their families, I offer my gratitude and affection.

Finally, I would like particularly to thank the families de Michelis, Elfer, Tevini and Gatenby who, as it will be seen, all played a fundamentally important in my father's eventual 'escape with his life'. They have shown me as much friendship, care and love as they showed him long ago, and my family and I will remain forever in their debt.

I have quoted from the following published and unpublished works, with kind permission from the publishers, or the families of the author, as follows:

Absalom, Roger, *A Strange Alliance – Aspects of Escape and Survival Italy 1935–45*, Accademia Toscana

Davies, Tony, *When the Moon Rises*, Leo Cooper

xii Escaping with his Life

Delaforce, Patrick, *Churchill's Desert Rats in North-West Europe*, Pen & Sword

Dunning, James, I*t had to be Tough – the Origins and Training of the Commandos in World War II*, Frontline Books

English, Ian, *Home by Christmas?* (privately published)

Foot, M.R.D. and Langley *J.M.*, *MI9 – Escape and Evasion 1939–45*, Biteback Publishing

Graham, Dominick, *The Escapes and Evasions of an Obstinate Bastard*, Wilton 65

Langrishe, Peter, *The Long Walk Out* (privately published)

Medley, Robin, *Cap Badge*, Pen & Sword

Moorehead, Alan, *The Desert War, Aurum Press*, part of the Quarto Group

Newby, Eric, *Love and War in the Apennines*, Harper Collins Publishers Limited

Ross, Michael, *The British Partisan*, Pen & Sword

Tudor, Malcolm, *Beyond the Wire*, Newton Emilia Publishing and *Among the Italian Partisans*, Fonthill Media

Watson, Peter, *Mountain Highway* (privately published)

Queen's Royal Regiment, History of, Volume VIII 1924–1948, compiled by Major R.G.C. Foster MC

Bedfordshire and Hertfordshire Regiment, History of, Volume II, 1914–1958, compiled by the History Committee of the Royal Anglian regiment

I have also quoted from these private accounts, by kind permission of the authors or their families: David Coles, James Darville, Charles Gatenby, Mike Howard, Dougie Turner.

I am most grateful for the permissions I have received to use the photographs in the plate section and on the jacket. Unfortunately, my best endeavours to track down the copyright owners have proved unsuccessful in one or two cases, and to them I offer a sincere apology and a promise to acknowledge them in future editions, if so requested.

List of Maps

Prologue

It was pitch black and icy cold as they crawled on hands and knees out of the minefield. In the lead, the two young Italians inched forward cautiously along the road. A few yards behind them was Leslie, an Englishman, ears pricked to catch any sound up ahead. Following him was a New Zealander called Charlie, and a young Italian girl, just nineteen years old.

They had spent all day in the village high on the rock behind them, looking out over the marsh and trying to work out the best route through the German lines and minefields towards Anzio, where British and American troops had landed two weeks earlier.

Intermittently, the crump of German guns pounding the tenuous Allied beachhead on the Italian coast split the night. From out at sea, warships returned the fire, making the ground tremble as shells crashed into the German positions.

Eugenio, a Jewish partisan aged twenty-three and the leader of the group, began to relax slightly. He turned to his companion, his sister's boyfriend Carlo, and smiled encouragingly in the darkness. Looking back, he could just make out the shapes of the two escaping prisoners of war and his sister Silvia.

So far, so good. Perhaps they were going to get through.

But time was getting on. To be caught where they were, in no-man's-land as it grew lighter, would be fatal. They had to move faster, maybe chance walking along the roadway itself rather than in the ditches alongside.

Eugenio raised himself into a crouching position and motioned Carlo to do the same. They moved on a few yards, then checked to see that the others were following.

Eugenio breathed deeply, slowly, in and out. Another step or two . . .

The crashing, chattering, shattering bark of the machine gun flailed the air and flayed their senses. Leslie hurled himself left into the ditch. Charlie went right, dragging the girl with him.

Another burst, then it was quiet. The minutes passed, each second a lifetime.

Chapter 1

To War — with the British Expeditionary Force in France

L eslie Charles Young was born on 24 March 1911 in Cheam, Surrey. It was the end of the Edwardian period in Britain – often depicted as a romantic golden age of long summer afternoons and extravagant parties, a time of enjoyment and some complacency after the awesome growth of the British economy and the empire under Queen Victoria. There was ballroom dancing, silent movies, early jazz, glamorous fashions and 'beautiful people'.

Leslie was the third of four children. His father, George William, was a big burly chap, aged about thirty-seven when 'Les' was born. The son of a policeman in Hampshire, he trained as a master builder and set up his own business in and around Cheam and Worcester Park. Leslie's mother, Nellie Agnes Baldwin, was – as I remember her – a tiny, deathly-white little old lady, who had trouble hearing and smelled of mothballs. She was from Hampshire, too, the daughter of a small-scale tenant farmer.

The Youngs were a comfortable middle-class family, living in a substantial house in Epsom, just off the Downs. G. W. Young (Builders) Ltd was a moderately successful local speculative building firm, with about 60 employees, which built much of the 'two-up-two-down', terraced suburban sprawl that lies to the east of Central Road, Worcester Park.

Leslie went to a private, fee-paying boarding school – Ardingly College, in Sussex. He did not altogether take to boarding school life and ran away a couple of times, to no avail and without attracting much sympathy from his father. Nevertheless, he settled down eventually and became confident enough to join the Ardingly College Junior Division Officers' Training Corps as a Lance Corporal.

In July 1929, immediately after leaving school, he transferred to the Supplementary Reserve of Officers for the Bedfordshire and Hertfordshire Regiment, as a Second Lieutenant. His name was published in the

London Gazette, and in *The Times* and the *Daily Telegraph*. His Commission from King George V reads:

> To our trusty and well-beloved Leslie Charles Young – Greetings! We, reposing special trust and confidence in your loyalty courage and good conduct do by these presents constitute and appoint you to be an officer in our land forces . . .

In the 1930s Leslie was leading a comfortable existence. Living at home in wealthy Epsom, working for his father and going to college to learn the building trade, he had money enough for a sports car and plenty of trips out with his friends and two sisters. He played a lot of cricket and football locally and went to the races on Epsom Downs, just up the road. He was a good-looking chap and had several girlfriends, something occasionally mentioned somewhat sniffily by my mother in later years.

Leslie also attended the annual training course for reservists regularly during these pre-war years, with his regiment. He was promoted Lieutenant in 1932 and in September 1935 he resigned his appointment in the Supplementary Reserve and gained a commission in the Regular Army Reserve of Officers, which was being built up at this time in response to growing fears about what was happening in Europe. Although money was tight, Britain's armed forces were being developed, with a focus on the Navy as our main means of defence, and the Air Force. For the Army, the build-up meant an increase in the Reserves, which grew to about 600,000 men.

In 1939, after the failure of Chamberlain's policy of appeasement, when war broke out and a general mobilization was ordered, the Bedfordshire and Hertfordshire Regiment, commanded by Lieutenant Colonel J. S. Davenport MC and part of 4th Infantry Division in the Second Corps of the British Expeditionary Force, was stationed at Milton Barracks, in Gravesend, Kent. Officers received their postings, and Lieutenant Leslie Young was posted to B Company, 2nd Battalion, as second in command. He arrived in Gravesend on 5 September, just as the silver in the officers' mess was being packed up and despatched for safe keeping to Lloyds Bank in Dunstable – a solemn moment, this must have been. The next day, enemy bombers were sighted over the town.

In those days the officers' mess must have seemed pretty daunting to a new recruit. Lieutenants were almost the lowest form of life, and the commanding officer was like God. Davenport was a career soldier who had been severely wounded in the arm in the Great War, so he may have had little time for raw recruits. Discipline was strict, and all the formalities were observed and enforced. A lieutenant was paid about thirteen shillings (65p) a day, but with beer at fourpence a pint and ten cigarettes for twopence, life wasn't so bad. The entire focus was on 'polishing up, and getting ready for war'.

On 20 September the entire Battalion (about 600 men) was drawn up for inspection on the football field ('an inspiring sight'), and the Colonel, accompanied by the commander of 4 Division, Major General D. G. Johnson VC, DSO, MC, addressed them. He was loudly cheered, and took the salute at the ensuing march past.

On 23 September the Regiment left Gravesend in two trains, bound for the Corunna Barracks, Aldershot in Hampshire. The people of Gravesend were sad to see them go and gave them a great send-off, with the Mayor and Town Council lined up at the station to say goodbye.

Aldershot was the centre for the British Army, with dozens of Victorian barracks. On 27 September the King and Queen visited the town, spoke with the officers and drove past the Battalion parade. This must have been an incredibly stirring moment for a young man of twenty-eight, on the eve of war.

Three days later, the Battalion left Aldershot by train for Southampton and embarked on board TSS *Biarritz*, a former Channel steamer, bound for Cherbourg in northern France with a convoy of other ships.

As the *Biarritz* pulled out into a Solent sunset that September evening, it's easy to imagine the sense of nervous anticipation on board, as the Isle of Wight dropped astern and the convoy headed into the night and across the Channel. The crossing was rough and uncomfortable, and they docked in Cherbourg at 0640 hrs on 1 October 1939 under cold grey skies and drizzle. Second Lieutenant Robin Medley describes in his book *Cap Badge* how 'the rain dripped off the steel helmets and on to the open gas capes' as the troops from a number of ships moored alongside the quay tramped down the gangplanks and lined up on the dock awaiting orders.

They were to form part of a continuous line of Allied soldiers deployed along France's north-eastern frontier with Belgium, and from the southern end of the heavily fortified Maginot Line in Switzerland to the sea east of Dunkirk. The British sector of this line ran north from Lille to the coast, curling round to Armentières, a distance of around 60 miles. By the time 2 Battalion arrived at Cherbourg, troopships had been crossing the Channel for a month and there were more than 150,000 British troops on French soil.

Belgium was neutral at this time, though expecting to be invaded by the Germans at any moment. The idea was that the French and British forces would be dug in and ready to defend France from invasion on the French side of the border, whilst being prepared to advance into Belgium and Holland if need be.

One of the flaws in this plan was that, although the British soldiers now in France were all regulars, the cream of the British Army, they were in fact very poorly equipped and trained, mainly because the Government had delayed intensive preparations for possible war until February 1939. Transport was insufficient and made up mostly of commandeered Post Office and butchers' vans, and the Army's tanks had far too little firepower to combat the German Panzers.

No doubt in blissful ignorance of this state of affairs, 2 Battalion marched to the railway station, where they waited for several hours whilst English money was collected in and exchanged for francs. Finally there was a hot meal and time off in town for a bit of fun with the locals.

By midnight they were on a train heading slowly south, arriving at lunchtime the next day at Noyen, about 200 miles from Cherbourg, whence they marched to pretty Malicorne-sur-Sarthe. Here, Leslie's B Company was billeted in a restaurant called Le Fief aux Moines, just out of the town centre; he was lucky, as most of the Battalion was in rough farm outbuildings, school halls and the like. For a few days the focus was on fitness training for fast marching over distance, and anti-aircraft drill. The target pace for a fast march is 120 paces per minute with a full pack, and this must have come as a bit of a shock to some of the men. Anti-aircraft drill consisted of entire platoons firing their rifles in unison at passing German planes – shades of 'Dad's Army'.

The few days in Malicorne provided a good opportunity for the Battalion to settle into some sort of routine. As well as the training, the new officers had to learn about pay parade, for example, with the soldiers forming long lines whilst the officers handed out cash and recorded each transaction in the Pay Book. Censorship of mail was another duty, checking that, in a letter to a loved one, a soldier didn't inadvertently give details of the Battalion's position or plans. Medley recalls how envelopes were often sealed with coded greetings like SWALK (sealed with a loving kiss) or IIBOYLTOP (it is better on your lips than on paper). HOLLAND caused a problem once at HQ, until it was realized that it wasn't the name of the country, but stood for 'hope our love lasts and never dies'.

On 8 October, as dusk was falling, and to the cheers of the local population, the Battalion marched back to the station and, at 2200 hrs, left by train for Carvin. Travelling in trucks strewn with straw, and the officers six to a compartment, the train rumbled through the landscape, crossing the River Seine at dawn at Rouen, and on through the next day, passing as they went famous Great War battlefields such as Amiens, Arras and Albert. The Commanding Officer, Davenport, stood by the train window and pointed out places where he himself had fought twenty-two years earlier. As Medley remarks, 'it was a sombre moment'.

Eventually, and in pouring rain, the train stopped at Carvin, and the Battalion stood about in the pitch black of wartime France waiting for transport to the main square, whence they were shown to what was to be their accommodation for the next two months.

Carvin is a former mining town just south-west of Lille, a dull little place in the middle of a flat industrial landscape, its slag heaps still visible. The officers' mess was at the Railway Hotel, beside the local brothel, as they discovered when lascivious clients arrived at the hotel and had to be directed next door. The troops were bedded down in various schools and community halls, and the officers were in private houses. The men spent their time doing long training marches in the pouring rain, whilst the officers reconnoitred the surrounding countryside and worked out how best to establish a defensive line. There were hot showers once a week at the nearby coalmine.

Basically, the Battalion's task was to hold a section of line against putative German attack along the Bois de Phalempin from the village of Petit Attiches to a small hamlet called L'Offrande, about two miles south. B Company was in the middle of this line, just inside the wood. Instructions were given to cut arcs of fire for the Bren guns between the trees at the front of the wood, and then to start digging fire bays and defensive trenches. In the constant rain this was a dreadful job and, when the trenches started filling with water, the order came to build up earthwork ramparts instead, an equally taxing task in the thick mud.

The Battalion's War Diary (which every commander in the field was required to update daily) suggests that, despite the mud, morale was high. It rained continually; roads were regularly blocked by the mud and rubble, and bricks had to be laid down to keep military traffic moving. The digging continued, interspersed with training and marches. There was church parade every Sunday, films and concerts in town, and small local bars and brothels to visit – indeed, the latter became a problem and, all along the front line, officers were ordered to make sure the men were well supplied with 'French letters', as they were known.

But everyone was on the alert. Night patrols were organized, and all 'suspicious activity' was to be reported, including signs of undue interest shown by the local population in what the soldiers were up to. Two 'well-dressed women' were found loitering around the men's billets and asking questions 'of military value', so they were briskly interrogated. There was a great deal of activity in the air, with frequent air raid warnings and regular German reconnaissance flights low over the digging area. Occasionally there was the sound of distant gunfire. One morning, amidst rumours of the impending German invasion of Holland, the Battalion loaded their kit on to trucks and stood by until late in the evening when, as Medley put it, 'the flap subsided'. The CO met with the War Minister, who was over on a visit to inspect the troops, as was the Duke of Gloucester.

Eventually, after two months of digging in the rain, the order came for a move, and after dark on 30 November the Battalion loaded on to trucks, waved good bye to local friends and set off north towards the Belgian frontier, where they were to relieve a French unit. The lorries crawled along in the pitch dark, following a dim little red light on the rear of the truck in front – a long boring journey, as Medley noted – until they arrived at Roubaix, where they were billeted in the former Corn Exchange. The next day, the officers inspected the billets which were to be taken over from the French and then dined together at a local hotel.

By 2 December the Battalion had settled into its new billets, close to the Belgian border between Lys le Lannoy and Leers. The War Diary reports that, although the billets themselves were adequate, they 'had been left in a filthy state by the French'. Once again, the Battalion settled into a routine of digging and wiring trenches, and of patrols and reconnaissance. Concrete pillboxes along the border had to be manned, and some new ones were constructed and marked on maps.

Barely had they settled in when, as reported by Medley, he and Leslie, or 'Porky' as he had by now been nicknamed (like his older and larger brother Alan), received orders to attend a Junior Leaders School at Béthune, a few miles back from the border. When Robin Medley first wrote to me in 1993 he mentioned the Béthune course, something he had every reason to remember because it nearly cost him his life.

Neither of them particularly wanted to go, and they had to pack up their things in a rush, with barely time to grab a snack. Once aboard the 15-ton truck that was to take them to Béthune, they had a chance to sit back and look around as they drove across a flat, desolate landscape of tilled clay soil, interspersed with canals, graves from the Great War and derelict concrete blockhouses from the old Hindenburg defensive line. It can't have cheered them up, or made them any more enthusiastic about the course.

Once at Béthune, they moved into their billets (Robin was delighted to have his own bathroom) and started on the three-week course, which was intended to teach future platoon commanders about tactical weapon training, field engineering and patrol work. Béthune was a smart, lively town and, as the food in the officers' mess wasn't up to much, four of them (Robin, Leslie, and two lads from Gloucestershire, Peter Millward and Michael Arnold) soon sniffed out a couple of reasonably priced hotels to eat at and even a 'bonbon' shop, which they used to visit every evening to try out one of the mouth-watering chocolates on display. They quickly became firm friends and talked about life and girlfriends; Michael, who was the oldest, spoke wistfully about his wife back home.

On the first Saturday morning, 16 December, when they were due to be learning about digging trenches and anti-tank mines, Peter Millward asked Robin to change squads, as he wanted to talk to Michael about a dinner party that evening. Robin agreed and joined Leslie in the other squad, to learn about the Mark I Anti-tank mine. This was, according to Robin, 'a rather Heath-Robinson piece of kit' and, when the instructor offered to jump up and down on an armed mine, to show off its capacity to withstand small weights without exploding, they all shouted out that they were quite prepared to take his word for it and begged him not to jump. The squad then disarmed the mines they had been putting together and swapped places with the other group, who had been learning how to dig trenches.

Fifteen minutes later, there was a loud bang, and a cloud of black smoke emerged from the hollow where the other group was working. Robin and Leslie dropped their tools and ran; they found a harrowing sight. The entire twenty-man squad had been standing around the instructor when he did his jump on the mine – which then exploded. The full impact of the blast had caused terrible wounds to the legs, the groin area and the faces of the men, and every one of them was lying on the ground seriously wounded. The instructor's corporal was so upset at seeing his colleague with both feet blown off that he had to be restrained from putting him out of his misery on the spot.

Three of the young officers died at the scene, and two more later that night. Amongst the dead were Robin and Leslie's two friends, Peter Millward (who was just twenty years old at the time) and Michael Arnold.

Robin and Leslie's squad did what they could for the wounded, but no one had had any first aid training (it later became compulsory), there was no first aid kit to hand, and the nearest casualty station was several miles away over rough ground and cart tracks.

Leslie was sent off to report the incident and get assistance; then, on his return, he helped tend the wounded. When there was no more to be done, he took Robin off to the mess for several stiff whiskies, to steady their nerves.

The incident is mentioned in Field Marshal Lord Alanbrooke's wartime diaries, as he was commanding 11 Corps in France at the time and hosting a visit by Prime Minister Chamberlain. He set up a board of inquiry into the incident but acknowledged that it would be difficult to find out what happened, as most of those who were near the mine when it went off were killed. He put it down to faulty equipment. The day following the incident, which was 'bitterly cold and freezing hard', he went to Beuvry for the funeral of three of the young officers killed (including Michael Arnold) and visited one of the survivors at Béthune.

The course continued until after Christmas, when it snowed. General Brooke (as he then was) came back to give the closing address, an impressive talk about leadership, and then Leslie drove with Robin to rejoin the Battalion at Lannoy. The incident, and the loss of their friends, must have had a devastating impact. With another man called Buchanan, they were the only officers from the group of twenty on the course who survived the war.

*

Over the years, I met Robin, or spoke to him on the phone, many times, and he never failed to mention this terrible incident, and his gratitude to Leslie who, as the older officer, had been so kind to him at the time. It is telling though that Robin never once referred to the death of his two close friends, neither did he mention it in his book 'Cap Badge'. My father never spoke of the incident at all, not a word.

*

Back at Lannoy, the so-called 'Phoney War' was in full swing (if that's the right word), as the Allies awaited renewed German aggression. The Battalion was still at work digging defensive trenches and earthworks and laying barbed wire. More pillboxes were constructed, and there were regular patrols. There were weekly route marches to keep fit, with tactical exercises and weapons training to keep them busy as well. It was bitterly cold, and a nearby canal froze over. Sentries were issued with extra heavy overcoats. There was a 'flap' on 11 January, when the Battalion was put on notice ready to repel a German invasion of Belgium, but then, on 22 January, they moved to Fives de Lille for a consolidated period of further training.

It remained cold, and Robin was unimpressed by the prospect of crawling around in driving wind and snow across flat, muddy farmland. Leslie must have been relieved when he was given a week's leave. But the routine was broken for the whole Battalion one evening, when the officers were summoned to a local cinema to join their colleagues in the British line for an announcement by Brigadier 'Bubbles' Barker that the battalions forming part of his 10 Brigade would soon be taking over responsibility for guarding part of France's main defence – the Maginot Line.

The Line was constructed during the 1930s, a formidable barricade of concrete fortifications, obstacles and weapon installations that France built on its borders with Switzerland, Germany and Luxembourg, and which faced the German Western Wall, in some places only a short distance away. The French established the fortification to give their army time to mobilize in the event of attack, and to allow French forces to move into Belgium for a decisive confrontation with Germany. The success of static, defensive tactics in the Great War was a key influence on French thinking, and French military experts extolled the Maginot Line as a work of genius, believing it would prevent any further invasions from the east.

The fortifications, however, did not extend north right through to the English Channel, because the French military did not want to offend Belgium, with its policy of neutrality. While the Maginot Line was impervious to most forms of attack (including aerial bombing and tank fire) and had state-of-the-art living conditions for garrisoned troops, air conditioning, comfortable eating areas and underground railways, the gap to the north was to prove fatal in the forthcoming battle. It was this gap that the British Army had been filling since October.

Whilst the Maginot Line itself was controlled by the French Army, it had been agreed that, in order to give British troops front line experience, one division at a time should be attached to the French command. This was the opportunity that Brigadier Barker was announcing to his excited officers in February, raising the cinema curtains with a flourish to reveal large-scale maps and detailed descriptions of the ground, the positions they would be taking over, the layout of the wire, known German positions and their patrolling habits in the no-man's-land between the two lines. The Bedfords were to be the first regiment in the Brigade to man these key defences.

Early in the morning of 18 February, the day after Leslie returned from leave, the Battalion moved 240 miles south-east to the French border with Germany at the Saar, in cattle trucks spread with a little straw. Leslie travelled with his namesake Peter Young (later to distinguish himself during the disastrous raid on Dieppe), arriving in a small hamlet near Metz the following day, where they were disappointed to find themselves sharing accommodation with pigs and using outdoor latrines consisting of a rough plank over a hole in the ground. You can just imagine someone saying, 'You're in the Army now, my lad!'

After a few days they moved to Monneren, about eight miles from the frontier. It was quite literally a ghost town, as every village, hamlet and farm between the Maginot Line and the border had been evacuated – not a person or an animal could be seen, and an eerie silence had settled over the whole area. Several properties had been looted, and the pews from the church had been used for firewood.

Once again, their positions had been left in a disgraceful state. Some sharp-eyed British professional soldiers felt that their French counterparts occasionally exhibited a 'relaxed' view of proper Army discipline, drill and dress. There were stories of soldiers smoking on duty, and lagging behind on marches if they were feeling tired. It was even alleged that they had a 'live and let live' approach to sentry duties, allowing German soldiers to wander about at will in small groups, and rarely mounting night patrols. One British general claimed to have been treated to a French military parade where, to his eye, the troops were unshaven and untidy, the horses were ungroomed, the vehicles were dirty, and the men seemed disgruntled and lacking pride in themselves or their units: 'Though the order was given for "eyes right", hardly a man bothered to do so.'

The Bedfords set to and soon had the wire re-sited so that it would be less easy for hand grenades to be lobbed into the trenches, which were themselves moved and dug deeper to provide real protection. The sandbags were refilled – one of the bags left behind was found to be filled with straw and biscuits. The position was in rolling countryside interspersed with woods. On higher ground, they had good views forward to the German line about 1,800yds away, but the undulations meant dead ground, too, in which an enemy soldier could hide, so regular patrols were vital.

The Maginot Line itself ran along the hills behind Monneren, but it was difficult to see, even with binoculars, because it was so well camouflaged. One day, the officers were taken on a tour of one of the large forts on the Line, at Hackenberg, now a museum. The main entrance was a vast tunnel at the rear, with a railway line to take ammunition to the seventeen fortified gun emplacements covering the Moselle below and connected with each other by a large underground passageway. Most of the guns were hidden and would be raised only when ready to fire. The control room was about

200ft below ground, near a canteen big enough to cater for 1,000 men and a fully equipped operating theatre. It was all very impressive, but even young Medley noticed the lack of a supporting line or 'Plan B'; if the Maginot Line was overrun, there was nothing to fall back to.

Reading Robin's account of the patrols his C Company mounted, there is a sense of cat and mouse, each side testing the other, running patrols into no-man's-land, cutting wires, felling telegraph poles, firing little machine gun bursts at largely imaginary targets and generally being as much of a nuisance to each other as possible. Occasionally, the French would fire off a light artillery barrage, the Germans would respond, and then the Maginot Line 'heavies' would open up with a great boom, followed by a period of silence, then a whistling noise overhead and eventually a crump far behind the German lines. Sentries grew nervous, and there was a danger that they would fire at the slightest noise, real or imagined, provoking a dangerous response from an equally nervous German patrol. Every incident had to be reported and examined in detail, and this encouraged good fire discipline.

It was excellent experience of front line work, and must have come as an enormous relief after the months of training. But it was soon over, and time to hand on to another regiment for their turn. On 4 March the Battalion pulled back to Kédange-sur-Canner and then Waldweistroff, finishing up at Lorry-lès-Metz, where they enjoyed a good hot shower and general clean-up. By 14 March training had begun again, and two days later, they were back in their old billets at Lannoy and once again constructing pillboxes and digging ditches. That winter, the British Army constructed 40 miles of anti-tank obstacles, 59 airfields, 400 concrete pillboxes and over 100 miles of broad-gauge railway line.

Ironically, these defences were never used. The French Commander-in-Chief's plan was that, in the event of a German advance, the Allies were to leave their well-prepared positions and move into Belgium to cover the gap in the Maginot Line. He also calculated that the Germans would be unable to attack France through the thick Ardennes Forest, an area of extensive woodland, rough terrain, rolling hills and ridges in south-east Belgium, so it was only lightly defended. This would prove to be a fatal mistake.

At about this time Leslie was appointed Acting Captain and placed in charge of the Carrier Platoon, a key role in every battalion and part of the headquarters team. The Vickers-built Universal Carrier, also known as the Bren Gun Carrier from the light machine gun it carried, was used widely by the British Army during the war, mainly for transporting personnel, weapons and equipment, or as a machine gun platform. It is the most-produced armoured fighting vehicle in history.

With the spring came change. As the weather improved, work on the defences increased in pace. The popular second in command, Lieutenant Colonel J. C. A. Birch, took over as commanding officer from Lieutenant Colonel Davenport, who returned to the UK to take up another appointment. Leave was postponed indefinitely, and there were 24-hour guards on all vulnerable positions. Weapons skill training was stepped up, and practice route marches became faster and fiercer – 130 paces per minute, a rate that was maintained both on and off road and along the entire length of a column of troops. Officers engaged in 'sand table' exercises, learning tactics and discussing responses to attack, and reinforcements arrived from England. There was time for some relaxation, too, as concert parties of stars like Gracie Fields came out to entertain the troops, and there were also local amateur performances.

But still the Phoney War continued and, on 4 April Chamberlain was declaring that 'Hitler had missed the bus'. But five days later, the peace was shattered as Hitler invaded Denmark and Norway. The Norwegian campaign was a disaster for Britain and led directly to the collapse of the appeasement-minded Chamberlain government.

'You have sat too long here for any good you are doing,' Chamberlain was told by Leo Amery MP in a fierce debate in the House of Commons. 'Depart I say, and let us have done with you. In the name of God, go.'

Within days, on 10 May 1940, Churchill was Prime Minister, and the Phoney War was over.

Chapter 2

Retreat

On the same day that Churchill became Prime Minister, Hitler's 'blitzkrieg' invasion of Belgium began. At 0325 hrs on 10 May forty-two gliders and the planes towing them took off from Cologne, tasked with capturing three bridges over the Albert Canal in northern Belgium and the Belgian fortress of Eben-Emael. Within twenty-four hours German ground forces had stormed across the Dutch border and linked up with them. Stuka dive bombers destroyed airfields and caused widespread panic amongst the population, and Panzer tank and motorized

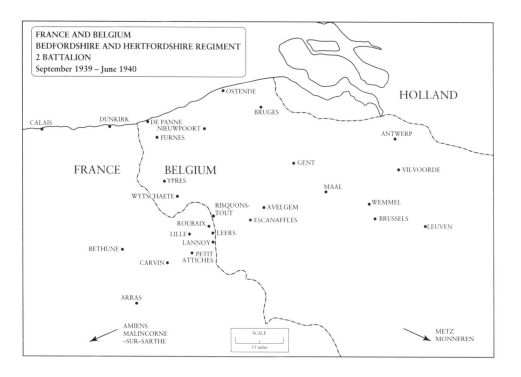

forces in their close-fitting black uniforms punched their way deep into Belgium. The Germans also attacked well to the south of Brussels three days later, through the supposedly impassable Ardennes Forest, and struck north-west towards the Channel, smashing through the French Army, crossing the River Meuse, outflanking the BEF and threatening to cut it off completely.

The new Battalion commander, Major Birch, was on leave in the UK at the time, so he dashed back to London as soon as he heard the news, catching the first boat out to Cherbourg the next morning. By the time he arrived, the Battalion, with the rest of 10 Infantry Brigade, had received a six-hour 'stand by' notice to implement Plan 'D'. This was the French Commander-in-Chief's agreed plan for the BEF to move straight into the gap at the northern end of the Maginot Line as soon as there was any sign of a German advance.

The Battalion was on high alert: there were frequent air raid warnings, and soldiers went about wearing steel helmets, respirators on their chests, gas capes ready folded on their shoulders, and goggles in case of gas spray from the air. Kit was being loaded on to lorries, and troop-carrying vehicles were lined up ready to go. There was the sound of bombing to the east, in the direction of the border with Germany, and reports of paratroop landings at Mons-en-Baroeul, a mile or two away. Medley recalls seeing tracer bullets from a Bofors gun streaking into the sky for the first time.

On 13 May an advance party from the Battalion, including some of Leslie's Carriers, moved across the Belgian border and, the next day, in glorious sunny weather, the remainder of the Battalion followed, travelling at 18mph and with a 300yd gap between vehicles in case of air attack. They crossed the border at Mouscron, north-east of Roubaix, and skirted the most heavily bombed roads, thanks to the assistance of some Boy Scouts, who showed them the way. It was here that they first saw endless streams of refugees going in the opposite direction: 'rich and poor, young and old, in motor cars, in buses, in carts, on bicycles and on foot'.

They debussed near Vilvoorde at teatime and, as they marched down the road, three German bombers swept along the canal towards them at 500ft. A Bofors gun opened up, and a wing was torn off one of the bombers. They arrived at their destination in the early evening, the roads crammed with some very tired-looking Belgian troops and horse-drawn artillery moving away from the fighting. Medley describes settling into his billet, in the house of a distraught local woman whose husband had been killed two days earlier.

A hot meal was prepared for the troops, as ack-ack barrages peppered the evening sky in response to constant air attacks. The Bren guns on their Carriers were used in an anti-aircraft mode, to prevent low-level bombing attacks on bridges and railways. The men had only just got settled when the order came for a move, and at 2230 the Battalion marched to Zaventem, arriving at 0300 on 15 May to take up a defensive position facing north and holding the railway line from Leuven in the east to Brussels to protect the right flank of the BEF, which was strung out along the River Dyle, between the Belgian army to the north and the French army in the south.

Birch sited his headquarters in a big tannery to the south of Leuven, near the railway line and just off the main road to Brussels. They were given the additional task of protecting Brussels Aerodrome – now the main international airport – only to discover Belgian troops firmly in occupation when they got there.

Here, as elsewhere, the speed and breadth of the German advance had completely overwhelmed the Allies. The German ground forces moved fast and were well supported by the Luftwaffe and by airborne troops, who parachuted deep into Belgian and French territory. The advance through the Ardennes, much further south than the French commander expected, was a brilliant stroke that threatened to outflank the French and completely undermined the success of the British in holding the Germans at bay in their northern sector of the defensive line. A massive Allied bombing raid on German bridgeheads in France failed miserably, with 85 of the 170 planes shot down.

The Battalion started work on its defensive positions, under constant air attack. Medley recalls seeing a German plane hit from the ground and the pilot jumping out with his parachute, only to be 'fired on by Belgian troops from miles around' as he landed. Later that day, he spotted eight Junkers bombers circling his position at 2,000ft and gave orders to open fire with the Brens, before the bombers were chased away by a squadron of Spitfires. The War Diary records an Army pilot making a forced landing, chased by nine Messerschmitts, and a dive bombing attack on Leslie's former colleagues in B Company.

Late that night, company commanders were summoned to an orders group meeting. They were given news which must have been unimaginable and completely devastating, after all the months of preparation and training – 'the BEF is withdrawing'. The Battalion was to hold its position overnight whilst 3 Division passed through, and then to start its own withdrawal at 0930.

The following morning, Robin, unable to grasp the speed of the Allied collapse, climbed a water tower at first light and was puzzled to see no sign of the German advance. As the Battalion prepared to leave, an angry old woman brandished her umbrella at them and swore that they were cowards.

By now thoroughly downhearted and depressed, and amidst feverish activity on the roads, they began the march west towards Wemmel, about 16 miles away, with Leslie's Carriers covering the retreat. They skirted Brussels to the north and crossed the Charleroi Canal over a pontoon bridge which was being held by troops from another regiment – Medley felt some relief to have other troops between him and the enemy. There were constant explosions as the Royal Engineers blew up bridges and holed barges and boats to impede the German advance. As they climbed a steep incline through a landscaped park they could see on a crest ahead of them long lines of men and vehicles, tanks and guns, all heading the same way, towards the Channel coast.

In the early afternoon they paused at Wemmel, for a meal. Boots were removed, feet were inspected and fresh socks put on. As they ate their meal, three Messerschmitts raced low overhead and everyone dived for the bushes.

But the respite was short, and at 2030 they were ordered to march through the night to Maal, about 25 miles away. The route initially was along narrow sandy tracks clogged with vehicles, so the soldiers were compelled to stumble about in the ditches until the blockage cleared and they could march in threes along the road. They passed through bombed villages, took wrong turnings, got directed and re-directed, drifted apart and became separated, but somehow arrived in Maal, more or less in one piece, at 0630. Temporary billets were allocated, and the officers set off for an orders group, but no sooner had the men lain down than an air attack forced them all up again and into defensive positions. By midday they were off once more, this time in Army buses bound initially for Knokke, then rerouted to the pretty little town of Avelgem, where they arrived exhausted soon after midnight. After a hot meal they collapsed on to their camp beds and slept for six hours. As Birch comments in his personal account of these days, 'It was dark, nobody knew the roads, and how it was accomplished I do not know.'

Communication between mobile units became impossible, other than through direct face-to-face contact. This was partly because, during the Phoney War, the BEF had kept radio silence in the interests of security. The radio network, which was thus virtually untested, now proved almost useless, and messages had to be relayed by despatch riders, who often found the roads clogged by refugees laden with their belongings, and by retreating French and Belgian troops with their horse transport.

The next morning, Leslie was ordered to take his Carriers across the river and hold an outpost position on high ground facing east near the Bois d'Enclus with three other companies. Medley's C Company was to hold the bridge across the River Scheldt at Escanaffles. This was part of a planned 'turn and face the enemy' manoeuvre, but it was soon abandoned. After a day spent working on defences and knocking holes in houses to give a better line of fire (to the intense annoyance of the inhabitants), the plan changed when the enemy was reported to be advancing a few miles away; C Company was told to hold the bridge until the other companies had crossed back over, and then blow it.

One and a half tons of explosive was packed around the bridge, and two companies crossed safely, but A Company was furthest away, and the minutes were ticking by. They eventually came into view on the other side of the river, closely followed by a line of refugees who, though warned of the danger, refused to turn back. The Company raced over the bridge, everyone ran for cover and, with a mighty roar, the bridge collapsed into the river amidst a shower of falling rock.

*

In the reports that I have seen, there is no mention of what happened to the refugees. I thought a lot about that as I stood by the bridge myself in 2006, trying to imagine the scene.

*

German reconnaissance parties arrived the next day, 20 May, and Leslie's best friend Tom La Fontaine was nearly caught on the wrong side of the canal, having misunderstood an order to 'go and have a see what's happening'. The Battalion found its positions overlooked, and sheets and blankets were erected to obscure the enemy's view. The Germans started sniping, pretty accurately, and B Company, which was in a very exposed position along the canal, suffered six casualties from shells and mortars. The Battalion returned fire and succeeded in destroying some vehicles with anti-tank rifles. The Carriers were moved forward to support B Company, and that night, fresh defensive positions were dug.

Birch was in a difficult spot. A German advance, with boats and across the rubble of the bridge, was clearly imminent, and the Germans held all the high ground. Avelgem was full of thousands of refugees hiding in a factory near the station and refusing to move. His men were relatively inexperienced, facing sustained heavy fire for the first time, and they were in an exposed position. There were several casualties that day, and one officer was killed. That night, just as Birch was waking from a short sleep, his headquarters was heavily shelled, twenty-five shells landing within yards of the building and completely destroying the office. Miraculously, no one was hurt. He decided to pull the forward companies back several hundred yards from the river overnight.

Within a few hours the Germans realized that the Battalion had withdrawn, and soldiers started crossing the river on foot two or three at a time to form a bridgehead on the other side. Birch sent Tom La Fontaine's D Company to counter-attack, with shell and sniper support from the other companies. The Carriers, according to Birch, 'did excellent work covering the flanks'. That night, 10 Brigade got the order to withdraw, the last to leave this part of the front line, and at 2200 they started falling back, with their wounded on an old tractor which had been commandeered (along with a goat for fresh milk), the Carriers forming the rearguard. They were all tired, in a long line of retreating soldiers, stumbling along country tracks at slow pace at dead of night, carrying all their heavy anti-tank weapons and ammunition – and in real fear of capture or worse. A soldier in the East Surreys, their neighbours in the line, shot himself in sheer desperation.

At first light on 23 May, and in early morning fog, Birch placed the Carriers on the east of the road, forward of the rest of the Battalion, to hold up the advancing Germans until the column had got on a bit. They arrived at the border between Belgium and France at 0900, after a march of some eighteen miles, and had breakfast. Medley recalls receiving a 'rocket' when his batman handed him a mess tin full of food before the men had all been fed. They started to dig in at their new positions, at Risquons-Tout (French for 'Let's risk it all', appropriately enough), near the national Range de Tir (firing range), just across the border in Belgium. They were overlooked by the Germans on the Mouscron Ridge and, somewhat surreally, by the inhabitants of a large block of flats nearby. The men were told there would be no withdrawal from this line.

Once again, companies were deployed in defensive positions, with the Carriers providing constant support and cover. Buildings were blown up to provide a better field of fire, new trenches were dug and old ones re-dug. Huge craters were blown in all the roads to the front to impede any German advance, and patrols were ordered by day as well as by night to try and dominate no-man's-land. Several enemy soldiers were killed. Medley describes taking a recce patrol out at night, moving forward gingerly in two groups of three, each group providing cover for the other, frightened of making too much noise with so much smashed glass all around, whilst enemy aircraft dropped parachute flares to light up the scene.

There were regular attempts by the Germans to infiltrate the British positions, and there were fears of 'fifth column' activity by the local population, many of whom had remained behind and were trying to continue normal life in the midst of all this. Each battalion in the line had to work closely with those on their flanks, since the join between the two was often the weakest point. The East Surreys were on the Bedfords' right, and the two battalions ran covering patrols for each other; the Surreys were badly mauled, with a major, a junior officer and several men killed and a Carrier destroyed. Later that day, Pincombe, the Battalion's Intelligence officer, looking for a missing fellow officer, found the burning Surrey Carrier and brought in the body of their major, under fire from the Germans. Pincombe received the Military Cross for his work that day.

By 26 May it was becoming clear that the BEF and the northern part of the French Army were cut off from the south, with their backs to the sea and with little chance of retrieving the situation. The Germans were at Boulogne on the Channel coast, the BEF was on half rations and men were told to conserve their ammunition. For Medley, 'things warmed up' as the Battalion came under constant shell fire, and the men were forced to stay in their trenches.

The next day, Birch was told that he was to lose his second in command Anstee to another regiment, and he wrote that he 'hated the idea of his going.' Later, he was ordered to start the withdrawal from Risquons-Tout, making as little noise and disturbance as possible; he was to leave part of the Battalion behind as a cover screen, in the hope of fooling the Germans. The Battalion was thus effectively cut in half, with the portion staying behind under the command of Major Ashby, supported by Pincombe, plus five platoons (including Tom La Fontaine and some of his D Company), and a few signallers and orderlies. One can imagine their feelings as the rest of the Battalion moved out that afternoon

They were heavily shelled through into the evening, and there were many casualties. The Germans used high velocity anti-tank rifles capable of piercing the steel shutters of pillboxes, and phosgene gas shells. Two officers were killed. Just before midnight, they were relieved by another regiment and were able to commence the 'long hard eight-hour' slog to Ploegsteert, where there was transport available. They then set off to rejoin the rest of the Battalion at Wytschaete.

Meanwhile, their colleagues on ahead were having a tough time too. Arriving at Wytschaete at dusk on 27 May, having spent the day struggling in the rain along clogged roads and through former battlefields of the Great War, they deployed immediately and started digging trenches along the road from Ypres to Warnetan. There was constant heavy shelling, with Verey lights illuminating their positions. Everyone was exhausted and jittery, and it wasn't long before a platoon opened fire when it heard movement out in front, only to discover that they were firing on a patrol from another British regiment, inflicting several casualties in the process.

At dawn it was still raining and cold, and the men had had a miserable night lying in wet ditches or digging in the rain. The Germans wasted no time in launching a stealthy probing attack, which was successfully repulsed; Leslie was ordered to position the Carriers to protect the Battalion's flanks and rear, for fear that the Germans might be attempting to infiltrate and attack from behind. The shelling grew heavier, making craters 5ft deep and 15ft across, earth shooting 20ft into the air on impact. All around, the fields were littered with the dead bodies of cattle in grotesque positions. The sounds of shell bursts in the trees, falling branches and the whine of shrapnel were frightening.

A counter-attack was ordered, then cancelled following a visit by the Brigadier, who commandeered one of the Carriers and set off with 'Porky' Young to see the situation on the front line for himself. Meanwhile, Birch was cheered to be greeted by his former second in command Anstee, whose new battalion was just back from the line. 'It was grand,' writes the sensitive Birch, 'seeing him at such a worrying time, and his usual calm self and full of humour.' He must have been relieved, later that afternoon, to receive orders to move back towards the woods at Dickebusch, where they were reunited with the other half of the Battalion.

But there was no time for celebration, as the Battalion was almost immediately ordered out on a night attack, with Birch rushing to and fro on foot in the dark, giving orders and gathering intelligence about the developing situation. He arrived back at the start line for the attack too late to see his men setting off, but was then astonished to receive further orders from Brigade calling off the attack. Poor man, he then had to run back to Battalion headquarters to check these orders with the Brigadier and give him the bad news that it was too late anyway, his men were already committed to the attack. Back he went to the front and, because he could find no one who knew the lie of the land well enough, he decided to push forward on his own to find his men and bring them back. Company by company, he somehow reeled them in without serious loss, finally tracking down Medley's C Company as dawn was breaking.

They then began the five-hour march back to the rest of the Battalion, Medley very reluctantly because, despite searching for some time, he had had to leave a missing soldier 'possibly asleep behind a rock'. There were burnt-out vehicles all along the road. When they eventually arrived back they were given their first hot meal in thirty hours, in a ditch, a treat unfortunately disrupted by a Bren gun going off accidentally and wounding soldiers on either side of where Robin was sitting. They were told to dispose of all excess baggage and papers – which were then chucked into a very green and boggy pond, weighted down with stones and accompanied by rude messages for the Germans.

Finally, at around 1400 hrs on 29 May, as the news came in that Belgium had capitulated, they boarded their transport and slowly followed the long column of men falling back northwards to Eikhoek, their path lit by the fires of burning buildings in Ypres. Birch comments laconically that, having fought for eight months around Ypres in the Great War, he hadn't expected to be back there under bombardment quite so soon.

Just outside Furnes, as a final indignity, orders were given by a slightly over-zealous military policeman to debus and destroy the vehicles, so they spent the next hour or so putting picks through tyres, draining oil from engines which were then left running, and collecting a few rations from a remaining NAAFI truck. Medley recalls wistfully that it was here that Spot the dog, who had been with them for months, was run over and killed.

It had been a terrible time, marked to this day at Risquons-Tout by a moving memorial to the dead of the East Surreys and the Bedfordshire and Hertfordshire Regiments. The Memorial takes the form of one of Leslie's Carriers, lovingly restored and repainted. In 2006 my son Tom and I marched in formation to this Memorial, with Robin Medley and other members of the Regiment, in the pouring rain, to pay our respects. The Last Post was played, and then we sang 'God Save the Queen' and, of course 'It's a Long Way to Tipperary'. I'm pretty sure I heard my father joining in.

Chapter 3

Dunkirk

As fierce defence gave way to headlong retreat, confusion set in, communications failed and the roads became hopelessly clogged by escaping refugees and despondent columns of defeated troops. The refugees were deliberately targeted by the German Stukas with their screaming engines, dive-bombing the roads and adding to the mayhem. Rumours spread like wildfire amongst the troops, and everyone with a foreign accent risked being taken for a 'fifth columnist'.

At his headquarters near Lille, the British Commander-in-Chief, General Gort, realized by 19 May that the game was as good as lost. The Dutch Army had collapsed, the Belgian Army was in desperate retreat, leaving a big hole on the British left flank, and the French High Command was issuing contradictory orders, causing yet more confusion. Gort started raising with Churchill and the War Office the possibility of evacuation. Churchill was appalled, and for several days Gort was compelled to continue planning and talking to the French about counter-offensives along various parts of the line. But by 24 May Hitler's troops were within fifteen miles of Dunkirk, and the serious risk that the entire 400,000-strong BEF might be lost was finally fully recognized and acknowledged. On 26 May the British Secretary of State for War, Anthony Eden, telegraphed Gort:

> The only course open to you may be to fight back to the west, where the beaches and port east of Gravelines will be used for embarkation. Navy will provide fleet of ships and small boats, the RAF will give full support.

The fear was that it was already too late – but fate played a hand, as the German troops, by this time only ten miles from Dunkirk, received orders to halt from Hitler, who was concerned that they had outstripped their supply lines and lost too many men. Hitler thought the task of finishing off the Allied armies could be left to the Luftwaffe, whilst German commanders in the field seem to have assumed that the Allies were about to capitulate. By the time they woke up to the fact that the defences around Dunkirk had been strengthened and the rescue armada was on its way, they had lost two vital days – and a golden opportunity to smash the British Army on the beaches.

Gort was, of course, unaware of this at the time, so preoccupied was he with what he saw as the likelihood of imminent defeat and the plans that had to be made for withdrawing a whole army, spread across a wide front, back towards the port and seaside town of Dunkirk – a task that must have seemed all but impossible in the time available.

Gort's strategy had two key features – two lines of defensive strong points to funnel the retreating troops down towards the beaches, and a strong perimeter defence around Dunkirk itself. The fighting around these strong points was fierce and brutal, and the courage and determination of the troops who manned them of an exceptionally high order. Many died, or were left behind to face certain capture, or worse. In a field near Wormhoudt, for example, the SS forced nearly 100 men of the Royal Warwickshire and Cheshire Regiments and some Royal Artillery into a small barn, then threw in hand grenades and finished off the survivors with machine guns.

On the Dunkirk perimeter the fighting was just as desperate, along a line 25 miles wide and 8 miles deep manned by troops already exhausted by days if not weeks of fighting, plucked from the beaches or from the units heading towards them through the defensive corridor and thereby required to give up their own hopes of imminent escape. The western sector of the perimeter was the responsibility of the French; the British took the east, from the ancient walled town of Bergues, along the canal to Furnes and then to Nieuwpoort, which was intended to be held by the Belgians – until their surrender on 27 May. The bravery of the men defending the perimeter, many of them giving their own lives so that others could escape, is almost impossible to exaggerate.

It was into this perimeter, and the gap left by the Belgians, that 2 Battalion marched on 29 May, along shattered roads lined with abandoned vehicles, under constant bombardment, machine guns chattering all around, and staggering with exhaustion and the weight of such equipment and stores as they had been able to salvage. To add to this, D Company had gone missing, and all attempts at finding them again had failed.

Birch and Pincombe went on ahead separately to reconnoitre the crossing of the canal, hoping to be able to use the bridge at Wulpen, opposite their allotted rendezvous point at Oost-Dunkerke. By the time they arrived, struggling against a tide of Belgian and French soldiers moving as fast as they could in the opposite direction, the bridge had already been blown, and it was the same story at Nieuwpoort further east. They headed back west, crossed the canal on a small barge which they then sank with anti-tank rifles, and proceeded towards Furnes where, at close range, Birch's car was hit twice and he 'went over a very high fence like a pole jumper'.

Birch was rightly concerned that the Germans were so close and formed the view that the canal at this point was not being defended. Deciding that he had to do something about it, he crawled out of the ditch he was hiding in and ran zigzagging up the road to report to the Brigadier, 'Bubbles' Barker, who put him in charge of a couple of stray companies from the East Surreys with the instruction to 'hold the canal'. They did so with distinction, under constant machine gun fire and sniping.

Having organized this part of the defensive perimeter, and still worrying about the missing D Company, Birch then made his way to Oost-Dunkerke and set about organizing his HQ in an abandoned house. Barker then reappeared and told Birch that, when his men arrived, he could get them under cover and let them have a good night's rest before slotting them into the perimeter line of defence. Birch had concerns about this because he realized that, if they were to survive the intense bombardment and almost hand-to-hand fighting that was going on all around, they would need the shelter of the hours of darkness to get themselves dug in and fully prepared. He therefore asked permission for his men to go into the line as soon as they arrived.

How this news was received by the men is hard to guess. Rumours had been spreading amongst them before they arrived at the canal that the BEF was withdrawing, and the second in command, Major Ashby, who had by now caught up with the rest of the Battalion, reported that there had already been some difficulty persuading them not only that they had to get out of their vehicles and destroy them, but also that they had to carry large amounts of extra gear and weaponry eight miles to Dunkirk, because there was still a lot of fighting to do. All of them, officers and men, were 'all really whacked', as Birch put it, and the news that their ordeal was by no means over must have added hugely to a sense of disillusion and despair for some.

They finally arrived at Oost-Dunkerke in the early evening, in the middle of a massive bombardment of the Town Hall, which was being used as a first aid post, and the main square. The Town Hall was wrecked, and with it one of Leslie's Carriers, which Birch feared, wrongly as it turned out, was the one being used by Pincombe. He commandeered a house as his HQ and began planning for the 'take-over' of their allotted section of the perimeter line, while the men had a meal and got themselves sorted out. Birch was annoyed that one of the companies had ignored his instruction to hang on to their digging tools, so replacements had to be snatched from nearby garden sheds, along with ladders to help cross a small stream that ran alongside the canal. Then the digging began.

Just before midnight, three companies were deployed left, right and centre along about one and a half miles of the perimeter. D Company had still not appeared, so Leslie's Carriers, who were 'excellent', had to carry on with their own job of transporting, covering and providing anti-aircraft fire, whilst also filling in for the missing company.

The next day, 30 May, brought continual sniping and prolonged heavy bombardment. The line was fluid, with frequent attacks on their right and left flanks, and Birch spent much of his day walking miles up and down his sector with 'Johnny' Johnson, the commander of C Company, who had been wounded in the face the day before, making recces for possible changes in the deployment of his men. Furnes was heavily bombed, and the Royal Berkshires and the Grenadiers lost many men. Birch was delighted to meet up at one point with Anstee, whose jolly 'There's no need to worry, sir! I have my Battalion behind you' must have cheered him no end.

On 31 May, just before dawn, the Brigadier came by again to say that the Battalion was to be withdrawn soon to the beaches, but Birch decided to keep quiet about this until the news was confirmed with specific orders. He briefed a couple of officers, in case he was hit, but told the men that they were 'certain to be there for a week if not a fortnight'.

That day in the perimeter, waiting for the order to withdraw, must have seemed to Birch to last for ever. He describes it in his report, with typical British understatement, as 'very trying'. For miles along the line of the canal German troops were making their way across, singly or in small groups, and then crawling along the ditches and through the long grass to harry the British forces. In Birch's section of the line the mortars had run short of ammunition, but they managed to scare off those they saw with small arms fire.

Shelling from the other side of the canal was continuous, and Birch was forced to move his HQ back a bit, to the only area apparently not subject to enemy fire – a potato field. Ashby lectured the HQ Company about diving for cover too often, and was promptly blown into a ditch by a high velocity shell – 'You chaps just ain't quick enough' was his laconic comment as he crawled out.

'Porky Young's Carriers', as Birch described them, now down to five in number, several having been destroyed or lost their tracks in the shell holes around, did sterling work protecting the Battalion's flanks and firing off their guns at the large number of 'Boche' aircraft attacking overhead. They all cheered as forty Blenheim bombers flew over to attack the German positions.

Finally, as it was getting dark, the Brigadier arrived and took Birch to the East Surreys' makeshift field HQ near Nieuwpoort, where they sat in a tiny room lit by a smoky oil lamp as the orders for withdrawing to the beaches were given. Returning to the potato field with the Brigadier, they missed their way and found themselves heading straight for the Germans. A desperate three-point turn and they were racing back in the right direction, the dust from their car against the setting sun making a prime target for enemy machine guns – putting 'Bubbles' Barker 'in high good humour' as the bullets spurted around them. Boy's Own stuff.

Back at the potato field, Birch and his officers could hardly keep their eyes open as they discussed the plans. Birch had to slap one of them to keep him awake – and promptly fell asleep himself. Only a tirade from Ashby about 'losing grip' jerked them back to life, and the plans were laid. The whole of Barker's Brigade was to vacate its position in the line and fall back beyond Oost-Dunkerke by 0130 hrs, leaving Medley's C Company and Leslie and his Carriers to hold on to the town for an hour. C Company was then to withdraw in some form of motorized transport in their turn, covered by the Carriers. They were all to re-muster at De Panne and be led down to the beaches.

Just as the withdrawal commenced, there was a frenzy of German heavy artillery fire, and Birch immediately handed over the large bag of regimental money to one of his officers, while he supervised the withdrawal. A platoon from A Company had been missing for eighteen hours and was now finally given up for lost. As C Company pulled out, Birch followed in his car with Pincombe, whilst Leslie and the Carriers covered their backs.

They passed through an awesome scene. All around them on that summer night houses were tumbling and glass was flying as the German guns pounded the route to the sea and escape. Birch said it was terrifying, in the dark, to see sparks and splinters flying in all directions. Medley describes one group of houses being hit by German shells at regular two-minute intervals, his men scurrying past them between salvoes. Many of the fleeing soldiers were hit, and some of the Bedfords did great work, amongst the crash of explosions and the crackling flames, bandaging them up and putting them on a commandeered French lorry.

The tempo increased as they neared the beach road, with a salvo every minute now. Still the men tramped steadily on, without excitement or fuss, until they approached De Panne. Birch describes the streets of this smart little seaside town as 'an amazing sight'. The roads were jammed with every conceivable type of vehicle, with movement in any direction almost impossible, and were becoming more so with each passing minute. Houses were crashing down under the shelling, and the streets were littered with electric tramway cables and their supporting standards. Most civilians were sheltering in their cellars, but some emerged to hand over wounded soldiers whom they had been looking after. Lorries were on fire, and ammunition was exploding all over the place as the shelling continued.

That day, Saturday, 1 June, at 0500 hrs, two or three hours after the Battalion had pulled out, the Germans deployed a massive four divisions against the six thinly-spread battalions defending the canal. The German troops were well equipped, battle-hardened and in vastly superior numbers. Fighting around Furnes was particularly intense, and it was on that day, after some incredibly brave conduct (which led incidentally to the first VC of the war, for Captain Harold Erskine-Evans of the East Lancashires) that the Germans finally succeeded in crossing the canal and forcing the remaining British and French troops down to the beaches with their backs to the sea.

It was clear to Birch that if there ever had been an orderly plan for this stage of the retreat it had long since been abandoned. The rest of the Battalion, under Ashby, was up ahead somewhere, and so Birch continued forwards with Leslie and a few other officers. They trailed along the road for a while, completely lost and at one stage apparently heading inland and across the border into France.

Meanwhile, Medley with the remains of the rearguard from Oost-Dunkerke had arrived at De Panne. He and the men with him rushed through the beach entrance in bursts, between salvoes from the German artillery, and came upon a sight that must have stopped them in their tracks.

The clear night sky provided just enough light for them to see, stretched out before them, the flat, wet sands of De Panne at low tide. The sea was still, with barely a ripple. Down the beach, long black lines of mostly silent men laden with kit snaked to the water's edge, looking out across the Channel at the ghostly silhouettes of warships awaiting their precious cargo.

German barrages crashed along the high water mark, whilst Royal Navy shells screamed overhead. There were tens of thousands of men, and Medley could see that, with only a handful of small craft available to ferry them from the beach to the ships half a mile offshore, the evacuation was going to be a long slow process – and time was running short.

Chapter 4

Operation Dynamo

In spite of the pressure he put on Gort to continue fighting, Churchill had in fact been considering the possibility that a wholesale evacuation of the BEF might be necessary as early as 14 May. Vice Admiral Bertram Ramsay was put in charge of planning, and an appeal was issued on the BBC Home Service for 'owners of craft 300 to 100ft in length [to] send all particulars to the Admiralty within fourteen days'. At this stage there was little real sense of urgency, and no thought at all that a complete evacuation of the entire 400,000-strong BEF (and a substantial part of the French Army) might have to be attempted.

Ramsay's team barely slept for days as they struggled to put the rescue fleet together and worked out where to moor it; how to supply it; how to collect spare parts, fuel, medical kits; where to find enough maritime charts; what route to take to which French ports and how to protect them from enemy air attack, submarines and floating mines along the way; how to provide trains for the troops once back in England. And, of course, they needed men to make all this happen.

At this point, for the British Army, all hung in the balance. For the British public, meanwhile, life went on pretty much as normal for early summer: the newspapers had carried news of the fighting in France and Belgium, but with no sense at all of the approaching debacle. Even the troops on the ground seem to have had no premonition of disaster, dug in as they were in their defensive positions along the Maginot Line. But in Whitehall there was a growing sense of unease and looming disaster and, on Sunday, 26 May, the day Medley was reporting that things were 'warming up' at Mouscron, the order was given for Operation Dynamo to commence.

Ramsay wrote to his wife:

> I am directing one of the most difficult and hazardous operations ever conceived and, unless the good Lord is very kind, there will be many tragedies attached to it.

Monday, 27 May became known as Bloody Monday, because of the vast number of explosive and incendiary bombs dropped on Dunkirk, reducing huge swathes of the port to rubble. The RAF was doing its best, but it was losing aircraft at an alarming rate, and Air Chief Marshal Sir Hugh Dowding refused to release more for the defence of the beaches, for fear that there would be none left – so the Luftwaffe ruled the skies. On that day 7,669 troops were evacuated as the rescue effort began.

On 28 May a few more Navy ships reached the coast but could get no nearer in than a mile because of the gently shelving shoreline. Even at this distance, they could see the lines of troops waiting on the sand. They used their lifeboats to reach the shore, but the mad scramble to get aboard resulted in groundings, swampings, overturnings, lost oars, clogged motors and fouled propellers. Many more small boats were clearly needed. Along the length of the South Coast, boatyard owners were hauled from their beds and yacht clubs were raided for more craft. Naval crews were assembled (sometimes including the boats' owners themselves). Objections were simply ignored. The evacuation gathered pace, and the legend of the Dunkirk 'little ships' was born. But that day, only 5,930 men were hauled off the beaches.

Meanwhile, in Dunkirk itself, troops were crammed into cellars, hiding where they could to avoid the savage bombing, some of them anaesthetizing themselves with the abundant supplies of wine and champagne kept by French families and café proprietors.

The bombing was mostly concentrated on the docks, leaving two long breakwaters or 'moles' that formed the entrance to Dunkirk's harbour relatively untouched. The moles comprised a wooden walkway just 3ft wide on top of concrete piles, stretching nearly a mile out to sea. They had not been built as jetties, but it was thought they would be strong enough for large ships to tie up to and take troops off. Now there was a viable alternative to the chaos of the beaches.

By 29 May the East Mole had become the main embarkation point, with destroyers, minesweepers and an assortment of ferries and steamers lining up to take men off. The Luftwaffe soon saw what was happening and managed to sink two ships and damage several more that day, as well as the Mole itself. But the terrible scramble for places on the few small boats working the beaches began to ease slightly, as word got round and thousands headed for the Mole, where tight discipline and iron control was needed to regulate the flow of men on to the breakwater with the arrival of the rescue ships. That day, 13,752 men were taken off the beaches and an amazing 33,558 off the Mole.

By 30 May these efforts were paying off, and an extraordinary armada of boats started to make its way across the Channel – yachts, paddle steamers, fishing smacks, cabin cruisers, an Isle of Wight ferry, a sailing cargo barge from Ipswich, even the cockle boat fleet from Leigh-on-Sea – more than a hundred all told, none of them armed and most of them on their first trip across the Channel. From the Mole 45,072 men were taken off, and another 29,512 were rescued from the beaches. It was only that evening, as men clambered off the boats at Dover and other ports, clutching whatever they had been able to salvage on the beaches, and boarded trains for London or elsewhere, that the British public was told what was happening on the other side of the Channel.

All that night and the next day, the makeshift rescue fleet hurried on towards the beaches, on a flat sea and with the benefit of a protective heavy mist that denied the Luftwaffe the opportunity to strike. Once close to the coast, their job was to act as ferries from the crowded beach to the larger Royal Navy vessels standing to offshore. It was tough work, with German shelling almost continuous, frequent breakdowns and minor collisions, men to be picked out of the water, injuries to tend, men desperate to be on their way home to be managed. A further 47,081 men were taken off the Mole and another 22,942 off the beaches, and the rescue was almost complete, with troops at the eastern end of the perimeter expected to be clear and on the beach ready to go that night. But it was at that moment, on 31 May, that the order came through from Churchill himself that they were to rescue as many Frenchmen as possible – 'an equal number' – and of course that meant not just continuing operations on the Mole but also on the perimeter, holding the Germans at bay the while.

On 1 June, as dawn broke and the mist cleared, the Luftwaffe renewed its attacks in the early morning sunshine, strafing troops on the beach and in the water, bombing the Mole and the rescue fleet, sinking or putting out of action sixteen ships in a day. Although more than 29,000 British and 35,000 French were rescued, it was a bad day . . . as Leslie and the rest of the Bedfords slipped out of the perimeter line and began to arrive on the beach.

Chapter 5

A Day at the Beach

By the time the men of 2 Battalion arrived on the beaches, early on Saturday, 1 June, the evacuation was drawing to its close – most of the BEF had been rescued, the perimeter was collapsing and the Germans were closing in. The main body of Bedfords, under Ashby, arrived first at the small Belgian seaside town of De Panne, today a smart tourist resort, its beaches overshadowed by high-rise apartment blocks.

In the early days of the evacuation they would have joined what was, to a considerable degree, an ill-disciplined, frightened and completely dispirited rabble. Although some units were able to maintain their integrity, many were not. Men became separated from their officers, military discipline broke down and a mood of 'every man for himself' began to spread. Of course, there were also many examples of individual bravery, and of men sacrificing themselves for others in greater need of a place on a boat – but the overall impression was one of chaos.

Some headed down the wide, gently sloping sands to the sea, where they stood, as the tide came in, up to their necks in water for hours at a time, waiting to be picked up by the pitifully small fleet of ship's tenders and life rafts plying between the shore and a handful of naval vessels out to sea. When a boat appeared, there was often a terrible mad fight to get on it; boats overturned or became swamped, men drowned in their desperation to get aboard, or in isolated cases were shot, or threatened with shooting, by officers fighting to maintain some order and save the lives of those already on board – and their own. The sea was awash with discarded equipment and dead bodies, and vital time was lost clearing propellers or organizing men to balance the boat and row in time.

Others decided to wait it out on the sand, or broke into beachfront homes and cafés and got drunk on whatever booze they could lay their hands on. There was little or no food beyond the small amounts that men had been able to grab as they retreated, begged or looted from local people. Fresh water ran out early on.

And all the time, German shells rained down, and Stukas, their sirens screaming and flying directly over the men's heads, ravaged them with their machine guns, as thousands more shambled on to the beach from the fighting inland. There were few spades to dig with, so men burrowed into the sand with their bare hands to try and find some measure of illusory protection. It was a scene from hell.

By 1 June, however, when the Bedfords arrived, order had been restored, relatively speaking. Most evacuations were taking place from the East Mole in the harbour at Dunkirk itself, where it was easier to control the flow of men and where larger boats could come in close and tie up. However, Dunkirk was an exhausting 14 miles' walk away across the border into France. The men had to labour through soft sand and dunes, or dodge along a road heaving with abandoned vehicles and equipment and fleeing refugees, under constant fire and shrouded in acrid smoke.

For those who chose to stay on the beaches, lorries had been run into the sea and disabled, to form ramshackle jetties from which men could, with difficulty, clamber aboard the armada of small ships that had crossed the Channel from England and which were now struggling through the waves and the flotsam of floating bodies and equipment to reach them.

The Regiment's official War Diary, written in Pincombe's hand and signed by him, records that the Battalion 'was of necessity split up . . . and embarked from De Panne and neighbouring beaches, others from Dunkirk and Bray-Dunes.' He describes the scene on the beaches and the difficulties of escape in short, clipped sentences and with masterly understatement, but both Birch and Robin Medley, in command of a platoon from C Company, have left personal accounts that give a bit more colour.

Birch in his staff vehicle arrived at De Panne after the main body of his men and could find no sign of them on the beach. As he was trying to work out where they were and what to do, he met up with 'Porky' Young and a handful of others, and then started trudging westwards along the coast, first on the beach and then on the road inland, until they were overtaken by the resourceful Pincombe in a Ford delivery truck loaded with wounded. They clung on to the sides of this truck until they got to Bray-Dunes, about seven miles along the coast, where they came upon 'an extraordinary sight':

> The tide was out. There were two piers of lorries running out to sea. There was a paddle steamer aground. Alongside the piers were grouped troops in close order, but elsewhere on this vast expanse of wet sand were small parties of troops of three or four

or individually seemingly with no object in view. Small boats, most of which were wrecked, were strewn over the sand. At a few places small queues were wading chest deep into the water to be picked up by only a few boats. Further off, about two miles out, were many vessels from destroyers or small cargo ships to lifeboats. Some were already moving away. Here and there were the blast marks of anti-personnel bombs and a few dead . . . just as we arrived there was a dive-bombing and machine-gunning display and every soul seemed to start shooting his rifle or automatic into the air.

Birch had about a dozen men with him by now, and they wandered about for a while looking for the rest of the Battalion. They found some 'excellent bread and bully' and examined an abandoned lifeboat and a partially sunken 'folding boat' as a means of getting off the beach. One of the 'Beachmasters' (who all wore red armbands, a sign of the improved organization and discipline), told them that the paddle steamer they had seen was to be used as an embarkation stage, so they waded out to it and found it crammed with soldiers, many of them wounded and some of them from the Bedfords. Birch made his way to a cabin and talked to some of them, then Pincombe astonished him by producing a glass of beer from some bottles he had found in the hold. Birch wasn't sure if Pincombe was a magician, or if he was himself delirious.

He watched enemy planes bombing the ships at sea and saw small boats sinking; then he saw the larger ships heading back to England and wondered if some of his Battalion were on board and how long it would be before the ships returned. He went on deck at high tide and watched two soldiers rowing a small boat round in circles, as one of their oars was far longer than the other. They came near and offered to take some of the wounded to Dunkirk.

In a display of extraordinary courage and leadership, Birch jumped in himself to help them come alongside, but found himself trapped in the paddle wheel, whereupon he struggled into their small boat to discuss their somewhat over-ambitious idea and ended up helping them row men ashore instead – 'But I was far too weak and tired, and was soon of little use.' Once back on the beach, a Company Sergeant Major and another man took over the rowing, while Birch and the original two lifted the wounded men along the sand, where they eventually found an ambulance to take them to some kind of field hospital.

A weary Birch then set off alone along the sand dunes towards Dunkirk. Shortly before reaching the town he was hailed by 'Bubbles' Barker, who was resting on the sand with some of his HQ team. Barker was covered in blood and weighed down by a pile of kit, including a large wireless set from which he refused to be parted. He had apparently amputated a man's arm that afternoon with a penknife. Birch had left all his kit on board the paddle steamer, so he offered to help out, and they moved off companionably towards the Mole, meeting up with Leslie along the way. They took comfort from seeing some French troops lounging about coolly, waiting to have a crack at the Germans, and Birch was pleased to hear from 'the Brig' that at least eighty of his men had already got away.

Finally, finally they came to the Mole. The first thing they saw was a destroyer being attacked by a squadron of bombers:

> It was an unforgettable sight . . . each salvo of bombs dropped by each diving aircraft seemed to blow the destroyer to bits but as the smoke and water fell away she was seen to be still steaming but each time slower and slower. The guns on board kept hitting back, first at rapid fire and then gradually less rapidly and less often till the guns were silenced and, steaming slowly in a circle, she seemed to be sinking.

Nearly twenty ships were sunk or badly damaged that day, including several destroyers. From the timings, it is possible that what Birch witnessed was the sinking of the French destroyer *Foudroyant*, on duty and waiting to escort out to sea and relative safety the few boats left alongside the Mole.

The attack was deeply alarming to the men remaining on the narrow planks of the Mole, at the end of a long day and with rescue at hand. There wasn't much for Birch and Barker to choose from – a 'small dirty and crowded trawler' or the *Ben-My-Chree*, a stylish and elegant steam packet from the Isle of Man, built in 1927 – but they took their time deciding which to board, opting eventually for the larger boat and its promise of greater comfort.

In fact, this might have proved an unfortunate or at least an uncomfortable choice. The unarmed *Ben-My-Chree* had already made two previous trips to rescue troops at Dunkirk, and its merchant sailors were frightened and exhausted. The ship was a big target and had no protection from German warplanes or artillery shells. According to some reports, back in Folkestone after the second trip, the crew lined the railings shouting that they were not going back and threatening to leave the ship. They were turned back on the gangplank by an armed naval guard marching towards them with fixed bayonets. A relief crew eventually took over, and the ship sailed again, for the third and last time that morning.

Robin Medley, with his platoon, had arrived at De Panne a little after Birch, around first light. Like him, he saw 'vast numbers' of soldiers on the beach and was immediately witness to the terrifying spectacle of thirteen Messerschmitt 109s overhead. They peeled off in line astern and then came sweeping back down along the beach with guns blazing, at a height of about 12ft. The men had no cover.

He was ordered by a naval officer to take over a 20ft-long beached lifeboat, which had to be manhandled afloat in the rising tide. With thirty-five Bedfords, and a couple of dozen others, Medley managed to get it moving, the men sitting opposite each other and turning the propeller by alternately pulling and pushing on rods running the length of the boat. At least the exercise got them dry and warm, and they set off for two destroyers about 1,600yds away offshore. They had come within 400yds when a squadron of Stukas split into smaller groups and dived vertically down on the ships from all directions. The planes were close enough for Medley to see the faces of the pilot and gunner. In his own words:

> One of the destroyers took a direct hit – there was a blinding flash followed by an explosion. When the smoke cleared there was no destroyer. It had all happened so quickly, the mind could hardly take it in.

Accompanied by some other small boats, they headed for the second destroyer, which had survived the attack and headed further out. But once again the Stukas dived as they drew near, this time singling out boats like Medley's and attacking them too. They decided the safer course was to head back to the beach and take their chances on the sand. There, Medley was comforted by the sight of a troop of Coldstream Guards being formed up, for all the world as if back on the parade ground. Then he set his own platoon off marching in the hot morning sun towards Dunkirk. By 1000 they were at Bray-Dunes, where the thick soft sand of the dunes slowed them down badly. They met up with a hundred or more Bedfords and stopped to watch one of the constant Stuka attacks on shipping out at sea and an RAF counter-attack – and Robin promptly fell asleep for three hours.

Eventually, in the early evening, they arrived at the end of the East Mole at Dunkirk, past a long line of German PoWs and burning oil tanks belching black smoke. Tied up to the Mole was the *Ben-My-Chree*, and Medley caught sight of Birch, with Leslie and the other Bedfords on deck. There was no room for him and his group, so they nervously clambered across two planks that were bridging a gap in the Mole caused by an earlier bomb, and gratefully boarded the fishing trawler that Birch had spurned.

Robin somehow found a space to sit down on deck, leaning against the side of the boat, and fell asleep watching a flight of Spitfires clear the skies. The next thing he knew, the trawler was docking at Ramsgate, and his ordeal was over.

Birch, Leslie and the others landed at Folkestone, and were put on a train for Yeovil. Birch wrote:

> It was Saturday evening and the folks at home were all out looking so happy and cheering as the trains went by. It seemed another world.

*

Years later, in 2006, I visited those beaches with Robin Medley and my son Tom. My abiding memory of that deeply moving trip is of Robin, his back to the sea on the beach east of Dunkirk, wearing his Army beret against a blustery cold wind. He told us what he remembered of the last time he had been there, sixty-six years earlier, and then he went quiet, remembering perhaps stories that were too hard to tell, and friends that he had lost, and feelings that went too deep for tears. It must indeed have seemed like another world.

*

Chapter 6

With the Commandos – Weymouth

B ritain had had a lucky escape, a very lucky one. Although it had lost most of its stores and equipment, its Army was still more or less intact and in a position, eventually, to fight another day. Men had died, more than 12,000 of them, with 14,000 severely wounded and another 40,000 captured, but 350,000 fighting men were safely back in Britain. On the other hand, France and the Low Countries were lost and under brutal Nazi occupation, and Italy now entered the war on the side of a triumphant Germany. In a very real sense, Britain stood alone, fearing imminent invasion.

Hitler ordered his generals to draw up plans for a cross-Channel assault, and launched wave upon wave of Luftwaffe attacks on RAF stations, whilst Churchill warned that the Battle of Britain had begun:

> Let us, therefore, brace ourselves to our duties and so bear ourselves that, if the British Empire and Commonwealth last for a thousand years, men will still say, 'This was their finest hour'.

All over the UK, but particularly along the south and east coasts, preparations were put in hand to repel the invader. An appeal went out for 'local defence volunteers', and more than 1.5 million men responded; anti-aircraft batteries were constructed and installations were built for the newly-invented radar system; along the length of the coast, concrete anti-tank barriers were erected, beach exits were blocked with miles of barbed wire, and hundreds of concrete pillboxes appeared.

The Bedfords' 2 Battalion re-mustered at Yeovil in Somerset. Their losses had been light compared to some of the other infantry battalions which had fought in France – but still five of the twelve platoon commanders had died and a further two were wounded. Birch calculated that nearly thirty of his men had been killed in action, with forty or more wounded, another thirty or so taken prisoner and more than twenty 'missing in action' or unaccounted for. The last to die was Captain Geoffrey Onslow, who was killed on the beach at Dunkirk, having already suffered a severe wound to the jaw on the approach to the port. Medley notes that the quartermaster, Lieutenant Vosser, having spent most of the Great War as a PoW, was captured again at Dunkirk and spent the whole of the Second World War as a prisoner as well.

Brigadier Barker came on a visit and told them that 'in spite of all the difficulties, you did all that was asked of you.' He was a popular and well-respected divisional commander, who had stood shoulder to shoulder with his men throughout the campaign and had personally supervised every withdrawal. Spontaneously, the men cheered him to the rafters.

The Battalion's role was now to be 'Home Defence'; they moved to a tented camp at Fareham, and thence to Bognor Regis on the south coast, where they were to man defensive positions and keep a close watch for Germans parachutists as forerunners of the anticipated invasion. It was high summer and, whilst the beaches were out of bounds to the general public, watching from the esplanade as the soldiers dug ditches made an enjoyable alternative entertainment for holidaymakers.

Perhaps surprisingly, morale amongst the men was good. They felt they were better than Hitler's soldiers and, inspired partly no doubt by Churchill's stirring speeches, relished the idea of 'standing alone' following the defeat of France. There were nightly Luftwaffe attacks on Portsmouth, and the Battalion was either on watch, or training and exercising, or digging defences along the beach, virtually twenty-four hours a day. In the skies overhead the RAF was fighting the Battle of Britain, as the Germans sent wave after wave of bombers to attack Britain's airfields and other strategic locations in a failed attempt to destroy the country's air defences. Several aircraft were brought down in the Battalion's area, and the men cheered as one Stuka flashed at roof level over Bognor, hotly pursued out to sea by British Hurricanes.

Leslie, meanwhile, was getting restless, and put his name forward to join a new special force for use in defence 'to spring at the throats of any small landings', but also, and more importantly, to carry out 'tip and run' raids against German-occupied Europe, to inflict casualties and confusion on the enemy and to bolster morale and public confidence back home. These were to be 'specially trained troops of the hunter class who can develop a reign of terror down the enemy coast'. They were 'the Commandos', named after the guerrillas who fought so effectively against the British in the Boer War.

On 8 July 1940 Leslie was summoned for interview by Colonel 'Percy' Legard (of the 5th Royal Inniskilling Dragoon Guards), the commander of one of the twelve new units. After a talk with Legard he was invited to lead F Troop of the 400-strong No 4 Commando. He accepted with alacrity, even though it meant a drop (having been given the acting rank of Major in France) back to Captain. Two days later, he was on his way to Salisbury Plain, where he established his 'headquarters' at the George Hotel in Amesbury and then 'set out each morning on the important task of finding the right men', from the 2,000 or so who had volunteered.

Leslie wasted no time in appointing his second in command, Second Lieutenant Hutton of the Royal Tank Regiment, who had been recommended to him by Legard. Leslie liked his bearing and took him on 'without much ado'. He soon found that, despite his youth, Hutton was keen and willing to learn, and the two men quickly enlisted the remainder of the Troop. Legard helped find a second officer, introducing Leslie over lunch at the Royal Artillery Mess at Bulford to 'a young fellow named Munn of the Gunners' who impressed him straight away: 'I asked him my rather stereotyped set of questions, but I knew that I would have him in my Troop if he would come.'

This relatively simple and informal process was typical of the Commandos. Although there was a set of guidelines for recruitment, and some criteria such as 'able to swim, not prone to seasickness, prepared to parachute or travel in a submarine and able to drive a motor car and ride a motorcycle', these were interpreted by the troop leaders according to their own beliefs and instincts and service background. Leslie's namesake, Peter Young, for example, when asked about his method of selection, said, 'You look at them, don't you? You talk to them a bit, make up your mind if he's a bull-shitter or has something to contribute . . . you can tell.' Roger Courtenay, another Commando leader, had a preference for former Boy Scouts and Army bandsmen, believing that the latter were 'naturally good at doing several things at once'. He also liked 'studious and artistic types because they were super-sensitive'. Bob Laycock recommended choosing 'your other ranks more carefully than you would choose your wife . . . tolerate no creepers.' They all seem to agree that they didn't want 'swaggering tough types, whose toughness was mostly displayed in pubs'.

Munn accepted the invitation to join F Troop 'almost greedily', and Leslie felt that the Troop had got off to a flying start. He had chosen a wonderfully eclectic and colourful group, with men from every walk of life, including a poacher, a colonel's son, a surveyor, a wall of death rider, a farmer, an international TT bike rider and an artist. As he noted in the F Troop diary – which he called *A True record of the Trials and Adventures of F Troop of No 4 Commando during the years when Great Britain alone fought for the Freedom of Nations* – the fifty men had 'volunteered not only out of a sincere desire to serve their country but also for the fun and adventure.'

One of his recruits, Jimmy Dunning (later to become Vice-President of the Commando Association) recalls meeting Leslie for the first time at Amesbury during this interview; he was impressed by 'his size and bearing, and his obvious desire to get at Jerry and beat him. I liked his offensive spirit and bright-eyed enthusiasm.' Clearly, F Troop was fashioned in Leslie's own image and likeness.

A week later, on Sunday evening, 21 July 1940, the men of F Troop arrived in their chosen 'home town' of Weymouth, where they were comfortably billeted in private houses; the officers were installed in their HQ at 20 Brunswick Terrace, right on the front, where they were 'very comfortably provided for by one Mrs Hart'. This in itself was a revolutionary innovation. The men would have been used to living in Army barracks, eating Army food, sleeping in dormitories in Army beds and spending much of their time performing routine and often irksome Army duties – on guard, domestic chores, admin, etc. In the Commandos, all that was swept aside, and the men were billeted with local people – families with a room to spare or seaside landladies eager to supplement their war-affected income. This arrangement had advantages all round – the men could focus entirely on their commando training and preparation, and the Commando itself had no need to employ the usual long tail of cooks, orderlies and administrators. The system fostered self-reliance, too, with every man taking responsibility for his own domestic arrangements – and for arriving on parade on time and properly dressed.

The men were paid at the going rate by their own regiments and retained their regimental cap badges. They also received a daily subsistence allowance of 13s 4d (about 67p today) for officers and 6s 8d (34p) for other ranks, plus a wartime ration card. The allowance easily covered accommodation, and the ration card enabled a landlady to buy sufficient rationed foods – meat, butter, cheese, tea, sugar – for two meals a day. For many of the (mostly young) men, this 'taste of home' brought other benefits, mental and physical – a friendly family or landlady to come back to after a hard day of mortal combat training; someone perhaps to wash your clothes or darn your socks; in many cases, a pretty daughter or a lonely widow to court; just a sense of being 'at home' during troubled times. Some of the younger lads no doubt benefited from a spot of 'mothering' – and the occasional verbal 'clip round the ear' for bringing muddy boots into the house or waving their rifles around (for weapons had to be kept close to hand at all times).

The next day, F Troop joined the other men of 4 Commando, in the exuberantly styled and recently requisitioned Weymouth Pavilion, for a welcome speech from their commanding officer, the dashing cavalryman, Percy Legard. Apart from his elegant good looks, he was also an Olympic pentathlete who had taken part in Hitler's infamous Berlin Olympics in 1936 and claimed to have given the dictator a V-sign during one of the parades. He is also credited with the design of 4 Commando's extraordinary 'death's head' badge that was issued to all officers in the early days.

After a bellowed 'Atten – shun!' from the new Regimental Sergeant Major, 'Jumbo' Morris, Legard wasted no time in assuring his men that their purpose was to go on the offensive. As Dunning describes in his book, *It Had to be Tough*, 'We would go out across the Channel in small boats to carry out raids on the enemy's coastline and start a reign of terror on the Nazis. We would hit first, hard and often.' There was a murmur of approval from the men. But first, they 'had to settle down, and start to get fighting fit'. The training would be 'demanding and tough', and anyone not up to standard would be 'returned to unit'.

Leslie wasted no time, and on the Monday morning he and his troop started training for their first mission. He devised a rigorous programme of 'fitness exercises, weapon training and elementary field work', which included 'marching at speed with full kit, cliff and mountain climbing, unarmed combat, seamanship, navigation by night and day, signalling and radio communications, demolition and sabotage, street fighting, occupation of towns, overcoming all obstacles, driving all types of motor vehicles, fieldcraft and first aid'. They started with marching.

Thirty-mile marches with kit sufficient for prolonged action were part of routine training, but there was also an emphasis on shorter distances and higher speeds, with a target of covering 'seven miles in an hour and [being] able to fight at the end of it'. Getting fifty men of differing heights and standards of fitness accustomed to a much faster pace than they were used to was quite a challenge in itself. There was lots of singing, an obstacle course or firing practice to look forward to and, if those didn't work, always the ultimate threat of an ignominious RTU (return to unit) to spur them along. Dunning acquired the nickname 'Double-Dunning', because if the men didn't sing up he doubled the pace.

Later that first week, Leslie organized a night exercise, with Weymouth Bay as the French coast and the Commandos mounting an attack on German troops forming ammunition dumps and preparing barges for the invasion of England. They were expected to get back to their destroyer by 0330 hrs, and he was pleased that they 'displayed very creditable zeal', despite some elementary mistakes like 'bunching at gaps, crossing the skyline, and failure of individuals to keep in touch with one another'. By the next night the men had learned from the earlier mistakes, and point section, led by Hutton, managed to work right round the objective without being observed by 'the enemy'. They also discovered that the 'nightingale' signal they were using was a bit of a giveaway if used away from woodland, so they reverted to good old 'tu-whit tu-whoo' instead.

The weekend saw some light 'normal' training, and swimming and sunbathing for the men on Sunday, whilst Leslie attended a Troop Commanders' Conference and prepared for another night exercise the following week – attacking and destroying a lightly-guarded enemy ammunition dump – and a lengthy route march. Already, Leslie could see signs of improvement in his Troop, though the section leaders needed to exercise more hands-on control and issue clearer orders. He was delighted when the Troop won the route march, though he felt they needed more cross-country running as a team.

With a German invasion still actively awaited, the training exercises were deliberately realistic, with lights blacked out, signposts removed, bridges and other key installations actively guarded and the coastline regularly patrolled. There was blank ammunition and thunderflashes to simulate gunfire, grenades and explosives, and 'plenty of scuffles and fights when the action was at close quarters'. A healthy dose of inter-unit and indeed inter-service rivalry and competition, with each 'side' determined to 'put up a good show', helped as well, whilst climbing walls and fences, jumping streams and ditches, wading through rivers and generally overcoming obstacles of all shapes and sizes was felt to be much more useful for getting the men fit than any amount of PT.

On Thursday, 1 August all the officers were taken out by the Colonel on a 'night scheme' to attack Wormwell Aerodrome from four different directions, successfully as it turned out, despite a strong RAF guard. 'Excellent. Just what I want', is Legard's comment in the margin of the Troop Diary. So useful was this exercise felt to be that the whole Commando repeated it five days later, with F Troop ordered to blow up two bridges after a fast approach across broken country, using rubber-soled shoes rather than boots to deaden the sound of their approach. Leslie was disappointed to report that they had had to wait at the objective for several of the men to catch up – 'special training' for them in future. Later, the officers were treated to tea in the RAF mess and 'an interesting hour inspecting planes and articles from destroyed German planes in their museum'.

Thursday, 8 August marked the start of a change in the routine, when normal training was interrupted to announce four days leave for the Troop, to commence the following day. In fact, the first half of that day was taken up with PT and preparations for the CO's inspection at midday at the Pavilion, in full marching order. This didn't take long, and most of the Troop managed to catch the 1325 train to London. Leslie must have set off in great good humour, as both he and another Troop leader were presented by Legard with special Commando daggers for the performance and turnout of their men over the two weeks. The daggers were specially designed for surprise attack and had a slender double-edged blade with a sharp stabbing point and good cutting edges that could 'easily penetrate a ribcage' and make a clean and effective cut to a main artery. Leslie's mother and sisters may well have had mixed feelings when he brought this knife home that summer as a 'present from Weymouth'.

Four days later, they were back, for 'the most strenuous week's training we have done'. This included rowing ('improving well'); long distance running ('good'); 300yd swims by day ('whole troop except six completed the course') and by night ('quite a weird experience but as the water was warm the men thoroughly enjoyed it'); rock climbing ('I was incapacitated after the three miles yesterday having strained the tendon in my left leg'); a night exercise ('too much noise made . . . by men coughing and they must be taught to control this sort of thing'); and finally a fifteen-mile route march completed in just under four hours ('the troops were prepared to march on rather than stop').

The next weekend was drill parades and the Sports Meeting – 'a grand show it was'. F Troop's hopes were pinned mainly on Corporal Nunn, who was strongly fancied to win the 100yds Sprint. Unfortunately, he fell at the start of his heat, though he made up for this catastrophe later with his performance in Grenade Throwing, where he came second with a throw of 57yds. The Troop also did well in Accuracy with a fourth, a third place in the Three Mile race and a creditable seventh in the One Mile Bicycle Race.

After all this excitement, it was back to work, with a week of night and day exercises designed to test the Troop in its defensive role against German invasion and in attack mode against the Germans across the Channel. In the first of these, they camped at Blandford, where they were immediately fired on by a bunch of pretend enemy parachutists. These they quickly rounded up in a fierce frontal attack led by Dunning, and Leslie was pleased with the prompt way his junior officers put his plans into action. His main concern was that 'few of them know how to give a fire order and consequently our fire lacked control.'

During the first few weeks at Weymouth weapons training was limited. They all had rifles, and every officer had a pistol, but that was about it, apart from a few Bren guns, which were in such short supply that they were kept under lock and key at the Colonel's HQ. The rifles were Short Magazine Lee Enfields (which had been in service since 1895), with an eighteen-inch bayonet attachment – 'They don't like it up 'em, sir', as Corporal Jones used to say in 'Dad's Army'. Thanks to a special screw-on attachment, the gun was also able to hurl a grenade at an enemy operating behind cover. The officers' pistols were either Webleys or Enfields and fired a .38 calibre round from a six-round chamber. At first, there was virtually no spare ammunition – most of it had been left on the beaches at Dunkirk. The men were allowed only twenty-five rounds each on their Troop's first firing experience at Lulworth, with a couple of magazines left over for two junior officers to fire the Bren gun at a 4ft target.

A couple of weeks later, the Troop had a go with a Boys anti-tank rifle, also kept locked up at HQ and issued for training on a rota basis. This 5ft-long monster fired .55 calibre armour-piercing shells, using a tripod or rest, and gave the operator a nasty kick in the shoulder. The bullets tended to bounce off most of their intended targets as tank armour was strengthened, so it was of little practical use except against pillboxes, gun-emplacements, etc.

Towards the end of August, Leslie started preparing his Troop for its week as 'Duty Troop' guarding sensitive local installations and possible invasion landing sites. Tension was high, for the month had seen a massive intensification of German bombing raids on RAF stations, as a prelude (it was feared) to the intended invasion. Mortifyingly for Leslie, F Troop did not distinguish itself at guard duty. 'A very Black Day for F Troop' is the diary entry for 31 August. A trooper was found asleep on guard duty, and was then charged, brought before the CO and 'naturally returned to unit'. His section leader, Corporal Nunn, who was the Guard Commander that night, was also charged and ordered to be RTU'd. This gave Leslie a problem – Nunn was his sports day champion grenade thrower, amongst other things – and he must have been relieved, after an interview with the CO the next day, when Legard 'was very decent over the matter, and has allowed Nunn to stay in the Troop. I am sure Nunn has learned his lesson.'

'Three Days Country Life' is how Leslie labelled the next section of the diary, as troops were sent to various parts of the surrounding countryside and given specific targets to attack at different times, with instructions to 'live as far as possible on their wits'. Given three days to get from Blandford Forum to Verwood Station, 20 miles away, F Troop set out merrily in buses 'well prepared with snares etc', marched with full kit the ten miles to Witchampton and there made bivouacs 'out of branches of trees and various oddments that we managed to find'. Then they took up the defensive positions required by the exercise, sending out patrols throughout the night who worked on compass bearings which they had taken during the day.

The country boys amongst the troopers set the snares overnight to see if they could catch some supper, but these 'did not prove very successful'. However, half a dozen dead chickens miraculously appeared in the camp that morning, and Leslie managed to borrow a twelve-bore from a friendly farmer and bag a hare for the pot as well. They struck camp and marched the six miles to Woodlands, where they set up their second camp, sent out a foraging party and started to prepare for a 'Big Troop Supper'. With a stew of hare, chicken and rabbit, and 'every variety of vegetable', cooked by Corporal Shepherd, this was pronounced a great success and provided a good foundation for an inter-section night stalk.

On the last day, and in good time, they marched to Verwood, where they carried out a 'very realistic anti-parachutist scheme' on the heathland near the station, surrounding and taking into captivity an alleged parachutist who bore a surprising resemblance to Colonel Legard.

The diary contains some wonderful pictures of the men preparing the bivouacs, climbing trees, rounding up fifth columnists, raiding 'enemy' orchards and preparing their bag for the pot – but the exercise had a serious side, too, and Leslie was pleased to note that the Troop was 'quick and able' to adapt itself to changing conditions, and that 'every man seemed well able to look after himself for food'. However, 'marching in a full pack on a hot day is very exhausting work.'

After this rural adventure there was an opportunity to practise another beach landing, this time at Elwell. Dunning notes that it had become clear fairly early on that 4 Commando was being trained up specifically for seaborne assaults rather than airborne (for which only 2 Commando was being prepared). Unfortunately, spare landing craft to practise on were in short supply, just like the guns, so they had to improvise, using rowing boats and motor launches borrowed from civilians locally, or get what practice they could with spells of duty on board Royal Navy vessels based at Weymouth or nearby ports.

These landings from the sea had to be practised by day rather than at night, to avoid the risk of alarming the local population about an imminent invasion. It was during one of these daytime practices that the Troop nearly lost a man. Having completed a 'raid' inland, the Troop returned to its requisitioned motor launch, only to find that the boat was unable to come close enough inshore for the men to wade out. They therefore had no alternative but to swim out, in full kit – a distance of about 200yds according to the Troop diary. Unfortunately, one of the men got cramp halfway across and had to be towed to the launch by his section leader, whilst several others got into difficulties. 'I want to do more deep sea swimming', came the order from Troop Leader Porky Young, the next day.

Then, on 7 September, a Saturday, came a real emergency. Everyone was off duty, back in their billets or in the cinemas and pubs around the town; there was only a skeleton staff on duty at Commando HQ in the Pavilion. Suddenly, the order came through for the whole Commando to muster in the car park 'in fighting order'. This was no easy matter to organize – with 500 men spread around the town, the only way to contact them was word of mouth. It took hours, and was made more difficult by the blackout and the constant nagging of Air Raid Wardens to 'put out that light'. By 2300 hrs most of the men were finally mustered, whereupon church bells started ringing out. This caused more chaos – church bells had been silenced throughout the land since Dunkirk and were only to be rung in the event of an enemy invasion by sea or air.

Immediately, the word went around that, as Dunning put it, 'Jerry has landed – but where, and what were we going to do about it?' According to his account, no one had actually stopped to imagine this scenario and prepare a plan of action. There was no information, no contingency plan and no ready orders. They just had to sit in the car park, rifles and grenades at the ready, and wait. Midnight came and went, and the long night dragged on until finally, as dawn was breaking, the order came to 'stand down' – 'Sorry chaps, false alarm.' Nevertheless, the Commando had to 'stand to' again the next two nights, once in the car park and finally, 'now that we were better organized', sleeping in deckchairs at the Royal George Hotel. This must all have put a terrible dampener on Sergeant Llewellyn's wedding that Saturday, notwithstanding the Troop Guard of Honour and 'canteen of cutlery' that was his wedding present.

Only years later, reading Churchill's memoirs, was Dunning able to discover what had happened. General Headquarters of the Home Forces had received information, backed by aerial photographs, that the Germans had stepped up their invasion preparations – barges had been assembled, and enemy soldiers had been seen practising the embarkation of troops and equipment at several places along the French coast. These stories gained added potency when four German spies were captured after landing near Dungeness on Romney Marsh in Kent. They eventually confessed to being on a spying mission and confirmed that German troops were ready to invade. (Three of these men were subsequently hanged, and the fourth, having given evidence against his colleagues, was imprisoned for the rest of the war).

GHQ had no alternative but to conclude that an invasion was imminent and, at 2000 hrs on 7 September, issued the code word 'Cromwell' to home commanders, the signal to get ready to fight. The word was passed down the chain of command to all units with electrifying speed, church bells rang out across the country and chaos reigned. Neither Churchill nor his Chiefs of Staff had been informed that the code word had been issued, and one can imagine that his reaction on finding out would have been 'interesting'. The next morning, a new system of graduated warnings was instituted, so that on future occasions vigilance could be increased without causing nationwide panic – and 4 Commando settled down to ask itself some questions.

As Dunning puts it: 'How can one have an effective mobile force if the force earmarked for this role [i.e. the Commandos] has no means of mobility apart from the CO's vehicle, the Admin 15cwt truck, a few private cars [including Leslie's] and 500 pairs of feet?' The answer, of course, was that you couldn't, and since most of the Army's vehicle fleet had been abandoned at Dunkirk, Legard instructed his troop leaders and their men 'to beg, borrow or scrounge' some transport.

Perhaps not surprisingly, the result was a small and bizarre cavalcade of cars, vans, motorcycles and several old bicycles, one of them with its trade plate still advertising Lipton's tea. Unfortunately, several of these vehicles arrived hotly pursued by their owners and the local constabulary and had to be returned whence they came, thankfully with 'no questions asked'. The bicycles had given Legard an idea, though, and on 11 September the diary records that the entire Commando embarked in buses for Tidworth and returned 73 miles and five and a half hours later on brand new khaki-coloured Army bikes, complete with special fittings for rifles to be strapped between the saddle and the handlebars. No gears, though.

It must have been quite a sight, five hundred Commandos cycling through the Dorset countryside in shorts and shirts. Many had never ridden a bike before, and no doubt there were plenty of sore backsides and bruises, not to mention surprised landladies who had to find storage space for the bikes amongst the best china and chintz curtains – but F Troop 'rode very well together' and, the next day, set off to practise 'cycling in tactical groups'.

At the weekend, F Troop and five others were sent off for a week's camping and 'living off the land' on the Ridgeway. Leslie was delighted when the CO gave him permission to use a couple of unoccupied huts on the site, and his car was used to ferry blankets, army greatcoats and other gear over to the camping site. Leslie clearly relished this opportunity to get to know his men better – though he was troubled by what he saw as a slackening of discipline 'owing to the comparatively easy time the men were having in billets'. He gave them a good talking to on the subject and felt that by the end of the week there had already been some improvement. They did lots of 'day schemes' (mock raids and sorties), map reading and 'plenty of cycling', but also enjoyed a 'well organized' camp, with an efficient kitty system ('audited and found to be correct'), and meals provided by 'a chirpy but capable RASC corporal [who] was installed as chief cook and bottle washer'. The food was so good that 'there was a protest meeting held asking for more'.

The men had a good hot meal at lunchtime every day; in the evenings they were on their own, working in pairs on what became known as the 'Me and my pal' system. From their makeshift bivouacs they set out each evening on 'nocturnal forays to forage [for] chicken, rabbits and vegetables from the neighbouring farmland, greatly assisted by advice and guidance from one Stan Harris, an ex-poacher and regular soldier from the Royal Tank Regiment. He showed them how to lay traps for rabbits and how to 'approach chicken coops', as well as 'other poaching ruses' such as how to overcome obstacles and deal with barbed wire without being heard.

When they returned to Weymouth at the weekend, it was to a visit to the Commando by Admiral of the Fleet Sir Roger Keyes. He was something of a hero to the Commandos. A serving naval officer in the First World War and commander of a battleship, he became an MP and, at the start of the Second War, a fierce critic of Chamberlain's government. He was a strong advocate of carrying the fight to the enemy as hard as possible and in June 1940 had been made Director of Combined Operations, responsible for implementing training plans for the Commandos and raids on the enemy coast.

Keyes lunched with the Troop Leaders at the Gloucester Hotel, inspected the Commando and watched some weapons training and the start of another exercise to round up parachutists. He was also treated by Legard, the former cavalry officer, to a 'ride-past' by two troops on their bicycles, an incident which led to 4 Commando becoming known as the 'Cavalry Commando' and being given a yellow and red lanyard to wear, the cavalry colours. Next was an extraordinary 'swim past' off Weymouth Pier. The whole Commando, dressed in denim and complete with waterproofed rifles, rounded the Pier in formation and swam breast stroke out to sea, then side stroke back to shore, where Keyes took the salute on the Pier.

All that week, the Commando was on high alert – as the 4 Commando War Diary reports: 'The enemy were supposed to be all ready with boats to come over.' Keyes reflected the concern in a letter to the Commando a couple of days after his visit, when he promised, 'Commando would soon be given the opportunity to perform the functions for which they had been formed', but emphasized that, in the meantime, 'It was essential to place their services at the disposal of Home Forces in the present emergency.'

In the last week of September the Troop started making plans for an extended week-long cycle tour. Initially, Leslie hoped to visit one of his friends from BEF days, his namesake Captain Peter Young, who was a Troop Leader in 3 Commando, stationed at Plymouth. Unfortunately, he was on leave, so they fixed instead on the pretty fishing village of Clovelly, 120 miles away in North Devon. Leaving Weymouth early on 23 September, they cycled 50 miles to Honiton Clyst near Exeter, where they pitched camp in a shady spot near a river and some of them enjoyed an evening in the local pub and 'a handsome meal supplied by a gracious hostess'.

The next day, they set off for Clovelly, Dunning going on ahead with the equipment in the accompanying lorry to recce the next campsite. He had done something to his foot and was in considerable pain – 'though he bore it with great fortitude; a good man is Dunning'. At Withleigh they did a 'job of good work for the amused villagers', reaching Clovelly ('a most delightful spot') at around 1700 hrs, where they were warmly welcomed at the Red Lion on the harbour wall by the proprietor and his daughter. The author of the Troop Diary was impressed at how quickly the daughter became 'Juni' to Captain Porky Young.

On the Wednesday morning the Troop's No 2 section was set to defend itself against an attack by the other section, and the ensuing bout of unarmed combat was 'so fierce as to leave doubt regarding the ultimate victory'. The morning's entertainment was completed with some inglorious shooting practice, which left a seagull 500yds away unharmed after a ragged bout of forty rounds' firing. After lunch they borrowed rowing boats from some local fishermen and managed to catch a fine haul of mackerel whilst practising their skills with the oars. In the middle of the afternoon the lifeboat was called out, the Troop helping to launch it in record time.

They struck camp on Thursday morning, and the villagers turned out to wave them off – 'including the landlord, his daughter and his daughter's most delightful friend' – then set off for Barnstaple, where they arrived about noon and stayed until the evening, enjoying some free time, before reconvening and setting off for a memorable night-time cycle ride in pitch black and pouring rain. They stopped for a sleep at 0300 hrs in air raid shelters at Taunton bus station, before starting out again 'damp and rather miserable' a few hours later. Dunning came to the rescue and managed to arrange a fry-up in a nearby café, whose owners frantically prepared eggs and sausages for fifty cold and famished soldiers – 'the most welcome meal we had eaten for some time'. It was just as well they had a good start, for another torrential downpour stopped them at a roadside inn in the late afternoon. Rather than camp as they had intended, the decision was made to cycle on to Weymouth, arriving in the early evening to the news that all leave was cancelled due to another invasion scare.

After spending the next few days coping with the invasion flap, the Troop spent a day honing their street-fighting skills. This included an exercise to occupy an empty house. Unfortunately, the scout picked the wrong house, which only became clear when they burst into a bedroom to find 'a beautiful damsel asleep in bed'.

On 4 October Keyes made good his promise that the Commando would soon be able to start doing the job for which it had been intended and announced that, with effect from midnight on 6 October, it would come under the direct operational control of the War Office, with instructions to be prepared to move at twenty-four hours' notice. The Commando would soon be moving to Scotland, and he sent them all off for four days of rest and home comforts.

Chapter 7

With the Commandos – Scotland

The arrival in Scotland must have seemed like a cold shower to the men after their interesting and amusing 'summer holiday' on the south coast. They fetched up at a railway siding on the Clyde at 0600 hrs, bleary-eyed after the long journey. What met them later that afternoon, though, was not another cosy, friendly billet, but HMS *Glengyle*, a converted merchant ship equipped with landing craft for amphibious operations.

The *Glengyle* had been built for trade in the Far East but was requisitioned soon after the start of the war along with her sister ships, *Glenroy* and *Glenearn*. The conversion to wartime use was pretty basic – there were some cabins set aside for officers above decks, but the men had to sleep in mess decks in the cargo holds, where the accommodation was sparse and cramped. The only furniture comprised tables and benches for eating, whilst the men slept in hammocks slung across the living accommodation – those who arrived early enough to bag one.

Before long, they heard the piercing noise of a bosun's whistle over the tannoy for the first time, and the words 'D'yer hear there – D'yer hear there?' blared out, accompanied by a stream of unfamiliar nautical jargon. No romantic Army bugle reveille, but rather a raucous chorus of 'Wakey, wakey – you've 'ad yer time!', followed by 'Lash up and stow!' as the hammocks were whisked down and the ship was made ready for the day's activities.

They were soon on the move, as the *Glengyle* edged down the Clyde, rounded the Isle of Bute, sailed up Loch Fyne and then anchored off Inverary, the ship dwarfed by the majestic peaks of the mountains of Argyll. Dunning's main concern was that they might well have to climb them – as indeed they did.

But the first task was to become familiar with the ten LCAs (Landing Craft Assault) on board. These highly regarded small boats were used throughout the war to ferry men and equipment from ship to beach. With their low draught and armoured sides they offered a good measure of protection against small-arms fire and could accommodate up to thirty-five troops, plus equipment. The men sat in three rows running the length of the craft and could be disembarked quickly down the ramp in the bows. Top speed was 8 knots, with a cruising range of about 50 miles.

The Commando was the first unit to board the *Glengyle*, so time had to be spent on such basics as working out how best to get troops from their mess decks to the boat stations on the main deck. Once all were aboard they were told to 'Lower Away!', then the craft lurched down to the water and, with a roar from their V8 engines, set off for shore. Here, speed was drummed into the men as an absolutely essential lifesaver. The natural reaction on landing was to drop to the ground if the beach was being swept by enemy gunfire, but the hope that this might reduce the risk of being hit was a false one. 'Out of the LCAs and split-arse up and across the beach – never, NEVER stop!' was the order of the day.

The days in Loch Fyne were easily filled. Landing practice first thing, followed by a long trek over the hills (many of them over 1,000ft), then perhaps some stalking, or an opportunity to practise with live ammunition. After supper, more night-time landing practice, with perhaps assault and re-embarkation training, or a night march over the trackless hills. Leslie was pleased that F Troop managed the night exercises without losing anyone, despite difficulties with night navigation and sub-section control.

After two weeks on board it was time to move on again. There must have been a certain amount of relief when they were ordered ashore for Oban, as both the food and the accommodation on board *Glengyle* had been pretty basic. Unfortunately, the advance party ruled the Oban billets out as unsuitable, so they spent the night in tents at Inverary. The next day, Leslie was ordered to march the entire Commando the sixteen miles to the railway station at Dalmally, where they were to entrain for Ayr. Again, fate wasn't smiling, and it bucketed down all day; to cap it all, there was no train waiting for them and very little shelter. When eventually they got to Ayr at midnight, there were only enough billets for just half the Commando, and the rest spent a damp and chilly night in the grandstand at Ayr racecourse.

This was an unsettling start to the remainder of their training, but worse was to come. On 6 November their charismatic CO Colonel Legard announced that his Commando was to be amalgamated with 7 Commando, to form No 3 Special Service Battalion under Lieutenant Colonel Dudley Lister MC, as part of a plan hatched by Churchill and Keyes to launch large-scale commando operations, now that ships like the *Glengyle* were available. His second in command, Major Kerr, would be taking over command of 4 Commando, which was to be re-designated No 1 Company. Reluctantly, Legard was returning to his regiment.

Lister was a 'character'. He was a regular soldier, not just a wartime recruit, and a veteran of the Great War, when he was awarded the Military Cross. Like Legard, he was an international sportsman and, as well as being Army heavyweight boxing champion, had represented his country at the 'Golden Gloves' contest in New York before the war. He was tall, well built and rugged, and a complete fitness fanatic, with a particular penchant for speed and endurance marches, which he led from the front. He firmly believed that fitness was the answer to everything, including fighting and success with the ladies.

Key figures in the training programme were the famous duo of Fairbairn and Sykes, who had previously worked together in the Shanghai Municipal Police and organized their riot squad. On the outbreak of war they decided to return to Britain, where they quickly became engaged in training Special Forces. In addition to pistol-shooting and sniper work, these two were masters of close-quarter fighting, unarmed combat and every known method of personal attack and defence. They were responsible for introducing a new spirit of ruthless personal aggression which, perhaps due to British notions of 'fair play', had only been evident up to that time (if at all) in the use of the bayonet. They tried to instil in the men the idea that, when dealing with an enemy who was prepared to kill at all costs, the only tactic that could possibly succeed was to be equally brutal. There was no room for concepts of 'fair play' or mercy, still less squeamishness or distaste – if you were going to win, you had to be prepared to fight and kill, not just with a gun but with knives, coshes, even your bare hands, however savage that might seem.

The courses taught by Fairbairn and Sykes included lessons on delivering blows without a weapon (using the edge of the hand, for example, or the chin); getting free from grasps or holds on all parts of the body; how to impose an effective hold (the thumb hold, for example, or the Japanese stranglehold); and how to disarm and throw an opponent. Sykes reputedly ended many of his lectures with the words 'and then kick him in the testicles' as a way of ensuring that, whatever tactic was used, the assailant would be in poor shape to fight back.

At the end of November the whole battalion was sent on fourteen days leave, and on returning to Troon they were told to pack and prepare for a move. Trucks arrived to take them to Gourock and the *Glengyle*, which soon cast off and sailed down the loch to anchor off the Isle of Arran, where it was joined by two more Glen ships and a troopship. Stores were brought out by lighter, and a host of small craft swarmed busily around the troopships. There were several exercises involving much larger numbers of commandos than hitherto, including one at night with landings on the east coast of the island. The Commando was abuzz with rumours of impending action.

But after two weeks the excitement fizzled out, and it was announced that the operation for which this large force of commandos had been training, the capture of the small island of Pantelleria off the coast of Sicily for possible use as a staging post in the Mediterranean, had been postponed.

The men were disappointed and, with Christmas approaching, some went AWOL for the holiday season – only to be RTU'd as soon as they got back. For the rest, billets were found on the Isle of Arran, and most enjoyed a pleasant Christmas with local families. Dunning remembers this as quite a jolly time, when the men were able to observe a very different way of life to the one they were used to and to mix with other Commando units, meeting well-known personalities like the actor David Niven (who wrote about the training in his autobiography *The Moon's a Balloon*); Churchill's son Randolph; and the novelist Evelyn Waugh, who depicted some of his experiences in his novel *Officers and Gentlemen*.

Back on board the *Glengyle* four weeks later, morale was at a low ebb. 'Shimi' Lovat, who had arrived in Scotland before Christmas as Keyes' representative for the training programme, writes in his memoir *March Past* of the poor relations that existed between the soldiers of Keyes' 'Cavalry Commando', as he still called them, and the naval types on the *Glengyle* under its captain, Lieutenant Commander Kershaw, who seemed to regard them all as a bit of a nuisance sent to make his highly-polished ship untidy. The combination of naval 'bull', the endless nautical jargon (which the soldiers enjoyed imitating), the frustrations of postponed operations, and the sheer collective stress of 400 fit young men cooped up at close quarters, was clearly in danger of causing an explosion. Keyes himself came up to give the men a pep talk and promised that he had no intention of 'allowing this bright sword to rust in the Highlands' – before sending them off on two weeks leave.

On their return, there was a call for volunteers to make up numbers for an operation to capture the Mediterranean island of Rhodes, and some did indeed sail in the *Glengyle* for final training in Egypt. But this operation had to be called off, too, when Hitler invaded Greece. The volunteers later took part in a raid on Bardia in North Africa in April 1941, but were then captured during the evacuation of Crete and spent the rest of the war as prisoners in Germany – as Dunning puts it, 'a disappointing end to an adventure that had started so hopefully in Weymouth'.

The rest stayed on with their landladies on Arran, and then returned to Troon to await events.

Chapter 8

The Lofoten Island Raid

On 20 February 1941 Leslie informed his troop that they were going on an exercise on the west coast of Scotland and that they would be away for about a fortnight. 'Yet another exercise' are the words that Jimmy Dunning used to describe the news. He can be forgiven. Throughout this early period in the history of the Commandos there had been a strong sense amongst the men that their senior officers had been 'making it up as they went along', and certainly both Lord Lovat in *March Past* and Waugh in *Officers and Gentlemen* confirm this impression. The watchword was 'Order – Counter Order – Disorder', and Dunning relates how, amongst the good folk of Troon (which was home to the Commando), they were known as the 'Troon BEF', BEF standing for 'Back Every Fortnight'.

Once again, the men grumblingly gave notice to their landladies – but this time, the rumours of 'a job' persisted, and they strengthened when, later that day, they were issued with sea kitbags and special commando 'fighting knives' and told to parade early the next morning in full marching order. They were quickly loaded on to requisitioned trucks and set off for the port of Gourock, where they found HMS *Queen Emma*, a converted cargo ship, awaiting their arrival.

They sat on the dock and waited dubiously for the order to board. By late afternoon they had embarked, been allocated troop decks and had set sail for Scapa Flow, Britain's historic naval base in the waters off Orkney, accompanied by HMS *Princess Beatrix* and an escort of destroyers. It is easy to imagine the sense of growing anticipation and excitement amongst the men of F Troop, especially when they heard – 'counter order' – that No 3 Special Service Battalion had now ceased to exist and was to be known as 4 Commando once again. What was going on?

At the end of the winter of 1939/40, while the British Expeditionary Force was in France fighting the Phoney War, Norway's strategic importance to Hitler as a source of iron ore had been recognized, and four destroyers had been sent to mine its coastal waters. But the move came too late, and

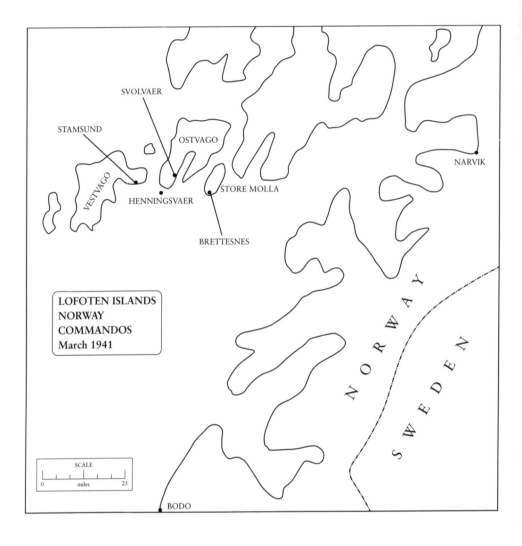

in April German troops started pouring into the country by sea and by air. King Haakon pledged resistance, and Britain promised help but could only spare a few half-trained volunteer Territorial battalions with little heavy weaponry, poorly organized supplies and no idea how to fight in Norway's mountainous and snow-bound countryside. A spirited and initially successful attack was launched against the Germans in Narvik, but by June King Haakon and his government had fled into exile in London, and the Germans had installed a puppet government in Oslo led by the Norwegian fascist, Vidkun Quisling.

Defeat in Norway was a significant blow to Allied morale and resources, with 4,500 men killed, 15 warships sunk and over 100 planes brought down during the early fighting. On the other hand, whilst Hitler had secured his iron ore supplies, and some naval and air bases that he could use later against Russia, the occupation involved the major drain on German resources of deploying 350,000 troops.

When, six months later, Keyes reported back to Churchill on low morale within the newly-formed Commandos, the idea of using them to launch a surprise attack on the Norwegian coastline was suggested. Churchill saw this as a means both of harming the German war effort and of contributing to the goal he had set for the Commandos of harassing German forces all along the North Sea and Atlantic coast of mainland Europe. He thought the raid would bring comfort and encouragement to the oppressed Norwegians, and that, by punishing a few 'quislings' (supporters of the puppet prime minister), the raiders might help discourage further collaboration. At its very least, it would give the Commandos and the Royal Navy something to do and show the British public that Britain was back on the offensive.

The suggested target for the raid was the Lofoten Islands, a small archipelago off the coast of Norway with a population today of about 25,000 people, 100 miles inside the Arctic Circle. These beautiful islands, with their dramatic mountains, open sea and sheltered bays, formed a key part of the Norwegian herring and cod fishing industry. Oil produced from the fish was being shipped to Germany to extract glycerine, a vital ingredient in the manufacture of high explosives. The oil was also a source of vitamin A and B for German troops. Four factories, one at each of the islands' ports of Stamsund, Henningsvaer, Svolvaer and Brettesnes, accounted for almost half of Norway's fish oil output, and it was all going to Germany.

The naval chiefs gave the plan the go ahead, despite their initial nervousness that it might divert destroyers from their vital task of escorting convoys in the Atlantic. The COs of the two Commandos selected for the raid, Durnford-Slater of 3 Commando and Lister of 4 Commando, were given a secret briefing and told to inform their men that they were going on another exercise. Only once they were in Scapa Flow, five weeks later, did Lister address his troop leaders and give them details of the plan and the training programme for Operation Claymore – the Lofoten Islands Raid.

On *Queen Emma* and *Princess Beatrix* the Commandos went into overdrive, for a week of intensive training. Men were shrouded in a complete security lock-down, with all shore leave and communication with families forbidden. The LCA drill took on a new sense of urgency, and each troop was rehearsed in its allotted part in the raid: establishing a bridgehead, securely cordoning off and searching key buildings, attacking potential enemy-held strongpoints, dealing with snipers, setting up road blocks and anti-aircraft positions.

There were talks and lectures below decks on key topics, and section leaders were issued with silk maps of Norway, for use in the event of their being captured or left behind in occupied Norway. The maps were to be sewn into the collars of battledress blouses, and a specially vetted East End tailor was brought on board to undertake the work and also to help attach special fly buttons that could be used as compasses. Such was the concern over security that the tailor was held for a while at the naval base when the ships sailed.

Volunteers from the exiled Norwegian Army were recruited to act as guides and interpreters, and they used their time on board to teach the men useful Norwegian phrases like 'I am a friend', 'Take cover' and 'Are you a Nazi?', which probably helped to pass the time, as did the evening sessions of 'housey-housey' (bingo), and the statutory naval daily 'tot of rum'. The weather was wet, cold and very stormy, which must have added to the dramatic atmosphere, as did the occasional visits from German reconnaissance planes before they were chased off by ship- and shore-based anti-aircraft guns.

On Saturday, 1 March, just after midnight, the *Queen Emma* and the *Princess Beatrix* slipped their moorings and, accompanied by the remainder of 'Rebel Force' (its codename), the five destroyers, HMS *Somali*, *Eskimo*, *Tartar*, *Legion* and *Bedouin*, headed north-west for the Faroe Islands. It is easy to imagine the atmosphere of pent-up nervous excitement on board, even if, for some, the glamour may have worn off fairly quickly; it was a rough crossing, and most of the men were violently seasick.

The Danish Faroe Islands, about 200 miles from Scotland, lie half way between Norway and Iceland, as the North Atlantic shades into the Norwegian Sea. They had been pre-emptively occupied by British troops in April 1940, three days after Germany's invasion of the Danish mainland, in order to strengthen British control of the North Atlantic. The flotilla docked at Skaalefjord for the destroyers to refuel at 1900 hrs, but nobody was allowed ashore; Operation Claymore was 'on', and the darkened ships were officially sealed.

Five hours later, Rebel Force sailed again, maintaining a course as far to the north as possible in order to avoid being spotted by the daily Luftwaffe weather flight. For this first part of the two-day crossing to Norway the sea was again very rough, with low cloud and frequent snow showers, and they had only fulmars and other petrels for company. One of the men who kept a diary of the trip, Ken Phillott, describes the discomfort of being crowded into a small ship 'with a very shallow draught and made top-heavy with landing craft. Anyone who knows the North Sea, even in summer, is aware of its roughness – but this was winter. That ship did everything but turn upside down, and I am sure that everyone was seasick – even the Captain.'

After two days of uncomfortable sailing, the weather eased as the Force started its approach to the Vestfjord and the Lofoten Islands, just after midnight, sailing in single line ahead and guided by the submarine HMS *Sunfish*. At 0430 hrs, when the Force split up, *Queen Emma* (carrying 4 Commando) headed in an easterly direction towards Svolvaer (the capital of the Lofotens) and Brettesnes, a small fishing village on the southern tip of the island of Store Molla, escorted by *Somali*, *Bedouin* and *Tartar*. *Princess Beatrix*, with *Legion* and *Eskimo* and carrying 3 Commando, made for Stamsund and Henningsvaer.

On *Queen Emma*, Lister and Kershaw, the ship's captain, were in a highly nervous state that night, brave and battle-hardened though they were. Neither man was in any doubt that the raid was viewed, at the highest levels, as an extremely significant one, with all eyes on their performance. They had had a difficult crossing, with the constant fear of attack by German U-boats or surface craft as they neared their destination; and, to make matters worse, there was disagreement about how to launch the raid itself.

Lister wanted the men to rest until 0400 hrs, with troops to be on parade on deck two hours later after breakfast, in the freezing cold, to await the launching of their landing craft two hours after that, with a final briefing for officers in between. His officers objected to the idea of exposing the men to the freezing conditions on deck for any longer than necessary. They were for launching the raid at dawn (around 0900) after a good breakfast, and allowing the men to stay in their hammocks fully dressed in the meantime. At midnight there was an uneasy compromise reached: to reduce the time to be spent on deck, but no full breakfast and no waiting until first light. Lister carried on firing off new orders, and the men were kept awake most of the night with a stream of loud 'D'yer hear there!' commands over the tannoy. Not a good start to the raid.

Lister's plan for 4 Commando's part in Operation Claymore was in fact quite straightforward, with a large margin of flexibility built in, as he had no idea whether they would meet substantial enemy opposition. He therefore kept troops in reserve to cope with unforeseen eventualities and to guard prisoners and quislings, or to distribute food to the islanders. He would lead the attack on Svolvaer itself in three waves, securing the post office, hotel, the mayor's and harbourmaster's offices, and a Luftwaffe wireless station first. They would then destroy a large fish factory and all the oil storage tanks. Meanwhile, his second-in-command, Major Kerr, was to lead another landing party (including Leslie's F Troop) to secure Store Molla, set up an anti-aircraft defence post, destroy the oil-producing and storage facilities on the island and capture any Germans or quislings. Durnford-Slater on *Princess Beatrix* had similar plans for 3 Commando at Stamsund and Henningsvaer.

In both ships, after the commanding officers' final briefing, the men were left alone with their thoughts, nervous, seasick and bored. Final letters to loved ones back home and last diary entries were written, then the long period of waiting to be tested, a period that began back in Weymouth in the summer, was at last coming to an end.

'Wakey-wakey, rise and shine!' The cry can't have come too soon for anyone on board. By 0400 hrs everyone was up and about, hammocks were stowed, tea and a bite of breakfast had been hurriedly swallowed by those that could, and the men were soon out on deck into the night, wearing two of everything against the sub-zero temperature, with water bottles filled and emergency rations (sufficient for 48 hours) packed. They were all wearing tin helmets, but the sensible ones had woolly hats as well to protect their ears from the intense cold. Lights were twinkling along the shore, but there were no warning shouts or shots, and it seemed that the vital element of surprise had been maintained.

The landing craft for Svolvaer were lowered and pulled away first, under the stern of HMS *Tartar*, at 0530 hrs, half an hour early in fact, as they were so close to the shore. F Troop and the others had to sit shivering in their LCAs as they watched them set off, whilst seven miles west along the coast, the parties for the other islands were following a similar pattern. Soon they were all in the inky, icy water and on their way, one destroyer following each party as it headed in towards the shore, halting a mile offshore because of the relatively shallow waters. The Commandos were on their own.

At 0610 hrs the raid began in earnest: HMS *Somali*, with Brigadier Haydon, the overall Force commander, on board with his staff, had peeled off from *Queen Emma*, *Bedouin* and *Tartar* just off Store Molla and, because of the radio silence, sailed west for Haydon to have a look for himself at how the other landings were going at Stamsund and Henningsvaer, 15 miles away. On the way over, a trawler (later found to be an armed German patrol boat, the *Krebs*) was spotted about two miles off, coming out from Svolvaer. The trawler was hailed off the bridge by a Norwegian speaker yelling 'Aloo! Aloo!' across the water, but she made off, and *Somali* opened fire. The trawler was hit but returned four rounds from a small gun in the bows. Three more shells from the *Somali*, one in the ammunition store, one in the wheelhouse and the third in the boiler room, finished her off. As smoke poured from the hull, and the boat drifted out of control, five survivors were seen in the water and were soon picked up: the first captives of the raid.

Meanwhile, at Svolvaer the landings were led by Lister himself in an LCA containing a handful of officers and junior officers, twenty-eight other ranks, six Norwegians including a pilot, and two Royal Navy signallers, accompanied by HMS *Tartar*. A second LCA followed on towards the west side of the harbour carrying an officer, fifteen other ranks, nineteen more Norwegians and Keyes' personal representative, 'Shimi' Lovat. As they headed in, arms at the ready and expecting a volley from the shore at every moment, the *Krebs* passed them, on the way to her fatal encounter with HMS *Somali*.

In almost complete silence, bar the occasional whispered command, the small flotilla moved slowly away from the *Emma*'s protective shelter. Across the water, the outline of mountains could just be seen against the sky, at their base the silent, sleeping town. Carefully, silently, they approached the jetty across the inky black water. As soon as they touched, the first men sprang up the iron ladders, those without gloves tearing their skin on the freezing rungs.

They climbed up on to the quayside, studded boots slipping on the icy surface which was covered with cod heads and other leftovers from the nearby fish-processing factory. Not a sound greeted them; the surprise was complete. Lister set up his headquarters in the harbourmaster's office, whilst the men went about their appointed tasks, occupying the hotel and the post office, pinpointing the installations marked for demolition, wrenching open factory doors and laying their charges. Within an hour explosions rocked the town, and all the main buildings had been secured. Several German ships in the harbour were destroyed, either by gunfire from the *Tartar* or by boarding parties from the shore – and, on one occasion, to the alarm of the Commandos, by both.

Three more LCAs landed, this time on the east side of the harbour near the 'Cuba' herring factory. They heard the shots that sank the *Krebs* out in the fjord. The Norwegian fishing fleet put to sea, with hundreds of small smacks and puffers dodging about offshore casting their nets into the icy sea, cheering and waving Norwegian flags at the friendly invaders.

The Commandos at first went about their work cautiously and efficiently, trained to be prepared and take no chances. But there was little or no opposition, and soon their activities were being followed by a growing crowd of jubilant Norwegian spectators, who hoisted flags and brought out refreshments to celebrate their short-term liberation. Lister distributed papers from the office of the harbourmaster, a suspected collaborator, to the crowds outside, and soon it became clear that old scores were being settled as quislings were pointed out to the invaders and arrested, and fires started mysteriously in buildings not listed amongst the official objectives.

Lovat records the gradual relaxing of tension as the morning wore on, and with it the dangers of relaxed discipline. Troops left their allotted posts on roadblocks and rooftops, the locals produced cakes and coffee, and something of a holiday atmosphere prevailed. Lovat's concern was that, had a German motorized column descended on the town at that moment, the Commandos might have given a poor account of themselves, so he was somewhat relieved when a Norwegian liaison officer spread a rumour that there was a German garrison just around the corner, and a force to neutralize this threat was quickly put together.

They set off in a makeshift convoy, led by a fish lorry with a Bren gun mounted on the cab, and the force leader, Lovat, and the Norwegian officer Linge with his revolver drawn, crammed inside. They were following the twisting road beside the fjord when, to their astonishment, around a blind corner, they ran into a column of Germans. The Norwegian's revolver went off, narrowly missing Lovat's knee cap, the lorry swerved and hit the side of a low bridge, the Bren gun crew were thrown off into the snow, and Lovat was hurled from the cab. The Germans took one look and fled, or put their hands up and surrendered in amazement.

But they weren't all prepared to give up without a fight, and one of the Germans was seen to drop a canvas satchel full of papers over the side of the bridge into the stream below. Lovat was furious and launched a ferocious chop at the neck of the German, which hurt Lovat's hand more than it did the man's neck, followed by a swinging left that knocked him over the parapet and into the water with the papers. A skirmish ensued, conflicting advice of all kinds was offered to the man in the water, the Bren gunner had to be forcibly restrained from taking a pot-shot at him, and the German was eventually hauled back on to dry land with the dripping papers, to the jeers of his comrades.

The small force then divided, half being sent back to Svolvaer with their prisoners, whilst the remainder set out to find the alleged garrison, which turned out to be no more than a small barracks, with signal station attached and swastika flag flying, near the village of Kabelvog, on the slope of a hill overlooking the road. Some local kids assured them that there were only a few technicians inside, so they set up a Bren gun about 300yds away and opened up with tracer at the door and upper windows. The inmates came bundling out of the back door – straight into the arms of the remainder of the group, who had skirted round behind to cover the rear exit. They were soon disarmed, told to pack kit bags for prison camp and left shivering in the snow under guard.

Inside the building, one of the group set to with a crow bar to smash up the array of high-frequency wireless equipment they found, whilst the remainder helped themselves to whatever they thought might be of use to the boffins back home, whose job it was to analyse what the enemy was up to – and any personal souvenirs they could lay their hands on.

With a bottle of schnapps to fortify themselves against the cold, and time running short, they set off back to Svolvaer in great spirits, arriving at the quayside in time to help load the last of the landing craft with nearly a hundred quislings and captured Germans, and a similar number of Norwegian volunteers keen to join the war effort in England. As they set out from the quayside at 1230 hrs, the local people roared abuse at the departing German prisoners, and three red Verey lights signalled to the *Somali* and Brigadier Haydon that the withdrawal on Svolvaer was complete.

In the meantime, the *Somali* had not been idle. Having, it was thought, disabled and probably sunk the *Krebs* earlier that morning, Haydon was surprised, on returning from the landing at Stamsund, to find that she had apparently refloated and was now drifting towards the centre of the fjord, with a white flag being waved from the deck. A boarding party was quickly despatched in a Norwegian fishing boat which had volunteered for the job, and they found five wounded sailors on board the stricken ship, two of them in a serious condition. The ship was searched; the wheelhouse had received a direct hit and nothing there was salvageable, and the captain and one sailor were found dead at the wheel. The ship was on fire below, and any further search was impracticable. As the boarding party returned to *Somali*, small fishing boats came alongside and showered them with gifts of fish for the ship's company, receiving food and cigarettes in return.

It emerged only years later that the search of the *Krebs* was in fact more fruitful than had been revealed at the time. On board was an Enigma machine, the electro-mechanical cipher device that was used by the Germans throughout the war for the transmission of top secret military and diplomatic messages. The commander of the *Krebs* had managed to throw his machine overboard before he was killed by one of the opening salvos from *Somali*. He didn't have time, however, to destroy all the relevant rotor wheels (the code-making parts of the machine), or his up-to-date code books. These were found by the boarding party and taken to the British code-breaking station at Bletchley Park where, after three weeks of intensive work, British Intelligence was able to crack the codes and, for the next month, read all the messages sent and received in home waters by the German Navy.

Leslie, meanwhile, was on the island of Store Molla, about five miles from Svolvaer. F Troop had boarded their landing craft soon after 0500 hrs, though they had to wait half an hour or so hanging in mid-air over the side of the *Queen Emma* for the Svolvaer group to set off before they could be on their way. Everyone was tense and apprehensive, until the Troop 'clown' Easton started to sing very softly under his breath the popular Andrews Sisters hit 'Ferryboat Serenade'. As they were finally lowered into the water and headed for the village of Brettesnes, under the stern of *Bedouin*, the spray coming over the ramp of the landing craft dowsed the Bren gunner and formed icicles on his steel helmet.

While the two landing craft were heading towards the shore, *Bedouin* intercepted the *Mira*, a Norwegian *Hurtigruten* ship (a steamer for passengers and mail along the Norwegian coast), and fired a shot across her bows to stop her. This had no effect, so a second shot was fired into the bow, again with no result. *Bedouin* then opened fire in earnest and disabled the ship with a shot just below her funnel. *Bedouin* then returned to see the landing parties safely ashore, whereupon she went back to sink the *Mira*, whose passengers and crew were by this time in the process of boarding life rafts and making for Brettesnes. When this was completed, *Bedouin* opened fire again, and the ship slowly began to sink. Four civilians died in the attack, and a further three died later from their injuries.

Whilst this drama was unfolding, at 0640 hrs the two landing craft arrived at the stone quay at Brettesnes (population around 50) and the advance party comprising force commander Major Kerr (an Old Etonian professional soldier, good with his fists and a cricket bat), Leslie, and their thirty-odd men, scrambled ashore unopposed, closely followed by another thirty from the second craft (including a thirteen-man 'sapper' demolition squad). The tiny Post Office was immediately surrounded and secured, and by 0710 hrs Leslie was reporting that a protective ring had been thrown around this building and the quay head.

The next objective was the destruction of the oil and fish meal factory, and Dunning was part of a small three-man snatch squad, led by Hutton (Leslie's first recruit to F Troop) and detailed to go to the home of the factory manager and require him to return with them to the factory and open up for the demolition party. Led by their Norwegian guide, they quickly found the house and the startled manager, who was very happy to cooperate. The locals watching proceedings on the quay were advised to take cover as the search and demolition team arrived with plenty of explosives and set about removing any useful papers before blowing the place up.

The demolition was held up for an hour, though, because they first had to deal with the evacuees from the sinking of the *Mira*, who had by this time begun to arrive on the quay. They included a German officer and eleven German soldiers, who were all taken prisoner, as were five other people who claimed somewhat incongruously to be members of a travelling theatrical troupe. The officer and one of his men was despatched across to HMS *Emma* in a landing craft, whilst the others were sent off to *Bedouin*. The wounded (including two Germans) expressed a preference for being taken to Svolvaer, where there was a hospital, so they were put on board a fishing boat and taken round later.

With the prisoners and wounded dealt with, and the demolition of the factory complete, Kerr's group was now free to complete the remainder of its objectives on the island. Leslie and his men found and demolished a cod press (for oil extraction) near the quay, sabotaged a cod meal factory, destroyed all the oil tanks they could find and decided to leave undamaged their final objective, which had proved on inspection to be the main electricity generating plant for the village. The villagers had assured them that this could not in any way have been of assistance to the enemy, and were apparently very appreciative when Kerr agreed.

By 0930 hrs the raid on Store Molla was virtually over, with all objectives achieved, not a shot fired and eighteen recruits enlisted for the 118 ships of the Norwegian Navy (which was operating from British ports, having escaped the German invasion with their King in June 1940). Twenty minutes later, the men were back on their landing craft being cheered by the locals, who sang the Norwegian national anthem as the raiders pushed off from the quay. They came alongside *Queen Emma* at 1015 hrs, about four hours after they had set out.

Kerr warmly described the reception they had received from the Norwegians in his official report:

Throughout the operation, my Force was received with tremendous enthusiasm, and we had the utmost support. On embarking the German officer prisoner, the inhabitants expressed their feelings extremely openly. As the two LCAs left the quay, a cheer such as none of us will forget broke out, and followed us as we left the harbour. I know I can speak for the rest of the Force when I say that

this was unforgettable, as their factory which was in the immediate
vicinity of the quay was in ruins.

At Stamsund and Henningsvaer the story was the same – factories and oil
tanks blown up, prisoners taken, Norwegian volunteers recruited and no one
injured. A hundredweight of sweets was distributed to the town's children.
The telephone exchange was captured, and Lieutenant Richard Willis sent a
telegram: 'To A. Hitler, Berlin: You said in your last speech German troops
would meet the British wherever they landed. We are here. Where are your
troops?'

In his book *The Epic of Lofoten*, George Mikes, a Hungarian journalist,
paints a picture from interviews of how local people received the news that
the British had landed. Within a few minutes they had spilled out on to the
main street, cheering and laughing as the Tommies came ashore. Eagerly,
they showed the men which buildings to blow up and led them to the home
of the detested Chief of Police, who was promptly arrested, along with two
German oil experts who had been staying at the local inn. As the cod boiling
factory and its huge oil storage tanks exploded in a roar of flames and thick
black smoke, one of Mikes' interviewees rushed home to pack and say a
hurried goodbye to his fiancée so that he could join the Commandos for the
trip back to Britain, as a volunteer for the exiled Norwegian Army.

It was time for all of them to go home. The men clambered back into their
landing craft and were soon back aboard the *Emma* and the *Beatrix*, whilst
the destroyers lost no time in wheeling round, against a dramatic backdrop
of blue skies, mountains and the burning oil tanks, and set a course back
to Britain. The soldiers went through the humdrum routine of unloading
their weapons and defusing grenades, whilst the prisoners were crammed
down below in the hold and the officers started to tally up the results of
their mission:

18 fish–oil factories destroyed, with their storage tanks holding
800,000 gallons of oil
10 German or German-used ships sunk
213 German prisoners and 12 Norwegian quislings captured
315 Norwegian volunteers brought back to Britain.
An unknown number of German sailors killed.

'A highly successful operation with no casualties' was how the BBC described
it the next day, Thursday, 6 March, as the troops sailed back through seas

that were, to the relief of all, a bit calmer than they had been on the way out. As they came close to the coast of Scotland, the escorting destroyers altered course and turned away, crossing the bows of the troop ships in a silent gesture of farewell before heading back to the open sea.

The Commander-in-Chief Home Fleet led the way up the fairway, as *Queen Emma* and *Princess Beatrix*, troops and crew standing to attention, manned overall and with flags flying, sailed past the anchored battle ships in Scapa Flow, their crews cheering them on as they took up their moorings.

They left Scapa Flow next morning, after a heavy evening of partying with naval colleagues, and made for Gourock, where they were to disembark. A Royal Marine band played 'We don't want to lose you but we feel you ought to go' on the quayside and, despite their hangovers, the men were in a festive mood and in very good heart. This didn't last, unfortunately, as there was confusion about where exactly they were to dock, and their transport had been sent elsewhere. Their prisoners were led away, and the jubilant Norwegian volunteers were taken off to celebrate by some fellow countrymen, but the Commandos were refused permission to leave the ship until the following day when, to add insult to injury, they were required to surrender all their souvenirs from the raid. There must have been a strong sense of anti-climax, as they filed off the *Queen Emma* and boarded trucks for Troon.

The raid had been an undoubted success in propaganda terms, with Hitler forced to find alternative sources of fish oil in the short term and to reinforce the Norway occupation force, tying up men and materiel in the process. It had been good for morale in Britain, too, as the country began to recover from the shock of Dunkirk and consider how to fight back. For the Commandos, regarded as they were with some suspicion by senior officers of the regular forces, here was a demonstration of what could be achieved by a relatively small force, trained for the purpose and with the element of surprise on their side.

But somehow the sense of anti-climax that had begun in Gourock continued. To some of the Commandos, the immediate results of the raid on the ground barely seemed to justify the months of training beforehand and, with no new projects to get their teeth into and another reorganization in the offing, a sense of uncertainty prevailed. Sir Roger Keyes, early champion of the Commandos, was forced into retirement a few months later, though he used his position as the Member of Parliament for Portsmouth to deliver a characteristic broadside against the 'inter-services committees and sub-committees [who] have become the dictators of policy instead of the servants of those who bore full responsibility; by concentrating on the difficulties and dangers of every amphibious project . . . the planners have succeeded in thwarting execution until it is too late.'

In Troon, the civil authorities threw a party for all ranks and a dance in the town hall, but the spell had been broken for some, and Lister's relative unpopularity as a leader amongst his officers, Leslie included, meant that several used his reorganization of the Commando as an opportunity to return to their original regiments, where in any event the prospects of doing some real fighting were judged to be better. In the Bedfordshire and Hertfordshire regiment, for example, there was a new CO, and big exercises were in progress that seemed to presage new opportunities. As Dunning notes, all three of F Troop's officers left – Leslie and the two he had appointed during those first heady days setting up his troop in Amesbury, Hutton and Munn – and F Troop disappeared altogether.

*

I visited the Lofoten Islands in 2011, seventy years after the raid, and stayed in a small renovated fisherman's hut by a quiet creek in Svolvaer. It was summertime, and the town, with its white-painted cathedral, looked a picture against the blue skies and surrounding hills. Even today, the Lofoten Islands are about fish, and everywhere we went we found wooden A-frame structures beside the sea festooned with drying cod.

We soon found the Lofoten War Museum near the quay where the Hurtigruten boat docks. In 1941 it was the post office and telegraph station and the first building to be occupied by the Commandos, who landed just a few yards away. The museum houses an extraordinary collection of uniforms, photos, flags, pieces of old weaponry, scale models, swastika Christmas tree decorations, a rather chilling reconstruction of a Nazi commander's office, some water colours allegedly by Hitler himself, Eva Braun's purse, a porthole from the Mira *(the Hurtigruten boat sunk by HMS* Bedouin*), and a section of a fish-oil tank pierced by a British shell. There are evocative pictures of oil tanks in flames, the Union Jack flying in the main square and German prisoners lined up against a wall being confronted by 'Tommies' and an excited newspaper reporter.*

The proprietor, William Hakvaag, was delighted to give us a personal guided tour, picking out little treasures that we had missed, like pots commemorating the German occupation, each piece with a tiny brown blemish by way of deliberate local sabotage. He was interesting on the aftermath of the raid, too, describing how the Germans returned with orders to destroy the town as punishment. In fact, only seven houses were razed, but the town was heavily garrisoned, a network of underground tunnels and bunkers was constructed and a huge cannon was mounted on a hill with a commanding view of the harbour. Sixty-four prisoners were taken to a PoW camp near Oslo for the duration of the war.

Trying to work out how to get to Brettesnes on Store Molla, we drove into the yard of a small boat hire company, where a woman emerged from the office and just stood, looking at us expectantly. I told her my story.

'I'm Ruth. I come from Brettesnes,' she said, with a smile. 'You'd better come in.'

She told us that she was brought up on the island and had heard stories of the raid. She had a friend called Viggo who might be able to take us across in his small boat. For several days we waited for news, and the last day of our trip was fast approaching before Ruth called again – Viggo was busy, but she and her husband Torbjorn would take us instead.

The next day, we were up early and hurried down to the boatyard, where we boarded the tiny fishing boat Wito *and set off for Store Molla, threading our way through a network of small islets of rock and tufted grass adrift on an icy blue sea beneath the towering peaks of Little Molla. Ruth told us that her father had been a smallholder in the north of the island but had moved to Brettesnes in 1953 so that she could attend the village school, transporting his house piecemeal by boat around the tip of the island. She had met and married Torbjorn, a local cod and whale fisherman, as a teenager, and they lived a simple life together on the island until disabling migraines forced him to forsake the sea and start a new business in Svolvaer, renting out fisherman's huts.*

Soon, Store Molla filled the horizon, a patchwork of green and brown scrub and rock. We passed the spot where the Mira *sank, her hull still visible at low tide, and rounded the point to find the hamlet of Brettesnes, dwarfed by a high peak and strung along a pretty bay ahead of us, just as my father must have seen it seventy years before. To the left, a small dock and factory buildings; to the right, dotted houses and huts along the shoreline.*

We tied up at a pontoon, clambered ashore – and there I was, seventy years later, following in my father's footsteps. I felt an extraordinary elation and a strong sense of him there beside me. After a sandwich lunch in Ruth's old family home, now being lovingly restored by Torbjorn, we set off to explore, and soon found ourselves standing on the very same stone quay that Leslie must have climbed on to from his landing craft. The fish-oil factory, rebuilt after the destruction of its predecessor, is deserted now, but the oil tanks are still there, and it was easy to imagine the sappers going about their business, whilst F Troop stood around chatting to the locals, enjoying a warming cup of coffee and a glass of akvavit *as they waited for the explosions, in the bitter cold of that early March morning.*

All too soon, it was time to be off. I sat aft on my own, watching Brettesnes and the island drop behind in the late afternoon sun, until I could see them no more. I felt very sad, as if I was leaving my father behind there somehow.

Perhaps he had a similar sense of leaving something behind, as he set off from Troon to rejoin his regiment on 9 April 1941. He had put his heart and soul into the building of his commando troop and he must surely have felt sad to say goodbye to the men he had picked and trained.

Many in the Commando were sad to see him go. Amongst the few papers he left behind after his death was a letter signed 'Lovat' and dated 8 May 1942. Lovat by this time had been promoted to Lieutenant Colonel and was about to be appointed commanding officer of 4 Commando in succession to Lister. He had led a successful reconnaissance and 'smash and grab' raid on the village of Hardelot on the northern coast of France, and been awarded the Military Cross. He told Leslie that he had been making 'tentative enquiries' through various named Commando colleagues to find out if Leslie would be 'prepared to come back to this Commando', and suggested that perhaps his duties as adjutant in his regiment 'prevented an otherwise willing return of the prodigal son'. Lovat offered him leadership of another troop – 'I think this would make you senior troop leader, with every chance of fairly rapid promotion.' He pointed out that he had himself accepted a lower captain's rank in the summer of 1941, and suggested that 'with forthcoming attractions mapped out for this summer you might easily end up as the Brigadier!' He said he needed an immediate answer, hence his hand-delivered letter to 'an unknown spot somewhere in Kirkcudbrightshire', and signed off, 'Hope to see you soon.'

Was Leslie tempted by this offer, or was he quite content to stay where he was? According to his sister, my Aunt Mary, my father admired Lovat greatly, and Lovat had pushed hard for him to be given one of the Troop Leader posts during Lister's reorganization. It must therefore have been hard for him to turn this offer down. Perhaps he wanted to go but was refused leave by a possessive CO – by this time, regimental commanders had become rather tired of having their best chaps pinched by the Commandos, especially as they remained on the regimental payroll. Lord Lovat himself suggested this as a reason, when I wrote to him in 1989.

Who knows? Had Leslie accepted Lovat's offer, he would have gone straight into the controversial and ill-fated Dieppe raid, where there were 4,000 casualties, mostly Canadian – and where 4 Commando produced the only land success of an otherwise failed mission: 'a classic example of the use of well-trained military . . . and thoroughness in planning, training and execution'. Pat Porteous, a friend of my father's, who had taken over F Troop, fought incredibly bravely at Dieppe, was wounded three times but carried on hand-to-hand combat with the enemy, captured the objective and saved the life of at least one of his men – actions for which he was awarded the VC.

For Porky Young, a different chapter was about to begin . . .

*

Chapter 9

Return to the Bedfords

The War Diary for 4 Commando records Leslie as having left to return to the Bedfordshire and Hertfordshire Regiment on 9 April 1941, although it is clear from the records of his old 2 Battalion that he was in fact on duty sooner than that. On 3 April, for example, he was detailed as a member of a Field General Court Martial, and on 7 April he was working in the HQ Company as 'Captain of the Week'. The Battalion was by this time based at Totton, near Southampton, in the New Forest, and was under the command of Lieutenant Colonel Ernest Pepper OBE, a highly regarded career soldier who had joined the Army in 1918 and served in India before the war.

As the official regimental history relates, the Battalion had changed since Dunkirk. For most of this time it had remained based at Bognor, working on the coastal defences against the threatened German invasion. A year of general, individual and specialist training had improved standards and tactical understanding. Gradually, the Battalion was re-equipped with the weapons and ammunition that it had lost in the retreat, including Browning automatic rifles, two Vickers heavy machine guns and a 'six-pounder' anti-tank gun to strengthen the beach defences. Morale was improving after the debacle of Dunkirk, and it was felt that the Battalion 'could take on any enemy – anywhere'.

By this time, however, the Axis powers, Germany and Italy, had consolidated their hold, or were seeking to do so, on most of Europe and large parts of Africa. The whole of northern and western France had been occupied (including the British Channel Islands), and the German-puppet Vichy government had been established with nominal control over the whole country, although in practice, all of northern France was under direct German rule .

Hitler had shelved his plans for the invasion of Britain, after the failure of the Luftwaffe to defeat the RAF during the Battle of Britain the previous summer, but the Germans were still bombing London and other British cities almost nightly. Hitler's focus was now on the possibility of invading Russia, whilst Italy had occupied a large part of North Africa, in addition to Albania and Greece. Hitler's U-boats were patrolling the Atlantic, and having some success in hitting convoys bringing food and equipment from America and Canada to a beleaguered Britain. Japan had joined the Axis, spreading the impact of war to the Far East. Churchill was trying desperately to persuade President Roosevelt to do more than send supplies and to join the war effort as a full partner.

The British were fighting back, though, and bombing German cities daily in retaliation for the German attacks on Britain, whilst the Italians were being pushed back in North Africa and Greece. At Bletchley Park, Alan Turing and other 'boffins' were having increasing success in breaking, on a regular basis, the secret codes used by German and Italian forces – thanks to the capture of German Enigma code machines such as the one the Commandos brought back from the Lofoten Islands.

On 15 April 1941 Leslie was appointed acting Adjutant for the Battalion, reporting direct to Pepper and responsible for the administration of the Battalion and all written communications. A month later, the Battalion moved to Alresford in Hampshire, and Leslie's appointment as Adjutant was confirmed. He took over from 'Streaky' Yate-Lee, who had won the Military Cross in France and had recently been promoted to command the HQ Company.

Leslie was busy that summer, and the War Diary contains numerous examples of the orders and instructions he sent out:

> The jam ration is 2 ozs per week.

> Carving names on buildings, trees, etc must stop.

> The sounding of the Rattle denotes the presence of any gas other than aircraft spray. Those within hearing will hold their breath and adjust respirator.

> Are you doing all you can? Take waste paper . . .

> Civilians (including women) . . . are taking part in voluntary fire prevention exercises . . . and officers and other ranks . . . should join in any scheme organized in respect of the residential property which they occupy at night.

> There still appear to be some users of the telephone who do not realize that telephone conversations can be overheard.

The RAF has reported that electric torches are being carelessly used in Winchester, thus defeating the Black Out.

The Pavilion Dance Hall in Bournemouth is out of bounds.

Great care must be taken disposing of rhubarb leaves. They are poisonous and likely to kill pigs.

All that summer, there were working parties to draw up, parades and route marches to oversee, platoon and company exercises to lay on and sports competitions to organize. The Regimental Band arrived from Bedford and had to be accommodated. There were exercises with Winchester School OTC and the local Home Guard, and demonstrations of Bangalore Torpedoes (a tube filled with explosive and then pushed forward along the ground, used to blast holes in minefields or barbed wire defences) and Kapok Bridging (a floating infantry assault pontoon made up of compartments filled with kapok, a cotton-like fluff made from the seedpods of a South American plant). There was a great deal of experimentation going on at that time – Mike Howard, a youngster who had just joined the Regiment, remembers the Blacker Bombard, a mortar which hurled dustbin-sized bombs, and a mine swathed in sticky muslin for attaching to tanks. Churchill paid a visit, and was treated to a demonstration of an attack supported by artillery and machine gun fire.

On 18 August 'Battalion Holiday Week' began with a treasure hunt, and there were baseball and basketball competitions, a two-day camp at Lee-on-Solent with fishing and swimming, a fair and, to finish off, a concert organized by the Entertainment National Service Association or ENSA. These concerts, laid on by entertainers volunteering their services to amuse the troops and maintain morale, were a popular aspect of Forces life, and sometimes featured stars like Noel Coward, Gracie Fields and Laurence Olivier. The stars were stretched pretty thin, though, across the country and overseas, so the joke ran that ENSA stood for 'Every Night Something Awful'.

In September a series of exercises began, organized by Southern Command. The first was Exercise Author, a 24-hour test of aerodrome defences. The Battalion was to act the part of the German attacking force, assisted by a platoon of paratroops, all wearing soft caps with a piece of white flannelette attached. The Lysander aircraft were designated as British, with the rest all German. Artillery fire was to be represented by smoke generators, bombs and shells by thunderflashes, and small arms fire by blanks or 'rattling a tin with a stone inside it'. The orders, signed by Leslie as Adjutant, and no doubt with health and safety in mind, state firmly, 'Bayonets will not be fixed.' There were strict rules for which areas of the aerodrome were out of bounds, with 'no fighting among the huts'. A bridge that had been 'demolished' was to be marked with 'tracing tape' and red boards. Umpires were appointed to ensure that the rules were obeyed and to mark with labels all those deemed to be casualties.

Exercise Author was followed by a Combined Operations night exercise hunting tanks, a Brigade night convoy exercise and desert warfare training in the pouring December rain on Salisbury Plain, after which the Battalion moved to Barton Stacey for weapons training – and was warned to be ready for service overseas 'in a cold climate'. The warning proved to be somewhat premature, and the furthest they went was to Fleet, near Aldershot, in November, for more exercises.

Lieutenant Colonel D. S. W. 'Johnny' Johnson, who had been in charge of C Company when the Battalion was in France, took over from Pepper. Medley recorded that it was Johnson who had ordered that a mascot goat should be left behind at Dunkirk, to general dismay, until the Brigadier saved the day by putting the goat into the back of his own vehicle.

Leslie was promoted Major and took over C Company, and the Battalion moved to Scotland in March 1942, where they were housed in a mixture of tents, Nissen huts and private billets. They were based initially at Inverary in Argyllshire, where they learned all about assault landings, and then at Barony Camp near Dumfries in April. They spent a lot of time climbing down scaling nets from a ship anchored in Loch Fyne into landing craft, or attempting to jump impossible distances across rivers in wet, cold and muddy kit.

Mike Howard, who was also in C Company, remembers the constant rain at Inverary, and Leslie's toughness and professionalism: 'He led us on some demanding exercises, when some of the men "questioned his antecedents". He was competitive, and came down hard on defaulters, but he also gave praise readily. He would never ask you to do something that he was not prepared to tackle himself. He was well liked and admired as an officer.' Jimmy Darville, a member of B Company, remembers Porky Young, the former Commando, as the 'Mad Major', a bit of a disciplinarian, who never crossed a river by the bridge if he could lead his men through the water instead.

In January 1943 news of a third spell of 'embarkation leave' came through. After two years of training for operations that never seemed to come off, the men were bored and frustrated, despite the best efforts of their officers to keep them motivated. They were cynical, too, and according to the second in command, Bill Whittaker, had learned not to get too excited: 'Any undue enthusiasm [was] regarded as rather naïve.' They had crossed 'narrow rivers, wide rivers, slow, fast, deep and shallow rivers; we had landed from most types of landing craft on many different coasts, penetrating deeply inland. We had cooperated with artillery, tanks and aircraft; a twenty-mile route march was of course routine, whilst ten miles in two hours in full equipment . . . occasioned no undue alarm.' They had studied desert warfare on Salisbury Plain in mud and pouring rain, and captured most of western Scotland and southern England – and now they wanted to see the enemy, and fight.

They felt they had missed out on a great deal, spectators from a distance. By January 1943 Hitler ruled Europe from the Arctic to the Mediterranean, with no fewer than ten major European capital cities – Rome, Vienna, Warsaw, Copenhagen, Oslo, The Hague, Brussels, Paris, Belgrade and Athens – under German influence or control. In the process, he had already exterminated nearly four million Jews, in Poland, Germany and all over Europe, and launched Operation Barbarossa, the invasion of Russia, along a 930-mile front with nearly four million men, becoming bogged down in a winter stalemate that would lead eventually to a disastrous and costly defeat.

In the Far East, Japan, the third member of the Axis with Germany and Italy, had decided not to join them in the invasion of Russia but to move into South East Asia instead; before any declaration of war, over 300 Japanese bombers and fighters, launched from six aircraft carriers, struck at Pearl Harbor in Hawaii, the main American naval base, blowing up or seriously damaging eight American battleships and eleven other warships, and destroying nearly 200 planes. At the same time, there were Japanese attacks on three other American Pacific Islands, and on Burma, Malaya, Singapore and Hong Kong.

America and Britain immediately declared war on Japan and, on 11 December, in what was probably one of Hitler's biggest mistakes, Germany declared war on the United States, thereby drawing America into the European conflict as well. The Japanese captured Borneo, Java and Sumatra, and Britain's 'unassailable' fortress in Singapore, where they took around 25,000 prisoners, many of whom would die in Japanese camps in the following years.

Leslie and the rest of 2 Battalion returned from embarkation leave at the end of January 1943, and moved to nearby Carronbridge. More training, they thought. But then, out of the blue, the King visited them in February, and all of a sudden the men knew that this time they were off and that the months of waiting and training were over.

Whittaker's account captures the sense of anticipation:

> Enthusiasm was no longer naïve but natural and universal. The transport moved off on 26 February and on 11 March the main body of the Battalion left Carronbridge for Glasgow on the first stage of the journey. Our destination was of course secret, but as we had been part of the First Army and had originally been intended to land with them, only to have our place taken by Americans at the last moment, North Africa was a strong favourite, and so it turned out to be.

Chapter 10

The War in North Africa

*L*ooking back over the half dozen or so brief conversations that I can remember having with my father about 'the war', I cannot recall his ever saying anything at all about North Africa. He talked a bit about Dunkirk, and about the Lofoten Islands; he once spoke a little about his time in Italy; and I knew he had been involved in the Normandy landings. But of Africa, easily the most exotic of his postings, he said not a word, even though he spent, in effect, two years of his war preparing for it. When I started metaphorically following his footsteps through the battlefields, I didn't even know where in North Africa he had been – the original letter I received from the MoD with my father's war record referred elusively only to the fact that he had 'embarked overseas with 2 Battalion' on 11 March 1943.

The only small clue I had was a letter that I found amongst Leslie's papers, from his friend and best man Tom La Fontaine, dated 23 November 1983 – just a couple of years before Leslie's death. Tom was an artist, a good one, who painted Leslie's portrait when they were together in the Bedfords. My father and Tom had met up at a reunion, and Leslie had written to him afterwards. Tom responded pleasantly enough, saying how nice it was to see Leslie again and grumbling that there was never enough time at 'that do' to talk properly. He gave Leslie the address of Dougie Turner, another regimental chum, and expressed the hope that Leslie would visit one day.

Then came the clue, and with it a hint of fretful regret on my father's part that has haunted me ever since:

> Incidentally, I have never heard any blame lodged against the Battalion or B or C Company for the Tunisian do. No way can a razor back be held. Everyone knew that. It all seems a long time ago.

What was 'the Tunisian do' that La Fontaine was referring to, and what happened on that 'razor back' that was still worrying my father forty years later?

*

The 'Tunisian do' came right at the end of the Desert War, a conflict that swirled to and fro, through clouds of sand and dust, east and west, across nearly 2,000 miles of rough and often empty desert for three years, from June 1940 to May 1943. Why, with so much more apparently at stake in terms of people, resources and possessions in Europe and the Far East, was so much time and effort spent fighting over a wilderness of sand, scrub and rock?

Of course, it wasn't really the sand, scrub and rock that were important. It was the sea – the Mediterranean. At the outbreak of war, Hitler had no apparent intention of waging war in the Mediterranean or in North Africa and made no effort to commit resources there. But his Italian fellow-dictator Benito Mussolini had other ideas. Italy had seized the northern part of Libya in 1911 and spent the next twenty or so years exploiting it. By 1939 Libya had become 'Italy's fourth Mediterranean shore', and its menfolk a valuable source of forced cheap 'recruitment' for the Italian Army. Mussolini, in his most overweeningly ambitious dreams, saw Libya as the springboard for a campaign to turn the whole of the North African shoreline into an Italian possession, and the Mediterranean itself into an Italian lake.

The Allies, naturally enough, had a very different perspective. Britain had vital political interests in North Africa, particularly in Egypt and the Suez Canal, its trading gateway to colonial India and the east, and in the oilfields of the Middle East. Looking ahead, Churchill saw the Mediterranean and its North African shore as potentially a vital springboard for an eventual liberating invasion of mainland Europe via its 'soft southern underbelly'. The problem for Britain was that its regiments in Cairo and the desert, and its ships in the harbour at Alexandria, amounted to less than one-tenth of the forces Mussolini had amassed for his quest to capture North Africa up to the Suez Canal. Whilst pleading for reinforcements, Britain's military commander in Egypt, General Wavell, therefore embarked on a massive game of bluff to convince the Italians that we were much stronger than we actually were. Wavell's approach was to mount constant attacks by small units, irregularly and at night, so that the enemy had no idea what was going to happen next.

Then, on 13 September 1940, as Britain was still recovering from the shock of Dunkirk and stood alone facing the might of the Luftwaffe and the real possibility of invasion, Italian forces led by Marshall Graziani crossed the border between Libya and Egypt and raced along the coast road to within 200 miles of Cairo. There he stopped to consolidate his position, ready for the next phase of the attack.

Three months later, Wavell counter-attacked, captured an area the size of Britain and France and virtually wiped out the Italian Army. Hitler despatched the elite Afrika Corps, under its inspiring leader General Erwin Rommel, 'the Desert Fox', to reinforce the Italians and prevent an Axis rout. A fluctuating series of desperate battles for control of Egypt and Libya, in dire desert conditions, followed over the next eighteen months until finally, at the second battle of El Alamein in October 1942, Lieutenant General Bernard 'Monty' Montgomery led British Commonwealth forces in a decisive victory over the Afrika Korps and forced Rommel to retreat into Tunisia, a land of mountain ranges, fertile river valleys and arable plains.

Whilst Monty and his Eighth Army were fighting their way from the east across North Africa, the American General Dwight D. 'Ike' Eisenhower was putting together 'Operation Torch', the largest amphibious invasion force ever yet seen – 300 warships, 370 merchant ships and 107,000 men. In November 1942 Ike's invasion force landed at Casablanca in Morocco and Oran in western Algeria; and the new British First Army, including eventually Leslie and the Bedfords, landed at Algiers.

The Torch landings were quickly successful and, within seventy-two hours, on 11 November 1942, two days before Monty's men reached Tobruk, 900 miles to the east, the Allies under Ike took control of 1,300 miles of coastline in North-west Africa. The jaws of an Allied pincer movement, Ike with the First Army from the west and Monty with the Eighth Army from the east, were slowly closing around Rommel and his men in Tunisia. Rommel attempted two massive counter-attacks, in the north and south of the country, hoping to keep the jaws of the pincer open, but when these were repulsed, he could see that he was staring eventual defeat in Tunisia in the face; he surrendered his command and left Africa soon after.

Leslie, meanwhile, embarked on the troopship HMV *Orion* at King Edward V Dock in Glasgow on 11 March 1943 with the rest of 2 Battalion, Bedfordshire and Hertfordshire Regiment, part of 10 Infantry Brigade in the 4th Division of V Corps of the First Army, and headed for Algiers. Its mission was to help capture Tunis and finally push the Germans out of Africa. After two years of training and waiting in Scotland, it must have been an emotional moment for him and the rest of the Battalion.

The ship was crammed full, part of a large convoy of troop carriers accompanied by an impressive escort of aircraft carriers, battleships, cruisers and destroyers. They sailed around Ireland and out into the Atlantic, to avoid German U-boats. The passage was uneventful, with only more training to entertain the troops. The ship was 'dry', and the Battalion was under its new commander, 'Johnny' Johnson. Whittaker describes some of the personalities on board:

> Johnny had taken over from Colonel Pepper about a year previously; it is always difficult to succeed someone superlatively good at their job, but Johnny's terrific good humour and enthusiasm carried the Battalion through a period in which it might well have become stale. His energy and unwillingness to spare himself made everyone feel that the best they could do could scarcely be good enough. HQ Company was commanded by Streaky Yate-Lee; he seemed to have been commanding it for ever. Presumably there was a time when he took over, but whenever it was it was so lost in antiquity as to be unimportant. 'A' Company had been commanded by Rayner by this time for two years. About a year previously it had won an exhaustive competition as the best company in the Division. 'B' 'C' and 'D' Companies were commanded by Michael Lofts, Porky Young, with the same zest with which he did everything else, and Charkham respectively. There were many others I would like to mention, of all ranks, the only difficulty would be to know when to stop, but I will content myself with saying that a visitor who knew the Battalion in 1939 would still have no difficulty in finding plenty of faces he knew.

They sailed through the Straits of Gibraltar ten days later and, as the whitewashed walls of Algiers came into sight in the morning sunshine, every man on board must have been leaning over the ship's rails and speculating about what Africa held in store for him.

Chapter 11

Tunisia 1943

Leslie and the rest of 2 Battalion docked at Algiers and disembarked during the afternoon of 23 March, stretching their legs after the long journey with a brisk 17-mile walk 'in boiling sunshine' to their camp at Cap Matifou, a reception area north-east of the capital on a headland overlooking the Bay of Algiers. Only a few days earlier, two Royal Navy officers had visited the wife of the lighthouse keeper at Matifou and presented her with two ducks, to replace the birds killed by Navy shells during the opening stages of the Torch landings.

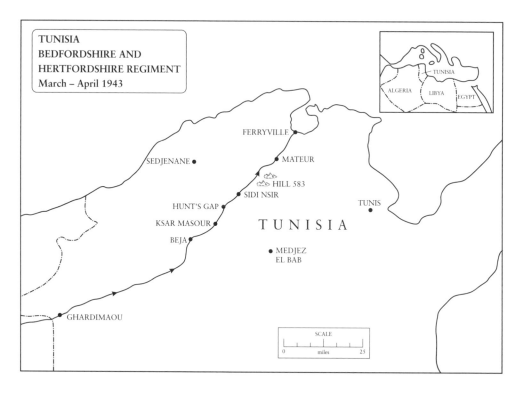

TUNISIA
BEDFORDSHIRE AND
HERTFORDSHIRE REGIMENT
March – April 1943

TUNISIA

ALGERIA   LIBYA   EGYPT

FERRYVILLE

SEDJENANE ●   ● MATEUR

HILL 583
● SIDI NSIR

HUNT'S GAP ●

KSAR MASOUR ●   T U N I S I A   TUNIS ●

BEJA ●

● MEDJEZ
EL BAB

GHARDIMAOU

SCALE

0   miles   25

Conditions at the camp were at best indifferent, but the Battalion's cooks, cleaners and sanitation experts soon made it habitable, and the Battalion was allowed a celebration swim in the Med on 24 March, Leslie's thirty-second birthday. The weather was fair for these first few days, but there was some rain at night and, by the time they received orders to move up closer to the front, it was raining incessantly, with some of the roads flooded to a depth of 4ft.

Five days later, they boarded a troop train for Bone, a coastal city about 260 miles north-east of Algiers on the border with Tunisia, but were diverted en route for the small and unglamorous village of Ghardimaou, a few miles inland, just inside Tunisia. They set up their bivouacs in an olive grove amongst the mountains and the hills that overshadowed the village on three sides, to await events. It was still raining and freezing cold as the men lay in their tents listening to the mournful cries of the call to prayer from a nearby mosque.

On the following morning 'Johnny' Johnson left the camp with Leslie and the other Company Commanders and, as Dougie Turner, a member of Leslie's C Company put it, 'we knew it wouldn't be long.' Sure enough, troop carriers started to arrive that day from Bone, some of them delayed by a fierce storm and the treacherous frozen roads over the mountains and, next morning, the Battalion set off for the front line 50 miles away near the small village of Ksar Mesouar in the mouth of the Sidi Nsir valley, about 10 miles north-east of Beja. Here, they were to relieve the 1st Hampshires. After a short night's sleep at Ksar, they set off again and by 0440 hrs on 4 April they were in position, at a feature called Hunt's Gap. C Company took over the Hampshires' position at nearby Montagne Farm.

As dawn broke over a wide open grassy valley, its sides rising gently to distant hills and mountains, they were unaware that, after the long years of see-saw fighting to and fro across the harsh North African landscape, the Desert War was at a crucial turning point. Indeed, that point had already been passed, and their predecessors in the front line, the Hampshires, had paid with their lives to help bring it about.

Five weeks earlier, the Germans had launched a massive attack against the advancing First Army called Operation *Ochsenkopf* (Bull's Head), along three valleys in the north of Tunisia. Its aim was to halt the Allied advance on Tunis and capture the towns of Sedjenane, Beja and Medjez el Bab; if successful, this would have left Rommel free to fall on Monty's Eighth Army in the south. The valleys, and the high ground that overlooked them, were the key to the battle in northern Tunisia – if you had anti-tank guns on the hills you controlled the valleys and the road and rail links along them.

Some of the fiercest fighting in the desperate Allied attempt to hold on to these three vital valleys took place around Sidi Nsir, a small and insignificant railway station at a crossroads about 30 miles north-east of Beja, and at Hunt's Gap, a narrow defile 20 miles back along the road towards Beja. So important was it to the Allied cause to hang on to Hunt's Gap that a 'no retreat' order had been issued.

The Germans had quickly overrun Sidi Nsir itself on 26 February, attacking the inexperienced Hampshire battalion with about 13,000 men and another 30,000 in reserve, but the Allied artillery on the surrounding hillsides held on, repulsing attack after attack. Another day passed, and the Hampshires were eventually forced to fall back towards Beja, having lost all but nine men from an original hundred and thirty.

A few miles down the road, near Ksar Mesouar, lay Montagne Farm, soon to be home to Leslie's Company. It was a settlement of small flat-roofed buildings on a slight rise jutting out into the valley, with commanding views and housing a battery of 25-pounders and heavy 5.5-inch guns. Here, a company of Leicesters was dug in and managed to hold out for a week, under virtually constant bombardment by heavy artillery and the bazookas of a German battalion dug in on the plain below. The pressure on the men was intolerable and unrelenting.

The Hampshires took over Montagne Farm from the Leicesters in early March, as they fell back along the road from Sidi Nsir. The German attacks continued, and the battlefield around the farm became an evil-smelling wilderness of mud-filled craters and wrecked buildings, littered with dead cattle, goats and pigs. It was this wilderness that Leslie and C Company were to occupy four weeks later.

The brave defiance shown at the farm allowed time for the Allied defences 10 miles away at Hunt's Gap to be strengthened. Intense fighting continued in the area, in atrocious fog and rain, until 5 March, when the Axis attack was finally blunted by Allied tanks and artillery. A series of RAF sorties along the winding road where the German transport was concentrated reduced it to a mess of bomb craters and burning vehicles. The Germans had to accept that Operation *Ochsenkopf* had failed.

The task now was for First Army to push the Germans back east towards Tunis along a broad front in the north of the country, whilst the Eighth Army fought its way northwards, containing the enemy in an ever-narrowing cylinder with Tunis in its north-eastern corner. The push in the north was to be led by V Corps, which comprised two divisions, the 4th (which included the Bedfords) and the 78th.

Arriving in the front line on 4 April, the Bedfords had what Whittaker describes as 'a relatively uneventful time' at the farm for a few days, 'smelly and unpleasant' though it was. There was regular shelling and mortaring, mostly aimed at the Battalion's HQ. C Company, which was in an exposed forward position at Montagne Farm, took some casualties from German snipers. Leslie himself, according to his friend Tom La Fontaine, trod on a German mine near the Farm but dismissed the experience with a shrug – 'Damn thing didn't go off. Can't have been much good!'

The main German resistance was further north, but the expectation was that they would eventually withdraw, and nightly patrols were mounted to test this hypothesis. On 9 April there was some unusually heavy shelling, and the next day patrols reported that the enemy had indeed abandoned their positions.

The way was now clear for 4 Division to push north and clear the road towards Sidi Nsir, whilst 78 Division advanced along a 10-mile-wide front through difficult mountain terrain to clear the main road from Beja to Medjez el Bab. Alan Moorehead describes the 'bitter hill skirmishing' that was involved:

> Yard by yard the infantry fought their way steadily upwards, through minefields, taking machine guns at bayonet point, rushing tiny upland villages with hand grenades, always going up and up until at last they stood on the crest. A whole division of men – fifteen thousand – was swallowed up in those hills, and they struggled on desperately among the crags and boulders, often without food or water or even ammunition. There was nothing wildly spectacular about it – no towns to take, no massed formations in pitched battle, no great hosts of prisoners. It was just a painful slogging fight that had to be fought before we could get at the last great obstacle on the way to Tunis – Longstop Hill. It was the slow contracting of the cylinder. (*The Desert War* trilogy book 3, *The End in Africa*)

The road from Beja to Sidi Nsir runs through a wide valley, and the Bedfords' orders were to advance to the south of the road, with a battalion from the East Surrey Regiment to the north. The general perception was that the enemy was in a weakened state, and it was therefore permissible in the interests of speed to take reasonable risks. The objective was Hill 609, about 7 miles from Hunt's Gap.

At first light on 11 April the advance began. The Battalion moved forward in two columns, with A and B Companies under the command of Whittaker on the left moving initially up the main road as an advance guard, with the anti-tank platoon, the Carrier platoon, two sections of the mortar platoon and some sappers for mine clearance. On the right, moving through the hills, were C and D Companies with Battalion HQ, under 'Johnny' Johnson.

The idea was that the two columns would link up at the crossing point of two tracks a few miles ahead. Within a very short time, however, it became clear that the road was still blocked with disabled tanks, and both the road and the fields to either side were heavily mined and booby-trapped (a German speciality). Mine clearance was slow, and a captain and five soldiers were injured early on.

Meanwhile, Johnson's column on the right was making better progress, although the terrain was rough and rugged, hard for the tracked vehicles particularly. The maps were inaccurate, too, with paths marked in the wrong place or not marked at all, and they lost a 15cwt truck in extensive minefields along the route. By 0700 hrs, however, they had reached the intended rendezvous and established contact with Whittaker's advance guard, still held up on the road. Johnson pressed on to recce the road, but by the early afternoon it was clear that it was effectively impassable, and it was therefore decided that the left hand column would turn off the road and follow Johnson's route through the hills.

Then, at 1530 hrs, disaster struck. Johnson's column came under heavy shellfire at a hill called Ben Hederich. Several soldiers were wounded, and Johnson himself was killed by shrapnel. By one account, this was friendly fire from a British artillery unit. Johnson's death must have been devastating for his men, at the very start of the campaign. Whittaker arrived on the scene an hour later, took command, and immediately decided to call a halt. Dusk was approaching, and the Battalion was widely dispersed, so 'the tail was drawn in' and a 'battalion fortress' was formed for the night, whilst engineers were sent back to repair and bring on those vehicles that had been damaged during the day.

Whittaker's mind must have been in turmoil as he tried to get some sleep that night on the bleak, cold hillside. He and Johnson, with Leslie, had fought in northern France as fellow officers; they had come back from Dunkirk in the same boat; and they had spent the two intervening years training in each other's company. Whittaker clearly had a great liking for Johnson, with his 'terrific good humour and enthusiasm', and had lost a friend as well as a respected colleague and commanding officer. Now he had to lead the Battalion forward himself in difficult and unknown terrain, and with the enemy all around.

The next morning at 0630 hrs, the Battalion resumed its cautious movement forward, in a shallow valley to the west of a hill called Djebel Aoud. 'Streaky' Yate-Lee had replaced Whittaker in charge of the advance guard (which comprised D Company, the Carrier platoon and some mortars), and he set off to recce the eastern flank of the hill, to the right. This is difficult, almost claustrophobic countryside; the steep, rocky hills rising up sharply several hundred feet from the valley base are topped with razor ridges, and there is little or no cover from enemy fire, either in the valley itself or atop a hill. It is tailor-made for ambush and nasty surprises.

The advance guard quickly came under intense mortar and small arms fire near the village of Haroun. They fired off some mortars and then attempted to move through and around the village, but were immediately subjected to further heavy shell and mortar fire and had to take cover in a small gulley just to the north. Yate-Lee tried to radio back to the main body of the Battalion, but the radio failed, so he sent off a runner and then deployed carriers to recce the village itself. On entering the village, some of the carriers were hit and disabled, one receiving a direct hit in the front seat according to the War Diary, and there were several deaths and casualties. Meanwhile, the rest of the Battalion was being shelled.

On hearing what Yate-Lee's runner had to say, Whittaker set off to recce the position, and the eastern slope of the hill, for himself. He ordered A Company to carry on to the east, towards the next series of hills, about half a mile to the right. They, too, came under shell and mortar fire and suffered casualties, but pressed on until they reached their objective, where they were held down by small arms fire. They reported that they could see enemy movement ahead, a number of 'Arab spies' and an observation post on a prominent hill to their left, but they were unable to estimate the enemy's strength or precise positions.

A patrol was sent off to make direct contact with Yate-Lee's D Company, to no avail, whilst Whittaker himself went forward to where A Company was sheltering, accompanied by Leslie and the B Company Commander Lofts. From there they could observe enemy movement and light machine gun fire on the hill ahead (Hill 583, according to the War Diary).

Whittaker needed to maintain forward momentum, but he had only sketchy information about enemy dispositions and strength to go on, and it was by now early afternoon. He knew that an attack on the enemy position by day would probably have been fatal without a preparatory artillery bombardment, a bombardment which would in any event immediately have given the game away for ground troops attacking up the steep hillside. Leslie, in the account he wrote of this incident a few weeks later, said that he believed Whittaker favoured staying put that night and sending out patrols to ascertain where exactly the enemy was. Brigade, however, had other ideas and, on returning to his Battalion HQ and reporting back, Whittaker was told that he had to 'push on with all possible speed'.

Whittaker then took Leslie, Lofts, the Intelligence Officer Douglas and the Gunnery Commander back to the A Company area for a further recce, and they decided that Leslie would lead C Company in a night attack on the hill to A Company's left (Hill 583), whilst B Company was to move along a high ridge to its right (Ridge 573). A Company thought that both objectives were lightly held and believed that the enemy was withdrawing. At the same time, D Company, which was still pinned down by fire from Hill 583, was to start moving forward again. Once the two hills had been seized, A Company was to send a patrol out to a small pass about 800yds beyond the two hills where enemy activity had been observed, and give early warning of any future enemy attack. Plans were made for artillery support if needed, on Leslie's command, though the intention was that the night attack should be silent.

Whittaker met with his officers in his tent at 2200 hrs for an O Group meeting to discuss and coordinate their detailed plans. Zero hour was set for 0300 hrs the next day, 13 April.

Through no fault of Whittaker's, the O Group turned into a shambles. Literally at the same time as Whittaker was addressing his fellow officers, further orders came in by radio from Brigade HQ for the Battalion to capture two additional features, Points 344 and 349, a mile and a half to the left of Hill 583 and closer to the road. Whittaker protested strongly that it was now dark, that he knew nothing of the ground over which the attack would have to be made, that there was no time to recce or make preparations and that it would leave the Battalion dangerously stretched over a wide area at night. Brigade insisted, whereupon Whittaker suggested giving up on his initial objectives, in order to concentrate his forces on Brigade's additional targets instead. 'No,' he was told, 'you must capture all four – by 0600 hrs.'

This was a tough message, and horribly undermining for Whittaker on the first day of his command.

They set to and made fresh plans. It was finally agreed that, once Leslie and his C Company had captured Hill 583 (with support from one A Company platoon), and B Company had captured Ridge 573, A Company, instead of patrolling ahead, would switch left and attack Point 344, whilst D Company, instead of moving forwards in the wake of C Company's attack on Hill 583, would also move left and attack Point 349.

Whittaker was clearly anxious – his Battalion would be dispersed across a mile of unknown, unfriendly and enemy-held territory. The East Surreys were three miles away in the hills on the other side of the valley beyond the main Beja–Mateur road, and on his right the nearest friendly forces were several miles to the rear.

Leslie was also worried. By now, with zero hour fast approaching, he had little time to brief his platoons, and he also had to deal with a report from his Company Sergeant Major that they had no grenades. With an extremely steep hill to climb, and the danger of grenades rolling back on to his own men, he dismissed this at the time – a decision he would come to regret the next morning. His plan of attack was to send two platoons forward in the assault, with two held in reserve under his second in command, Tom La Fontaine. He would lead the assault himself.

They crossed the start line at 0300 hrs, C Company on the left, B Company on the right. Leslie's notes on the action, written a few weeks later, read as follows:

> We had travelled about half the distance to the objective (about 1,200 yards) when the enemy opened fire on our left. The position was very obscure but, as my assaulting platoons were not under fire, I decided to continue on, leaving the 2 i/c and the reserve platoons to deal with this enemy as necessary. This meant that we had to do a wider detour to our right to get onto the objective, and we were not at the base of the hill until about 0400 hours. 14 Platoon were pushed up the hill to the right, and 13 platoon round to the left . . . and cleared out the observation point, and captured the two occupants. 14 Platoon searched their side of the hill, but discovered an enemy machine gun post . . .
>
> By this time, which was past 0430 and just getting light, 15 Platoon had arrived and parts of the A Company platoon. The hill itself was almost sheer rock, and on the right faced the ridge onto which B

Company were getting and apparently fighting as they went, and on the left it faced towards the high ground A and D companies were to attack later on.

Since he was now in possession of the hill Leslie made a quick recce to decide where best to place his platoons. He wanted to be in a position to support A Company when it launched its own attack on Point 344, a few hundred yards away to the left, but also, more urgently, he needed to ensure that his men would get as much protection from potential enemy mortaring as possible.

*

I have stood on this very spot myself; there was no protection. The top of the hill, a hundred yards or so across, is just bare rock, with a light covering of scrub and patches of dusty soil compacted into the cracks and fissures, and with occasional small boulders covered with yellow lichen. On that cold April morning it must have seemed a very bleak place indeed.

*

Mike Howard was a member of C Company at the time and remembers scrambling up the sheer hillside on to the barren rocky summit. He recalls someone peering over the edge of the hill and calling out agitatedly, 'Those people down there, they're bleeding Germans!' He piled up a few stones to make a *sangar* (a temporary shelter in ground where digging is impossible), slightly in the lee of an overhanging rock, whilst machine gun fire rattled overhead and German mortars thumped. To this day, Howard remains incensed that, thanks to the poor planning at Brigade level, there was only enough ammunition for each man to have ten rounds – nowhere near enough to defend the position. Food and water was short too.

The reserve platoons now arrived, having suffered more than twenty casualties, including the A Company platoon's officer, Lieutenant Carter, and Leslie's second in command, Tom La Fontaine, both injured and out of action. The two platoons were quickly slotted into the defensive position, with the A Company platoon back down towards the base of the hill, ready to get back to A Company if needed. The other platoons, 13, 14 and 15, were to the left, right and rear of the hill respectively. Leslie's HQ was in the middle.

He tried to get word back to his Battalion HQ, but his radio sets were not working, so word was sent back via the A Company platoon that C Company had reached its objective. The failure of the radios meant that messages between Leslie and his own platoon leaders had to be shouted across the hilltop. His report continues:

> There was no chance of digging in at all, with the exception of 13 Platoon who adapted the German observation post, and Company HQ which was on a small piece of grass with the whole hill behind. Platoons had to get as much cover as they could behind small boulders, which they formed in the shape of section posts.
>
> By this time it was quite light and B Company could be observed on their ridge, with two platoons facing our position and the third platoon presumably on the ridge itself. About 0600 we were mortared by light mortars, which seemed to be in a position behind a small hill facing the A Company platoon. 13 Platoon tried to get their two inch mortar on this position, but the range was too great, and shortly after this the heavier mortars opened up on us. It was absolutely impossible to spot any of these as they seemed to be firing by groups from three sides of us, and any movement on our part was greeted by machine gun fire.
>
> 13 and 15 Platoons soon had suffered casualties and I tried to move two sections of 15 Platoon to the other side of the hill, but gave it up as there was no better cover than where they were.

By this time Leslie had managed to get one of the radios working and asked Whittaker to organize an artillery strike on the enemy mortars and forming-up places. He was given the message from Brigade that they believed there were no German troops in the area, to which Leslie's response was 'Yes there are. I'm bloody well looking at them.' Brigade clearly knew better, and the artillery remained silent.

Suddenly, around 0900 hrs, a succession of Verey lights blazed in the sky and a company of crack German troops from the elite Hermann Goering Panzer Division, more than a hundred strong, started scrambling up the steep left flank of the hill, behind the platoon from A Company. Lieutenant Pat Lemon, a 'fresh-faced' 21-year-old, died in the assault, hit by a mortar round. Simultaneously, B Company on its ridge to the right of Hill 583 could be seen to be under attack on all sides by mortar and small arms fire.

The German attack developed with stunning speed on three sides and was supported by mortars firing shells that burst a few feet off the ground, spraying shrapnel in all directions. When 13 Platoon, facing the German position, came under fire next, its leader Crouch was wounded but carried on fighting; whilst 15 Platoon was fired on, too, both platoons losing Bren guns to direct hits from mortar fire.

Leslie then saw, to his horror, two men from 15 Platoon, behind him on the hill, standing up in their trench with their hands in the air. He scrambled out of his 'scrape' and threatened them with a rifle, bullets from a German automatic whistling around his ears from less than 30yds away.

The men in the HQ trench then opened fire and managed to hold the Germans back for a while, but ammunition was now running desperately low, and the lack of grenades that had been reported before they set off 'was sorely felt'. Once again, the radios failed, and it was impossible to alert Whittaker at Battalion HQ to the German counter-attack or call again for artillery support.

A junior officer called Bryant launched himself single-handed at a machine gun post, firing from the hip, and managed to put the post out of action, before being hit himself. The stretcher bearers were kept busy, and two of them were killed.

German losses, too, were heavy, but they had the advantage, and soon a section of the attacking force managed to work its way round to the left and behind the HQ trench. The Germans opened up with a submachine gun and killed two more of Leslie's men instantly (Privates John White and William Jenkins), whilst Private Broom was hit in the back and badly wounded.

In Leslie's own words: 'There was nothing to be done against this new threat, and I surrendered the trench.'

Mike Howard remembers a German soldier pointing his rifle at him and shouting '*Hände hoch!*' Mike helped carry Broom down the hill, and a German medical orderly gave him some morphine.

It remained only for the Germans to mop up 14 Platoon on the far right hand side of the hill. They had been providing support to B Company on the ridge but were now exposed to German fire from behind and had to give in. The Germans now held the high ground, and B Company on Ridge 573 was also overrun.

C Company's brief occupation of Hill 583 was over. As Leslie and his men were marched away, the German forming-up area beyond the hill was shelled – the long-awaited supporting artillery barrage had finally begun, about two hours too late.

Mike Howard saw Leslie at the base of the hill, and asked, 'Did we do all right, sir?'

'Yes,' said Porky Young, 'you did.'

The official history of the Bedfordshire and Hertfordshire Regiment reports as follows:

> B and C Companies had both been violently counter-attacked and suffered very heavily indeed. By the evening, the Battalion had lost about 234 men and Major LC Young and seven subaltern officers were missing. As far as was possible Major Whittaker then gathered the Battalion round the crest of Djebel Aoud where they took up defensive positions.

*

Nearly seventy years later, one day in early March 2010, I stood on Hill 583 with my wife and a Tunisian guide. We had spent the morning visiting the graves of Bedfords who died in the fighting. Colonel Johnson is buried in the Commonwealth War Cemetery at Beja, along with Pat Lemon and John White. It is a tiny cemetery, huddled in a space between three blocks of flats, just by the bus stop. It is not as grand as the majestically peaceful cemetery at Medjez, where William Jenkins has his resting place, but somehow the location seemed appropriate, amongst all the bustle of a busy Arab town.

After lunch, we set off to find Hill 583, driving east along the road towards the station at Sidi Nsir, past Hunt's Gap and Montagne Farm. We found the station easily, unchanged since 1943, and then turned right to see if we could identify 'Leslie's Hill'. I could barely contain my anxiety that it should be there and identifiable.

Suddenly, there it was, on our left hand side as we headed east, a steep grassy hillside leading to a razor-back summit. I leapt out of the car and raced up the hill – I felt literally dragged aloft and got to the top quite exhilarated by the climb. I stopped, aghast. How bare it was! How could anyone have survived there, under a barrage of machine gun fire, mortar shells and shrapnel? I was appalled to think of how vulnerable they must have felt on that cold April morning, and I just sat there on the top, the wind whistling about my ears.

My father never, ever mentioned that morning in April 1943 – not once. The first clue I had about it was that letter from Tom La Fontaine, written forty years later, a year or so before Leslie died:

> *Incidentally [Tom wrote] I have never heard any blame lodged against the Battalion or B or C Company for the Tunisian do. No way can a razor back be held – everyone knows that. It all seems a long time ago.*

It must have haunted my father for forty years, his defeat on that hill top and the fact that some of his men died whilst he survived.

I met Tom and asked him about the letter. Yes, they had met up at a reunion. Tom had been surprised to see Leslie there. They had met only rarely since the war, and my father had never been to one of the annual reunions. Shortly afterwards, Tom had received a letter from him, asking about Tunisia. He said, 'Your father had no reason to feel guilty. He was set an impossible task, and did his absolute best to achieve it. No one could have done any more. He was a completely first class person.'

*

Chapter 12

Into Captivity

Leslie and the survivors of C Company were taken down the hill by the Germans and held under guard with their colleagues from B Company. Later that day, they were all put in trucks and driven north to Ferryville, where Leslie was interrogated. Their first night in captivity was in the squalid local jail. The next day, they were driven south to Tunis and held in a filthy PoW compound at a rubber shoe factory. Jimmy Darville from B Company, when I met him in November 2000, remembered Leslie's greeting at this point: 'Hello Jimmy. Don't say they got you too?'

Dougie Turner of C Company later recorded in his 'Wartime Log' his surprise at being handed over at this stage to the Italians, with eight other officers including Porky Young and Jimmy Darville. They had been defeated and captured by German not Italian troops, of whom they had a rather poor opinion. He recalled Leslie objecting strongly to being asked to fill in a notification form naming the Italians as their captors. But there was nothing they could do – almost all Allied troops captured in North Africa, whether by the Germans or the Italians, were held in prison camps in Italy, by agreement between Hitler and Mussolini.

Within a few days they were marched down to the docks in Tunis, where they spent the night with hundreds of other prisoners in a large cage surrounded by impenetrable barbed wire fencing 12ft high and 3ft wide. Tony Davies, who passed through this transit camp around the same time, describes the scene in his book *When the Moon Rises*:

> Few sights can be more pathetic than that of some hundreds of fit, active young men, formerly members of an efficient fighting force, disarmed and herded together like so many cattle at a market. I know my own feelings at this time were of intense misery and despair. The determination to seize the chance of making a break – a chance which never in fact came – gradually gave way to desperation as the hours before embarkation slipped away.

After a wash in a mobile bathing unit, they were herded aboard the captured French ship *Fort de France* ready for the journey across the Mediterranean to Italy. Turner recalled that they were all amused at the shouts of 'Gangsters!' as they were marched through the crowded streets, whilst Darville remembered Leslie kicking up a fuss because initially they were locked in the ship's hold.

'We're British officers,' he said. 'We don't go in the hold.'

Eventually, the Italian commanding officer appeared and apologised, whereupon they were transferred to quarters just under the ship's guns – which Darville thought was not much of an improvement.

The two-day passage must have been an anxious and uncomfortable one. At the time, some 50 per cent of Italian shipping in the Mediterranean between Africa and Sicily was being sunk by the Royal Navy and the RAF. Had the *Fort de France* been hit, there is little chance that there would have been any survivors.

On 21 April they docked at Naples early in the morning, and in the afternoon were taken by train to PG (Prigionieri di Guerra) Campo 66 at Capua, 30 miles to the north-east, where they arrived at 2000 hrs. Capua was a sprawling transit camp on a flat plain at the foot of the Apennine Mountains where thousands of officers and 'other ranks', captured in North Africa, were accommodated in separate wired-off compounds of wooden huts, awaiting transfer to more permanent prison camps. The officers' compound was small, about 75yds long and 30yds wide, with four 90ft long huts – three for sleeping and one as a mess. Each sleeping hut held upwards of thirty 'beds' (three planks laid between iron uprights), each with a straw mattress and two smelly blankets.

The next day, Leslie filled out a small brown card, a *Carta di Cattura per Prigionieri di Guerra*, giving his regiment, rank and number, and stating that he was well and in captivity. The card also gave his father's name and home address, and all this information was repeated on a tear-off portion of the card which was sent back to his parents. The original card is now lodged in the headquarters of the International Red Cross Tracing Agency in Geneva, which houses the records of all prisoners of war who have been formally registered with it, as required by the Geneva Conventions.

*

I can still recall my excitement on first seeing this extraordinary document. 'Mr Young, I've found him!' called Madame Scheinberger, Head of the Tracing Agency in Geneva, when she caught me just as I was leaving to catch my plane after a day of Red Cross meetings. I was working for the British Red Cross at the time, and had casually mentioned my father's time in a PoW camp in Italy to one of my Swiss colleagues. A few hours later, I was holding in my hands that card from fifty years previously, with my father's instantly recognizable handwriting on it. I could see him at once, in my mind's eye, in the camp, so irritated at his plight and at having to fill in this prosaic little form (with all that it implied), yet thinking also of home and his worried family – and the equally mixed feelings of his parents in comfortable Epsom, as they read sadly of his capture, but with relief that he wasn't injured or dead.

It was around this time, in Capua Camp, that my father started keeping a diary. It is a small pocket notebook, with a scuffed magenta cover, its lined pages filled with a haphazard collection of notes of briefings and occasional jottings, a draft report on his capture, some lists of fellow soldiers and quotes and ideas from books he had read. I found it in a drawer in his bedroom, a day or two after his sudden death from pneumonia in 1986, and put it to one side to read later. It was some time before I picked it up again and discovered that, beyond the jottings, and starting on the last page and working backwards, in tiny cramped pencil scribbles, was a day-by-day account of his captivity.

I was baffled. My father had never at any time mentioned the existence of this diary to me, or to my mother. Indeed, he hardly ever spoke about the war at all. I was aware that he had been a PoW, but he had never told us the story properly and, to my eternal regret, I never asked him to do so. And now he was dead, and it was too late. But he left us the diary and, as I squinted and peered at the crabbed script, I realized that I had a job to do – to work out his story for myself and to bring it to life for my own children.

The diary entries are brief – a couple of lines for each day – but they paint an extraordinary picture of life as a PoW in Italy: the daily routines, the sporting and social activities that helped the hours to pass, books read and friends made, the little glimpses of life outside the narrow world of the camp itself. Some of it I found hard to understand, until I was able to track down fuller accounts written by other PoWs which made it all much clearer. I feel extraordinarily lucky to have been able to follow the story in my father's words through the pages of his thin little notebook.

*

As soon as Leslie had finished filling in his small brown *Carta di Cattura*, the diary records that he was plunged straight into some of the tedious realities of prison life – he was taken off for a bath, and his clothes were removed for de-lousing in a hot oven. Prisoners had to wear a large red patch on their backs, so that had to be sewn on, and Leslie cut down his thick battledress trousers to make shorts.

Every morning, at around 0830 hrs, the men were summoned by the interpreter Magione for roll call. They would shamble out of their huts in dribs and drabs and then hang about in the yard until everyone was assembled and the Italian second in command could begin the count. But there were always delays – some found it hard to get up at all, and others appeared but then wandered off to wash or start preparing breakfast if nothing seemed to be happening. If the count appeared to be short of a man or two, then the Capitano, or Deputy Commandant, would go into a huddle with the Senior British Officer, to try and work out what had gone wrong; then there would be a recount, or all the names would be read out one by one and ticked off in the register. But not until the roll call was completed to the Capitano's satisfaction could coffee be served and the day's activities begin.

Food quickly became a constant obsession, because there was nowhere near enough of it for fit and energetic young men. Breakfast was a cup of black coffee made from dried lupin seeds; lunch was a plate of macaroni soup with a roll of brown bread; tea consisted of another cup of coffee, with some cheese and a few dates. And that was it. To stay at all fit, or even alive, the men depended on a regular weekly food parcel from the Red Cross, made up by volunteers in Britain, Canada and other countries, shipped to Marseilles, taken by train to Geneva and then distributed from there by the Red Cross to prison camps all over Europe. But Red Cross parcels were often in short supply at Capua, with one parcel, (usually comprising tinned meat or fish, cheese, powdered milk, sugar, tea, chocolate and dried fruit, as well as soap and cigarettes) having to be shared between two men.

The food provided by the Italians was eaten communally in a Mess Hut; but for the food in the Red Cross parcels the men divided themselves into 'syndicates' of five, who would cook for themselves. Leslie was in a syndicate with Dougie Turner. Fetching the weekly parcels for each syndicate, preparing supplementary meals with the contents, dividing the tiny portions exactly equally between the five famished syndicate members, and then wolfing it down, became a main focus of activity.

But first, the syndicate had to build its own stove, out of tins from the parcels and mud from the prison compound. Then they had to collect wood and shavings for the fire, usually from the primitive furniture in their huts, or by using odd pieces of wooden equipment carelessly left lying around by the Italian guards. Once they had got the fire alight, the syndicate members would share out the tasks of blowing on the embers, opening the Red Cross tins and stirring, frying or toasting whatever there was to cook, then dividing the result into five tiny but equal portions. Leslie, ever the builder's son, made a tin stove on his second day in the camp, Good Friday, as his contribution to the syndicate.

There was also a small canteen, set up at the far end of one of the huts and managed by Magione and one of the guards. Magione bought food items and kit like razor blades and pencils off the local black market and sold them to the PoWs, no doubt at a profit to himself, the prisoners paying with lire chits from their weekly allowance. There were often long queues, especially when fruit or cakes were in stock, although some of the men became adept at making their own cakes, avidly watched by the other members of their syndicate, mouths watering and proffering (usually unwelcome) advice or encouragement.

There were regular squabbles – about how best to squeeze an extra cup out of a teabag or how to divide a piece of chocolate or cake into five. Some were better at cooking, or less clumsy than others, or had a better eye for dividing the portions, and petty jealousies and suspicions easily became magnified out of all proportion in the cramped and frustrating conditions – but at least it occupied the time and kept them from starving.

Health and hygiene were also constant concerns, with about 150 men living at close quarters in three huts and sharing six latrines, often with no water available for flushing. Baths or showers were infrequent – Leslie had three in the six weeks he spent in the camp. Everyone had intermittent diarrhoea, or 'squitters', but there were also more serious outbreaks of diphtheria and jaundice, which caused several deaths. Bugs were another source of regular discomfort, and prisoners spent hours scouring their huts and bed boards with flaming sticks and boiling their clothes to try and eradicate them. There were clouds of flies everywhere.

In Capua discipline was fairly light-touch, perhaps due to the naturally easy-going temperament of the Italian guards (who were not front line troops), and the inclination of the prisoners themselves (encouraged by the Senior British Officer, who was responsible for the safety of the men and for maintaining Army discipline) to keep everything on a reasonably even keel, in the interests of peace and harmony. Occasionally, prisoners would be sent off for a spell of solitary confinement in 'the cooler', but men took this in their stride as part of 'the game' they played with their captors.

The handsome interpreter Corporal Magione was a key figure, a likeable rogue who was in some ways seen as the true commander of the camp. He spoke English well and had an intelligent, good-humoured approach to mundane tasks like taking the roll call, organizing meals, dishing out post or making sure the men had reasonably regular baths. He was also willing, at a price, to run errands for the prisoners or buy little 'illegal' extras in the town – a trade which quickly developed into a major business, with two or three cartloads of contraband goods making their way into the camp every time he went out. He was a fixer, who endeared himself to the men as a result.

So life in the camp was reasonably stable and manageable, even if crowded and uncomfortable. The diary shows that Leslie engaged in a wide variety of social activities – keeping fit with regular PT, playing football and table tennis, losing money (usually) at poker and vingt-et-un, sitting in on lectures and gramophone and band concerts (instruments sourced, no doubt, via Magione), taking part in a play (*And Now Tomorrow* by Rachel Field), having lessons in bridge and Italian, studying *Builders Estimating* and *Architectural Building Construction*, writing letters home (though he didn't receive any), taking part in quizzes, debates and spelling bees, attending Church services regularly – and reading and reading and reading. The camp had a small library (thanks in part to the Red Cross) under a bed in one of the huts, with boxes for fiction, biographies and 'heavyweight literature and improving works', and Leslie lists in his diary all the books he read while he was in the camp.

He also went on several 'walks'. How could you go for a walk in a prison camp, I asked myself. But they did:

Saturday, 1 May – cold better, change of sheets. Walk in afternoon 5 miles glorious feeling

Monday, 3 May – House planning and designing. Walk to Church in afternoon fine view. English parcels received

Thursday, 13 May – Wrote to Mum and [sister] Muriel. Very good walk to mineral springs

The men were occasionally allowed out in groups to get some additional exercise, escorted by a couple of guards and having given their undertaking not to try and escape. The two-hour walks were very popular as an opportunity to stretch one's legs and to see something of the surrounding area – but also to have some fun at the expense of their guards by striding out at route march pace, leaving the less fit captors struggling along behind. In groups of fifty or so at a time, they would set off from the main gate at a great lick, only to slow down suddenly to look at the wild flowers or admire a particularly fine view – and then speed up again to 'get a bit more exercise'. Singing was popular but discouraged.

They kept up to speed on the progress of the war, as far as they could. On Saturday, 8 May, Leslie's diary recalls that the Senior British Officer announced the fall of Tunis; this must have been bitter-sweet news for all those captured in the fighting in Tunisia. There was a well-established wall newspaper in the camp, called *Clickety-Click* and composed of handwritten sheets of notepaper gummed side by side on to an Italian newspaper, which was then pinned up on the wall with barbs twisted from the barbed-wire fence. There was usually a leading article, a detailed summary and critique of the war news as given in the Italian papers and snippets of home news culled from letters from England. There was also a strip cartoon, odd features and recipes, a gossip column and spoof adverts.

Some took to the cheek by jowl existence in camp better than others. Many had been psychologically bruised by their capture and found it hard to show trust or share wholeheartedly in the life of the camp community. Michael Ross, in *The British Partisan*, talks of the dramatic changes in social behaviour in the early days of captivity:

> Personal relationships, previously normal, suddenly showed strain. Individuals became markedly insular, withdrawing from larger groups and associating strictly in twos or threes. These small groups kept entirely to themselves to the exclusion of others. Strangers were shunned, and absolutely no attempt was made to form new friendships.

This produced 'an atmosphere of mistrust and suspicion', and Ross goes on to speculate that it was deep-seated insecurity that led to these behaviour changes, with men seeking the intimacy and protection of a small family-like group, plus the loss of 'any immediate purpose in life, coupled with fear for the future and the realization that one was powerless to influence it'.

There is little evidence in Leslie's diary that he was particularly prone to such thoughts. Certainly he brooded on his capture, since the notebook in which he wrote his diary contains a long analysis of how it happened, and the diary itself records that, very soon after arriving in Capua, he wrote to the parents of Private Pat Lemon, who died on Hill 583. He records several conversations with other individual officers – 'Talked with Ricketts. Liked him very much' and 'Long talk with Webb'. But he also seems to have enjoyed taking part in wider group activities, and shows a quite boyish enthusiasm for simple pleasures – 'Bought first cherries at canteen'; 'First performance by camp dance band. Very good'; 'Evening play reading good'. He says absolutely nothing about his mood, nor does he ruminate on his plight.

The diary is also, understandably, silent about the possibility of escape. It was the duty of every officer to try and escape, and for many this became their *raison d'être*, to the annoyance of some of their fellow captives who disliked both the disruption that preparations for an escape attempt caused to their daily routines and the trouble that resulted for everyone when an escape attempt was made. It was also a very dangerous business.

The lights around the wire were left on all night, except during an air raid, when anyone seen near the fence was liable to be shot on sight. Tunnelling was also impossible in the restricted confines of the Capua camp. Climbing the wire was out of the question, since the Italians were trigger-happy and regarded anyone who tried to escape as a dangerous lunatic who deserved to be shot, as some were. The effect on those who remained was distressing and chilling

Chapter 13

Fontanellato

Friday, 28 May – rumours confirmed. Am moving to Camp 49. All morning washing. Another touch of sun – did not feel too good at rehearsal.

Monday, 31 May – moving tomorrow. Wrote telegram. English parcel. Played in 'And Now Tomorrow'. Saw large numbers of English bombers.

Tuesday, 1 June/Wednesday, 2 June – spent morning packing few belongings and saying goodbyes. Left Capua about 16.00 hrs and travelled by train Rome–Florence–Bologna–Parma to new camp. Arrived Rome 23.00. Left 03.00 arrived Florence 07.00 hrs, Bologna 09.00 and left 15.00 hrs. Tony Emery and party got off at Modena. We arrived at new camp 19.00 hrs. Sharing room with Bill Caffyn Surreys.

*

Leslie's diary entries convey a small frisson of anticipation, even excitement, as he set off by train in a cattle truck from Capua for the new camp. For some time after my discovery of the diary in 1986 I couldn't work out the location of the new camp, save that it was obviously in the north of Italy. By chance, however, I took out from our local library the Eric Newby book Love and War in the Apennines, *and soon realized that he and my father must have been in the same camp – Fontanellato, near Parma. I wrote to Eric, who said that he had indeed known Leslie and put me in touch with Keith Killby, who was running an organization called the Monte San Martino Trust, set up by other former PoWs in Italy, many of them also from Fontanellato.*

A few weeks later, I was in the basement of a small Italian restaurant in Haymarket having lunch with half a dozen of these 'old soldiers'. Several of them had escaped from Fontanellato and had been helped whilst on the run by impoverished Italian farming folk (the contadini*). As a way of saying thank you, they had formed a small charity to bring young Italians from mountain* *communities to the UK to learn some English. This was the start of a lifelong association with the Trust, which I now chair and which has brought me closer to my father, the soldier, than anything else.*

*

According to Italian and Allied sources, 79,533 Allied soldiers, sailors and airmen were being held in Italian prison camps by the late summer of 1943 – 42,194 Britons, 26,126 from other Commonwealth countries, 9,903 from mainland Europe and 1,310 Americans. Almost all had been captured, like my father, in North Africa.

Around the same time, the British War Office identified 72 main PoW camps in Italy, 12 prison hospitals and 7 camps for civilian internees. There were also dozens of sub-camps, set up to house 'other ranks', for whom work was compulsory – officers were excluded from this requirement by the Geneva Conventions.

Fontanellato was a cut above most of the other camps. The prisoners were housed, not in huts within a barbed wire compound, but in a large new '*orfanotrofio*', or orphanage, just to the east of the town centre. The building, with its rather pompous 'Fascist sham-classical' façade, had been planned in the 1920s but wasn't completed until the early years of the war. It was built with funds contributed by pilgrims to the neighbouring shrine of the Madonna del Rosario, who was credited with a number of miracles in the seventeenth century.

The orphanage was built on three stories plus an attic, with a large multi-storey galleried central hall/chapel, wings on both sides and a basement. Despite its grandiose façade and marble staircase, the building was so unstable that, according to Newby, it seemed to wobble like a jelly if anyone jumped up and down on one of the upper floors, or even got out of bed heavily. The washing, toilet and cooking facilities were good and, though crammed in, the prisoners actually enjoyed the luxury of proper beds rather than wooden bunks, either in one of the light and airy 24-bed dormitories, or in a smaller 6- or 10-bed room.

In front of the main building was a large courtyard, and behind was a two-acre grass compound, the whole being surrounded by a barbed wire fence with watch towers at each corner. It was next door to the convent and church of the Sanctuary del Rosario, and just behind it was the town cemetery – so it was quite a busy corner of the town. The nuns in the convent did the men's laundry and would often exchange notes with the prisoners or undertake little errands for them in the town.

The town itself, which today has a population of 7,000, boasts a fifteenth-century moated castle called the Rocca Sanvitale and, facing it, a market square with deep shaded arcades of shops and cafés, as well as a small, ornate and very pretty eighteenth-century opera house. It is about ten miles north-west of Parma, in the fertile Plain of Lombardy, between the River Po and the busy main Via Emilia to Milan. To the south, beyond the road, are the Apennine Mountains, the spine of Italy.

PG *(prigionero di guerra)* Campo 49 housed, by the time of Leslie's arrival in June 1943, 540 prisoners – 502 soldiers, 28 airmen and 10 sailors. Of these 479 were British, 4 were American and the rest came from other Commonwealth countries. Most of the captives were junior officers, with a sprinkling of majors (of whom Leslie was one) and 114 'other ranks', who were paid ten shillings a month by the officers to act as orderlies and personal servants or 'batmen'. The Senior British Officer (SBO) was Lieutenant Colonel Norman Tyndale-Biscoe, a Great War veteran.

Guarding the prisoners were 70 Italian soldiers, commanded by Colonel Eugenio Vicedomini, also a veteran of the Great War, in which he had fought alongside British troops against the Austrians. He had a good relationship with his British counterpart, as did his second-in-command, Captain Mario Jack Camino, who had an English wife and had been in business in Slough before the war.

Fontanellato has been described as something of a 'show camp'. Philip Kindersley, who came with Leslie from Capua, described it as 'the Ritz Hotel of prison camps'. A report carried out under the Geneva Conventions in May 1943 by an attaché at the Swiss Legation in Rome reported that it was the best prison his team had visited in Italy. He found the lodgings 'clean and comfortable, the camp well organized and morale high'. The SBO agreed.

Leslie must have been counting his lucky stars as he unpacked his clothes and put them in his personal wardrobe in the room he was to share with three other majors, Laird, Duthie and Pyman. 'Weather glorious – much cooler – no flies', he noted on 4 June and, three days later, 'First walk at Fontanellato. Short but very enjoyable'.

The first thing he noticed was that food was organized on a collective basis. This was a significant change. The food in the camp was reasonable anyway, though limited in terms of variety, but there was also a fairly regular supply of Red Cross parcels, with tins of meat, real butter and dried milk to relieve the monotony of rice and pasta. Instead of being issued individually or in syndicates, all the cookable food was removed from the parcels and prepared in the kitchens, thereby obviating the need for hoarding food under beds or trying to cook it on open fires in or around the building.

The basic rations allowed by the Italians could also be supplemented, either individually or collectively, on the black market, using as currency cigarettes supplied by the Red Cross, or through the medium of an enterprising little business called Opps Limited, set up by a captured bomber crew member called 'Rainy' Rainsford. For a straight 10 per cent commission he would organize anything, from tailoring and watch repairs to special purchases and the rescue of cigarette lighters dropped down the loos – easily done as the toilets were of the continental 'squat over a hole' variety. Leslie was delighted to be able to buy 4oz of tobacco from him on his second day.

Leslie describes a 'typical day's feeding' in his diary:

> Small roll for breakfast, cup of cocoa at 11 o'clock. Plate of stew (no meat) with 4 small peaches for lunch. One Canadian biscuit and cup of tea for tea. Small quantity of fish pie, 2 potatoes (small) with marrow, rice and coffee for dinner.

Even alcohol was available: the Italians provided a daily ration of half a litre of the 'strange, dark and repulsive' local wine, heavily doctored with various chemical additives; but better wines, an excellent Vermouth and beer could also be purchased by the prisoners, and every man was entitled to a daily ration – and could buy more if he had money left over from his 'pay' (issued in the form of vouchers and based on the pay of an Italian officer of equivalent rank). Leslie helped celebrate Peter Laird's birthday on 24 June, no doubt contributing some of his pay or cigarette ration in order to buy more drink, and Newby describes a very successful party thrown by an elderly lieutenant colonel which ended with the tipsy host walking into a cupboard and shutting himself inside, in the mistaken belief that he was walking into his own room. Some of the prisoners also tried making their own alcohol in a bath in the basement, but it wasn't a success.

There was even a bar, in the 'minstrels' gallery' on the first floor, run by Tommy Pitman and open for business late morning and in the evening. The bar looked out on to the road into the town centre and afforded the prisoners a view of any local girls who happened to be passing by – but this was a dangerous business. The Italians had forbidden such peeking (and the whistling that frequently went with it), and the sentries in the watch towers beyond the wire would take pot shots through the windows (the glass had long since been blown out) to deter spectators.

The daily routine in Fontanellato was similar to Capua, with tedious roll calls morning and evening in the compound at the rear of the main building, after which the men were left to do pretty much as they pleased. As at Capua, there were lectures, voluntary classes, plays and play readings, a band, gramophone record concerts and sports, and games of chess or cards. Football became a big craze, with seven-a-side matches every day, morning and evening, attracting big crowds, plenty of barracking and a great deal of betting. There were also various clubs, including an angling club, without water, and a motoring club, without cars.

Leslie seems to have had a go at the lot:

> Thursday, 17 June – reading Buchan's 'The Dancing Floor'. Wrote to Mother. Lecture on Iraq Rebellion by Lt Col Everett – very good.

> Friday, 18 June – very good walk. Played basketball and lost 6–4 after two lots of extra time.

> Saturday, 7 August – played chess with Blake. Basketball against the Queens and won 16–2. Bridge – lost 6 lira, 46 lira in total

Others just wandered about in small groups and talked, or stared out of the window, often at the beautiful-looking Italian girls walking by in the street below on their traditional evening *passeggiata*, or on Sunday mornings when they would come cycling in from nearby farms to go to church in Fontanellato. They would stop at a hut opposite the camp to leave their bicycles and put on their stockings – an event that always attracted a large audience willing to risk pot-shots from the guards outside.

Men responded to prison in different ways. Newby got in with a bunch of 'upper class OK people' – 'the sons and brothers of peers and Highland lairds, young merchant bankers, wine shippers and gentleman jockeys' – accustomed to power and privilege whether inside or outside a prison camp, and for whom life in Fontanellato was in some ways merely an extension of public school. They tended to associate exclusively with each other, regarding the majority of other (mostly lower or middle class) prisoners with condescension or as a source of amusement. They occupied one of the dormitories as, to all intents and purposes, their private 'Gentleman's Club'.

The OK group in particular liked to gamble, and they set up a baccarat table in the basement. Backgammon was popular, too, and they also placed bets on cork races in a small stream which ran across part of the compound and on games of football or running races between members of the various armies represented in the camp. Leslie played cards, too, always for small stakes, which was perhaps just as well as he usually lost – 'played bridge and lost 12.50 lire. Total for month now 58.50 lire'; 'Lost at bridge again, 70 lire down'.

Inevitably, with large numbers of fit young men cooped up at close quarters in a confined space, some friendships became deeper than others. Dan Billany, for example, was gay, as were a small minority of others in the camp. In his book *The Cage*, written with his partner David Dowie, Billany tells the moving story of their developing but clandestine relationship while they were in the camp. They disappeared whilst on the run together later in 1943, and their bodies have never been found. Billany gave the draft of his book to a friendly farmer during the escape, and after the war the farmer sent it to his parents, who had it published to considerable acclaim.

Peter Watson, who had joined the Duke of Cornwall's Light Infantry and, before the war, gone to serve in India noted, in his account, *Mountain Highway*:

> I was an only child and rather small and, despite having commanded a company in action, still felt rather diffident among men who had a greater experience of the world than my own. It is difficult to judge oneself and how one changes, but [in the camp] I learned a lot about the world, beyond my own limited military experience, and expanded my ideas to encompass those of men who had had a very different upbringing and education in the world. Prison affected us all in various ways and I think that, in my case, it helped me to grow up.

Leslie's diary doesn't mention that he had any particularly close friends. Of the three majors he shared a room with, only Pyman (who led the Escape Committee and was therefore an important figure in the camp) gets a regular mention, mainly as a bridge partner, though one or two entries hint at a closer friendship:

Thursday, 29 June – Pyman gave me tobacco and saved situation.

Thursday, 6 July – nothing much to report. Pay for month 465 – drew 400 and paid debts. Collected 103 for card winnings. Annoyed Pyman very stupidly.

Above left: Second Lieutenant Leslie with his older brother Alan, photograph taken around 1929. (*Young family*)

Above right: Major Leslie Young, 1942, by Tom La Fontaine. (*By kind permission of the artist's family*)

Below: The bridge at Escanaffles after its destruction by the Bedfordshire and Hertfordshire regiment, May 1940.

Above: Painting of the beach at Dunkirk by Tom La Fontaine. (*Artist's family*)

Below: The East Mole at Dunkirk.

Above: The SS *Ben-my-Chree*, the ship that took Leslie home from Dunkirk.

Right: 4 Commando 'skull' badge, 1940. (*Author's collection*)

Below: Extract from 4 Commando F Troop Diary, 1940, showing 'Sunbathing Parade' on the beach at Weymouth and 'O.C. F Troop' Captain Leslie Young. (*Author's collection*)

SUN BATHING PARADE.

THE 'O.C.' F.

THE WAR

No. 74

3D WEEKLY

Incorporating WAR PICTORIAL

OUR BRILLIANT RAID ON LOFOTEN ISLANDS

Lofoten Islands Raid, March 1941
Above: The sea alight with burning cod oil. (*Dr G. Mikes*, The Epic of Lofoten, *Hutchinson*)

Left: Front cover of *The War* magazine, 21 March 1941, published by George Newnes Ltd.

British troops leaving one of the Islands with prisoners and Norwegian volunteers. (The War *magazine*)

The village of Brettesnes on the Norwegian island of Store Molla, where Leslie landed with his Commando Troop. Photograph taken from the sea in 2011. (*Author's collection*)

Hunt's Gap, Tunisia, 1943. C Company HQ 2 Battalion Queen's Regiment, pen and ink sketch by Tom La Fontaine. (*Artist's family*)

Hill 583, Tunisia, taken by Leslie's Company and subsequently recaptured by the Germans. (*Author's collection*)

International Committee of the Red Cross record of Leslie's capture in Tunisia, still held in Geneva. (*Author's collection*)

Above: Italian Prisoner of War Camp, Fontanellato PG49, near Parma, northern Italy – photograph taken in 2017. (*Author's collection*)

Below: Sketch plan of Fontanellato PG49 from *Home by Christmas?* by Ian English. (*English family*)

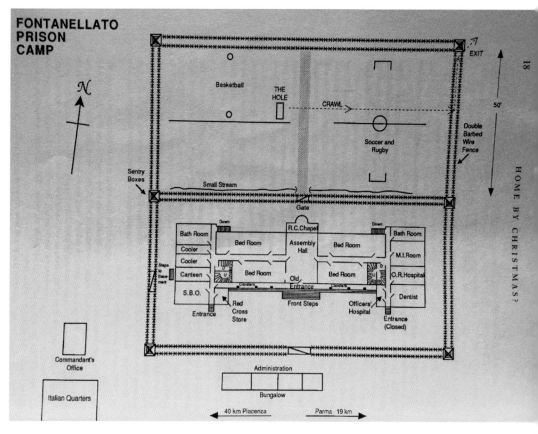

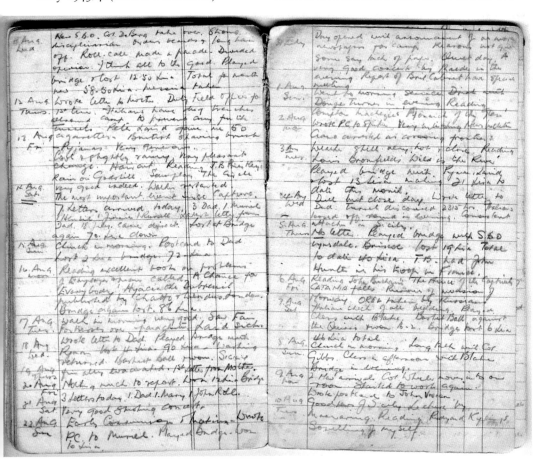

Right: Painting by Ronald Mann of the breakout from Fontanellato PG49, used on the front cover of *Home by Christmas?* (*Estate of Ronald Mann*)

Below: Extract from Leslie's diary, kept during his imprisonment and escape in Italy 1943/4. (*Author's collection*)

HOME BY CHRISTMAS?

edited by
IAN ENGLISH

The village of Banzola, near Fontanellato, where Leslie spent his first night 'on the run'. (*Author's collection*)

The Apennine village of Specchio, where 'half the village turned out to meet them', and local girls sang Ave Maria at the nearby shrine – one of more than forty villages in the mountains where Leslie spent a night. (*Author's collection*)

Above left: Pilot Officer Reg Dickinson, Leslie's first escaping partner.

Above right: The New Zealander Charlie Gatenby, with whom Leslie spent four months dodging German patrols. (*Gatenby family*)

German Wanted Poster, signed by the Supreme Commander of the German Forces, warning Italians that the Badoglio Government has 'treacherously released' Allied PoWs, some of whom are still at large 'breaking into your homes and looting your gardens and fields'. Suggesting that the escapees are 'still, as before, your enemies', the poster urges Italians to apprehend any PoWs they find, and to hand them over to the nearest German soldier. A reward of 1800 lire or £20 is offered. (*Gatenby family*)

Avviso per la ricattura di fuggitivi prigionieri di guerra inglesi e americani

Italiani !

Con disonesta e rea leggerezza il traditore governo Badoglio ha messo in libertà prigionieri di guerra inglesi e americani.

La maggior parte di essi è già stata ricatturata per mezzo di truppe tedesche. Una parte però si aggira ancora per le campagne, introducendosi nelle vostre case e saccheggiando i vostri orti e i vostri campi.

Italiani !

Guardatevi da questi evasi che ora come prima sono vostri nemici! Catturateli dove li trovate e consegnateli ai più vicini soldati tedeschi oppure avvisate dove tali fuggitivi si nascondono!

Io dispongo, per ogni riacciuffato prigioniero di guerra, una ricompensa di lire italiane 1800 o 20 sterline a scelta di colui che fa la cattura.

IL COMANDANTE SUPREMO
DELLE TRUPPE TEDESCHE

The village of Corvaro, where Leslie and Charlie hid from the Germans November–January 1943/4. (*Author's collection*)

Above: Peppino and Bernadina de Michelis, who hid Leslie and Charlie in their home and then in a shepherd's hut. (*Gatenby family*)

Below: Alexander Certificate presented to the de Michelis family on the recommendation of Leslie and Charlie and other escapers. (*de Michelis family*)

This certificate is awarded to ...Michelis Giuseppe as a token of gratitude for and appreciation of the help given to the Sailors, Soldiers and Airmen of the British Commonwealth of Nations, which enabled them to escape from, or evade capture by the enemy.

H.R. Alexander

Field Marshal,
Supreme Allied Commander,
Mediterranean Theatre

1939–1945

Questo certificato è rilasciato al

de Michelis Giuseppe

quale attestato di gratitudine e riconoscimento per l'aiuto dato ai membri delle Forze Armate degli Alleati che li ha messi in grado di evadere od evitare di essere catturati dal nemico

Il Maresciallo Britannico
Comandante Supremo delle Forze Alleate
del Mediterraneo

1939–1945

62535
15262

Right: The *casale* or homestead in the Valley of the Bandits – home to Leslie and Charlie during the worst of the winter of 1943/4. (*Author's collection*)

Below: Eugenio and Silvia Elfer hiking in the Abruzzi mountains, pre-1943. (*Elfer family*)

The grave of the Elfer family, Antonio, Elisa and their children, Eugenio and Silvia, in the Cimitero Monumentale at Verano, Rome.

Podere (farmstead) *355* and the ditch near Borgo Podgora, where Eugenio's body was found after the war. (*Both images from author's collection*)

Above left: Count Carlo Tevini, Silvia's companion, who helped guide Leslie and Charlie to safety and was wounded by a German patrol but survived. (*Tevini family*)

Above right: The author retraces his father's footsteps, leaving a 'thank you letter' in every village. A letter pinned to a tree near Castelcorniglio. (*Author's collection*)

Below left: A notice pinned to a tree near Vegheretto was seen by a member of the Bragagni family (pictured here), in whose home Leslie spent a night in October 1943. (*Bragagni family*)

Below right: Angiolina (née Bragagni), aged fifteen in 1943, who saw the notice and recognized Leslie from the photograph, with the author. (*Author's collection*)

Above: A tree planted in Leslie's honour in the orchard at Lucoli, with plaque. (*Emanuela Mariani*)

Below: Plaque in the orchard at Lucoli. (*Emanuela Mariani*)

GIARDINO DELLA MEMORIA
DEL SISMA
DEL 6 APRILE 2009

DONATO DA
MONTE SAN MARTINO TRUST

REMEMBERING IN PARTICULAR MAJOR
LESLIE YOUNG, WHO SPENT A NIGHT
IN LUCOLI DURING HIS ESCAPE FROM PG
CAMPO 49

GIUGNO. 2018

Noi X lucoli ONLUS

Above: The house on the Livarot–Orbec road where Leslie's HQ was attacked by a tank and he was wounded. (*Author's collection*)

Right: Letter from the War Office dated 30 August 1944 with news that Leslie had been wounded. (*Author's collection*)

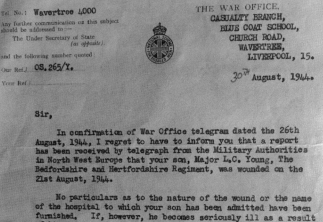

Tel. No.: **Wavertree 4000**

Any further communication on this subject should be addressed to :—

The Under Secretary of State (*as opposite*).

and the following number quoted :

Our Ref.: **OS.265/Y.**

Your Ref.:

THE WAR OFFICE,
CASUALTY BRANCH,
BLUE COAT SCHOOL,
CHURCH ROAD,
WAVERTREE,
LIVERPOOL, 15.

30ᵗʰ August, 1944.

Sir,

In confirmation of War Office telegram dated the 26th August, 1944, I regret to have to inform you that a report has been received by telegraph from the Military Authorities in North West Europe that your son, Major L.C. Young, The Bedfordshire and Hertfordshire Regiment, was wounded on the 21st August, 1944.

No particulars as to the nature of the wound or the name of the hospital to which your son has been admitted have been furnished. If, however, he becomes seriously ill as a result of his wound, you will be notified by telegraph. In the absence of such a communication, it can be assumed that Major Young is making normal progress in which event you will, no doubt, hear from him in due course, if you have not already done so, about his wound and progress.

Will you kindly notify this office of any change in your address, in case further reports are received.

I am, Sir,
Your obedient Servant,

G.W. Young, Esq.,
"Speldhurst",
St. Martins Avenue,
Epsom,
Surrey.

Above: The de Michelis family today, still living in Corvaro. (*Author's collection*)

Left: Leslie Young in 1980, six years before his death. (*Young family*)

Laird, too, another roommate, the one whose birthday party he had attended, was clearly a chum:

> Thursday, 12 August – Pete Laird gave me 50 cigarettes, British shaving brush, pyjamas. Very generous.

But Leslie was never a 'heart and soul of the party' type, and my guess is that he would have disapproved slightly of the OK group and their antics and casual approach. He was a soldier, somewhat reserved and always professional in his manner and bearing. He was, nevertheless, a reasonably sociable chap, who took part in and contributed to the life of the camp. He was also a dedicated self-improver:

> Sunday, 13 June – Whit Sunday. Holy Communion first thing. Talk with Laing RE whose building books I had borrowed.

> Tuesday, 15 June – hot bath. Work in morning and afternoon.

> Monday, 12 July – examination on hot water fittings.

Sensibly, he seems to have attended every lecture going, many of them about the wider strategy and progress of the war from senior officers who were able to give the men a broader perspective. Lieutenant Colonel Hugh Mainwaring, a veteran of El Alamein, gave an excellent series of lectures about the 1940–41 campaign in the desert against the Italians and 'was able to explain the reasons for actions which up to then had been something of a mystery to all of us' (Peter Langrishe quoted by Ian English, *Home by Christmas?*).

Leslie was also a regular letter writer, to family and friends, though he received none himself until late in the summer, and this clearly troubled him:

> Monday, 21 June – lots of mail in but none for me. Bad day. Started hot water fitting with Laing.

> Wednesday, 21 July – wrote letter to Dad. Saw SBO about mail from Capua.

> Monday, 26 July – letters for the subalterns but none for me.

> Thursday, 29 July – still no letters. Feeling bad about this. Have stopped working. Reading 'How Green was my Valley'.

> Saturday, 14 August – the most important event since capture. 7 letters arrived today, 3 Dad, 1 Muriel, 1 Hensie, 1 Jinnie, 1 Russell.

Latest letter from Dad dated 18 July came direct. Lost at bridge again, 70 lira down.

Leslie's parents kept all his letters home for years, though sadly they were chucked out when the family home in Epsom was sold in the 1960s.

Ensuring that the prisoners were kept up to date with what was happening in the outside world was the responsibility of Larry Allen, an American sailor who had been serving with the British Mediterranean fleet in HMS *Ark Royal* when she was sunk in 1942. He interviewed every new prisoner, pumping them for information about the progress of the war at the time of their capture, and scoured letters received from home for snippets of news that might have escaped the censors. Italian newspapers were rigorously analysed and interpreted, and the guards subtly interrogated for further information to add to Allen's regular news bulletins and 'flashes'. There was also a clandestine and very well-hidden radio set in the camp, made from Red Cross parcel tins and camp wire plus valves smuggled in somehow from the town.

Leslie's diary is peppered with references to these news bulletins, in which he clearly took a keen interest; but for some, the news from home was of passing interest only, so used had they become to the relaxed pace of life and easy atmosphere in the camp. In addition, there was a growing sense that an Allied invasion of mainland Europe was only a matter of time. For others, however, the daily news bulletins meant only one thing: the war was passing them by, and they became desperate to rejoin the fray.

Escape in Italy was by no means easy. There were obvious physical differences between the average Tommy and the average Italian, and few of the prisoners had more than a smattering of Italian, let alone the capacity to speak it with a believable accent, so they stuck out like the proverbial sore thumb in a land of sociable, observant people – particularly in remote rural areas, where everyone knows their neighbours and their neighbours' business.

Italy is, of course, surrounded on all sides by sea or by the Alps, so the physical mechanics of escape, even if you got away from the camp, were problematic, and there were no established covert 'escape lines' of sympathetic civilians or resistance workers willing to risk their lives by hiding escaped prisoners and helping them on their way to freedom, as there were by this time in occupied northern Europe. Furthermore, many of the camps were on the outskirts of towns in busy areas, with people passing to and fro all the time – PG49 itself was right in the middle of a busy town – so tunnelling was a huge risk; and, for all their weaknesses as soldiers, the 'Eyeties' were observant as guards, and sensitive to changes of behaviour or mood amongst the prisoners. Only six prisoners are known to have escaped successfully from Italy and got home before the Armistice in September 1943.

Nevertheless, attempts at escape were made from Fontanellato, though none of them were successful. Four PoWs managed to get out briefly by taking it in turns, two by two, to hide in a small trench which they had dug, under cover of some pitch-levelling operations and a rugby match, in the 'sports field' at the rear of the building. Once it was dark, they managed to cut through the wire, intending to make their way north to neutral Switzerland. Despite detailed cover stories, magnificently forged identity cards and other documentation, emergency rations and faked 'civilian' clothing, the two pairs were picked up fairly quickly and brought back to the camp for a spell in 'the cooler'.

The story of the two brave escapes, and the hilarious attempts by their captors to discover how they were made, are brilliantly told by Michael Ross and Toby Graham in accounts of their wartime adventures, and the way each describes his first moments outside the camp is worth quoting:

> Those thrilling first moments of freedom are something I will never forget. It seemed that the world had suddenly opened up before me and I felt intoxicated by the thought that I could now walk on and on as far as I wished, free of escorts and barriers. (Michael Ross, *The British Partisan*)

> It was a wonderful night and I felt so free and full of life that there was little room for gloomy thoughts about my failure to rendezvous with the others . . . the night was so fine and warm and I was so thrilled with life that the gravity of the situation did not dawn on me . . . Oh Purest Joy. (Dominick Graham, *The Escapes and Evasions of an Obstinate Bastard*)

Later, work on a tunnel from the basement dining room began, hindered regularly by the guards 'tapping each brick and prodding each crevice and floor tile', according to Tony Davies. This was quite a sophisticated affair, with bellows blowing fresh air to the digging face down a flue constructed from the KLIM (powdered milk) tins in Red Cross parcels, and a light supplied from an electric point in the dining room itself. Unfortunately, the tunnel was discovered when someone carelessly left the light on one night.

Then a second tunnel was started from the ground floor, digging down and through the thickness of the basement ceiling and the outer wall. The men managed to dig to at least 5ft below the level of the basement floor, but then the tunnel flooded, due to the high water table, and had to be abandoned.

Leslie shared a room with Pyman, the chairman of the Escape Committee, and his diary around this time evinces a sudden interest over several days in 'working on field – levelling running track' (Wednesday, 26 June), so presumably he played his part in these escape attempts. Two months later, his diary on Wednesday, 4 August reads laconically: 'Dull but close day. Wrote letter to Dad. Tunnel discovered 23.15 hrs'; and a week later, he records that the 'Italians have dug trenches all round the camp to prevent any further tunnels'.

*

Many years later, in 2003, when I visited Fontanellato with my son Alex, in a party of former PoWs and their families organized to mark the sixtieth anniversary of the Italian Armistice, we were shown around by the consultant in charge of what had become, by then, a clinic for patients with neurological conditions. One of the PoWs asked if we could be taken up to the attic – the consultant was surprised and puzzled, but she led the way up a small staircase to the attic void. On the floor, between the joists, were piles of earth.

'Dio mio!' she cried. 'What is this?'

'Ah', said Anthony Laing, one of Leslie's friends in the camp, 'that's our tunnel. We carried the earth up here in Red Cross boxes because we ran out of places to hide it.'

*

The last attempt to get out was by Jack Comyn, who had a job assisting one of the guards to look after clothing that had been confiscated out of parcels sent from England. He hit upon the idea of hopping out of a window in the clothing store on to the road, whilst one of his mates diverted the attention of the guard. All went to plan: he quickly changed out of his prison garb with the red patch sewn on the back and into clothes resembling an Italian workman, dirtied his face, grabbed a hammer he had found earlier and clambered out of the window. Brazenly walking along the road right past the front of the camp, he made it out of the town, only to be stopped by the commander of the local Carabiniere detachment, who popped out from behind a tree, saw through his disguise at once and ushered him back to the camp. The Commandant was astonished at his foolhardy adventure.

'But *Tenente* Comyn, my sentries on the wire might have shot you – and then what would your mother have said?'

Off he went to the cooler.

Chapter 14

Armistice – and Freedom

In Leslie's diary, the first sign that, after the years of fighting in North Africa, the Allies were at last in a position to carry the fight against the Axis back on to mainland Europe came on Saturday, 10 July – Sports Day in the camp:

> Walk, very good one. News of invasion of Sicily 2pm from Rome. Sports very good fun. Came second in Majors race. Boxing tournament in evening.

Two days later, the diary reports 'invasion going well', and the day after that, 'news of four more landings in Sicily and riot at Taranto' (the Italian naval base).

On Friday, 16 July Leslie records 'heavy air raid during the night on Bologna Parma and Modena', and on successive days thereafter there are mentions in the diary of further withdrawals in Sicily, the bombing of Rome, a meeting between Hitler and Mussolini and the evacuation of Palermo, Sicily's capital.

There was a general air of excitement in the camp, and Leslie was clearly swept up in it like everyone else. On 19 July he records: 'Bet with Fane-Hervey – £1 in England before end of October'. As it turned out, this was wildly optimistic on his part, and when I met Fane-Hervey's niece years later I was forced to stump up. They both spent Christmas 1943 stuck in Italy.

For a few days there was a lull. Leslie watched a performance of *Blithe Spirit* and did a bit of sunbathing. Then, on 25 July, Leslie notes, 'bar shut by Italians' and, on the following day:

> Mussolini sacked. Badoglio taking over and the Fascist party finished. Italians appear indifferent but rush to hear the news. Martial law plus curfew.

Ian English, in his book *Home by Christmas?*, describes how, thinking it meant the end of the war for them, 'the camp soldiery poured out of their huts, jumping up and down with delight, tearing the portraits of Il Duce from the walls and treading them underfoot.' Larry Allen announced Mussolini's departure to his fellow prisoners with the famously laconic 'FLASH: Benito Finito'.

Speculation about what would happen next was at fever pitch, and hopes and expectations of an early end to the war in Italy and a return home were high. Everyone was focussed on the news coming into the camp, from the Italians themselves and from Larry Allen's secret radio receiver.

> Tuesday, 27 July – news in papers of last Fascist meeting – called the 'fantastic epilogue'. Very bitter towards Mussolini.
>
> Friday, 30 July – Italians had special parade and Commandant explained the situation.
>
> Saturday, 31 July – day opened with announcement of no more newspapers for the Camp. Reasons not given, some say lack of paper.
>
> Monday, 2 August – very interesting news bulletin. Ciano [Mussolini's Minister of Press and Propaganda] arrested on crossing frontier.

Back in England, there was talk of persuading the Italians to change sides and join the Allies, so that Allied forces could land unopposed on the Italian mainland. But the Allies were insisting on unconditional surrender first, and the new Italian Prime Minister Badoglio, who wanted peace, was forced to announce that 'the war continues alongside our German ally', in an attempt to avoid the risk of the Germans seizing power while the exact terms of a possible surrender were still being worked out in secret negotiations in Spain.

Baking in the sultry heat of August, the camp fell quiet again. Leslie played cards and bridge – 'Played bridge with SBO Tyndale-Biscoe, lost 19 lira. Total to date 40 lira' – read books – Buchan's *A Prince of the Captivity* and Kipling's *Something of Myself* amongst others – wrote home, and started studying plumbing and quantity surveying again. Walks were cancelled. Letters from home suddenly started flooding in.

Leslie reports a frisson of excitement on 16 August with 'flying fortresses over – parachutes', while Michael Ross remembers 'cheering in the camp when vast formations of our bombers appeared overhead at high altitude'. Ross also records seeing one of these bombers shot down, and the appearance of two white parachutes. Later, one of the survivors was brought to the camp, but was then driven away shortly afterwards.

On 24 August Leslie attended the celebratory 'Sicily dinner', a seven-course extravaganza, for which the prisoners had been saving up their Red Cross rations for days. But generally there was an air of anti-climax.

In the meantime, the Germans started rushing troops south in order to be ready for the inevitable Allied landings; indeed, German troops were seen unnervingly close to the camp around this time. On Monday, 23 August Leslie reports, 'Walk cancelled. Germans passing through', and Ross remembers the Germans 'marching along the road just outside the building, singing Nazi hymns with much gusto, obviously for our benefit'. He speculates that 'most of them seemed to be passing through on their way to the newly opened front down south.' A little later in the day, the Germans returned, hot, dirty and bedraggled after a day of exercises, and were roundly jeered by the Brits, to the amusement of their Italian guards.

The appearance of Germans raised huge questions for the prisoners – what would happen to them if the Germans overran Italy before the Allies could rescue them from the camps?

The fate of the PoWs in Italy was in fact a key part of the surrender discussions, with Churchill insisting as far back as January, in conference with the Americans at Casablanca, upon 'the immediate liberation of all British prisoners of war in Italian hands, and the prevention, which in the first instance can only be by Italian hands, of their being transported to Germany'.

Thus it was that, when the Germans subsequently demanded that the Italians should hand over their PoWs, the new Italian Foreign Minister Guariglia refused point blank to do so. At the same time, however, steps had already been taken by the Italians to move prisoners out of the camps near Naples and the far south, where the next phase of the Allied invasion was expected, and these camps were now closed.

So far, so good – or perhaps not? The Italians were really in no position to convince the Germans that they were still effective and reliable partners in the fight against the Allies, nor was it at all likely that they would be fully trusted by the Allies if they attempted to change sides and join them against the Germans. In either event, the PoWs in their camps all over Italy would be in a highly vulnerable position, with ever more German troops moving south to protect the front line. It was inconceivable that the Italians would be able, or even willing, to defend the camps against the Germans, who would be keen to make good their hold on the prisoners, not least to prevent them operating as potential guerrilla fighters behind the German front line.

This very eventuality had already been considered by Montgomery, in April or May 1943, as he took up his next task as Commander of British forces for the invasion of Italy. In June he returned briefly to London from North Africa and, whilst there, it is said that he gave directions that Allied prisoners on Italian soil were to stay put in their camps until the advancing armies overran them. It was apparently his belief that the campaign in Italy would be brief and, with his tidy mind, he came to the conclusion that ill-planned irregular operations by small pockets of former PoWs would do little to help the Allied effort and could conceivably lead to unnecessary deaths. The direction was therefore passed to Norman Crockatt, head of MI9, the secret British service charged with supporting British prisoners in Axis hands, to transmit, via dozens of hidden radio sets and any other means to hand, to the SBOs in the camps in Italy. The order read as follows:

> In the event of an Allied invasion of Italy, Officers Commanding prison camps will ensure that prisoners-of-war remain within the camp. Authority is granted to all Officers Commanding to take necessary disciplinary action to prevent individual prisoners-of-war attempting to rejoin their own units.

This infamous instruction, known as the 'Stay Put' order, has been hotly debated ever since – as it was no doubt at the time. The dilemma is well described in Foot and Langley's book *MI9*:

> Crockatt was still enough of a fighting man to take in the military worth of groups fresh out of prisoner of war camp: it was bound to be low. Individually, many of them might be capable of some single astonishing, even heroic, feat; and collectively, in tunnelling squads some of them had acquired a strong sense of team unity. But in his judgement they were bound to lack that disciplined cohesion, born of months of training together and years of regimental tradition, by which a sound military unit imposes its will in battle. Besides, however willing, about half of them, airmen or gunners or tank crew or men from service units, had little or no infantry training, and only the sappers among them knew anything about demolitions; and they were unarmed. Montgomery did not relish the idea of having his future supply lines hampered by unauthorised bridge demolitions . . . and Crockatt had the foresight to envisage that, if his prisoners overreached themselves, they might all find

themselves packed into cattle trucks and sent off to extermination, Geneva Convention or no.

The original order has never been found, so it is impossible to say who actually did sign it off. In the light of the confusion and delays it caused, perhaps no one really wanted it to be found.

The Senior British Officer in Fontanellato at this time was Lieutenant Colonel Hugo Graham de Burgh of the Royal Artillery. Leslie's diary records that he arrived on 11 August – 'Strong disciplinarian. Orders beards and long hair off. Roll call made a parade. Divided opinion. I think all to the good.' Aged forty-nine, de Burgh was an experienced soldier who had fought with distinction, and been wounded twice, in the Great War. During the current conflict he had served in India and North Africa, where he was captured in 1942. Before arriving at Fontanellato, he had been SBO at three other camps, most recently at Lucca, and was described by Peter Watson in *Mountain Highway* as 'a stocky unsmiling man with a harsh voice and a bad limp . . . he pulled us together and did much to sustain our morale.'

Arriving as he did at a time of such uncertainty, de Burgh clearly saw the need to instil a sense of purpose and discipline into the rather relaxed inmates of PG Camp 49 – in their 'lackadaisical, demilitarised state' as Newby describes it. In addition to the 'beards off' order described by Leslie, he set about organizing the camp along the lines of an infantry battalion in five companies of around one hundred men, four of officers and one of other ranks, each commanded by a lieutenant colonel. There were drills and duty rosters, and punishment for anyone caught breaking the prisoners' accepted code of behaviour (by stealing the food of another prisoner, for example). For the denizens of the bar, or the mini-casino in the basement, this regime must have come as quite a shock, just when freedom seemed around the corner.

De Burgh also took great trouble to maintain good relations with the Italian Commandant Colonel Vicedomini – a man already seen as 'all right' and a 'good chap' by the prisoners, despite being an 'Eyetie'. The relationship between these two 'old soldiers' was to prove of vital importance for the men of PG Camp 49 in the days ahead.

On Friday, 3 September Leslie's diary records a 'rumour of landing in Italy'. The diary entry for the following day reads:

Rumour confirmed. Landings at Calabria and at Naples. Party with Kitson, Graham-Campbell and Keay. Game of bridge. Stormy day with wonderful sunset.

Even before the Allied victory in North Africa in May 1943, there had been disagreement between the Allies about the next steps. The Americans wanted a full-on invasion in Northern Europe as early as possible; Churchill favoured a more indirect 'soft underbelly' approach, beginning in the Mediterranean, to weaken the enemy in stages before launching a frontal assault. The compromise eventually adopted was for a relatively small-scale Italian campaign, to knock Italy out of the conflict quickly and enable the Royal Navy to dominate the Mediterranean and communications lines to Egypt, the Far East, the Gulf and India – followed by the invasion of France in early 1944.

After four weeks of preliminary bombing attacks on airfields, ports and industrial targets on the mainland and offshore, the campaign proper began on 9/10 July 1943, as reported in Leslie's diary – 'news of invasion of Sicily 2pm from Rome'. An Allied amphibious force ('Operation Husky') stormed ashore on the south-eastern and central southern shores of Sicily, led by Montgomery and his Eighth Army to the east and the American General Patton to the west. The Italians and Germans mounted a strong defence and, although they were unable to prevent the stronger Allied force from capturing the island (which they did on 17 August), they did succeed in evacuating most of their 300,000 troops and other personnel to the mainland.

Whilst the fighting was going on, there had been discussions between Italian and Allied leaders about the possibility of an Italian surrender, discussions which both sides were desperate to keep secret from the Germans. Timing was key, as the Italians wanted to try and ensure that they had some guarantee of protection for their leaders and institutions of state against the inevitable German onslaught as soon as the surrender was announced. The Italians were also keen to maintain a shred of dignity by ensuring that no announcement was made until after the Allies had invaded the mainland itself.

Thus it was that, at 1400 hrs on Friday, 3 September, as Montgomery's Eighth Army landed in Calabria, on the very toe of Italy, an American and an Italian general signed an armistice agreement at Cassibile in south-eastern Sicily, under which both sides agreed to stop fighting each other and Italy agreed upon an unconditional surrender – to be announced, at Allied discretion, following a landing in central Italy.

The armistice was announced five days later, on 8 September, as reported by Leslie in his diary:

> Walk cancelled because of Italian fiesta. This followed usual lines.
> Church bells ringing very early in the morning. Hundreds of people

cycle into Fontanellato – most girls – walk about village – come to have a look at us – the whole show fizzles out at lunchtime. Marvellous day this. Armistice at 2000 hours – just after dinner – sitting down to write to Mother – Italians throw hats in the air. SBO gives very good talk.

Peter Langrishe, in his account of the moment, writes:

I had come back to my room after supper and was chatting with two or three others when the serenity of the summer evening was shattered by a growing hubbub from the direction of the village. We went to the windows and soon were astonished to see a large crowd of villagers, joined by our guards, come hurrying down the road, some on bicycles and some on foot shouting, singing, cheering and throwing their caps in the air. '*Pace, pace*' they cried, suiting the action to the words. The soldiers threw down their rifles, jumped on them and called out to us that we were now their friends.

Our first reaction was perhaps one of numbness. Here was the thing we had all been waiting for, and what were we to do? Were we free to leave the camp? Would our troops be with us in the morning? How would we be sent home? These and a hundred other questions sprang into our minds until through the chatter of excited conversation came the order that the Senior British Officer would address all ranks in the main hall immediately.

Malcolm Tudor quotes directly from de Burgh's talk in his book *Beyond the Wire*:

Gentlemen, I have been informed by the Commandant that the Italian Government has asked for an armistice. Beyond that I know nothing, but he has promised to keep me in immediate touch with the situation. In the meantime, it is absolutely essential that everyone remains perfectly calm and behaves like a British officer. No one is to look out of the windows or make demonstrations of any kind with the civilians. No one is allowed outside the building. Everyone will parade in the courtyard at nine tomorrow morning, when I will give you further details of the situation.

Lookouts were posted, and the men went to bed that night in a state of barely controlled excitement. The bar did a roaring trade.

The following morning, they awoke to the extraordinary sight of Italian guards removing the wire at the far end of the playing field and digging trenches and constructing machine gun posts along the perimeter of the camp.

At 0900 hrs the men were summoned to parade on the courtyard outside the main building, and de Burgh addressed them from the steps. According to Watson, 'He stared grimly down at us . . . [and] spoke slowly and emphatically in his rasping voice.' He told them about the Stay Put order, but said that he did not believe that it reflected the situation on the ground and that accordingly he viewed it as being out of date. He told them that the Germans were known to be in Parma, and that the likelihood was that they would soon arrive at the camp with the intention of transporting all the prisoners back to Germany. He noted that Vicedomini had said that (in accordance with instructions issued by the Italian Government) his men would defend the camp, and the village, from the Germans. De Burgh had considered offering the support of the prisoners, but had decided that this might embarrass the British Government.

Accordingly, by agreement with Vicedomini, Italian sentries had been posted on all the roads approaching the camp to watch for any German advance; in the meantime, the men were to change into battle dress and boots, and pack a haversack with necessaries and twenty-four hours' rations. A bugle would sound three Gs as a warning note and, upon hearing it, the men were to parade on the field in companies, ready to evacuate through the gap that the Italians had made in the wire and march to a pre-selected hiding place nearby.

The parade dismissed while de Burgh conferred with his company commanders, and the men collected their rations – one tin of bully beef, one of biscuits, some chocolate and a few raisins – and packed their haversacks. They were issued with small sums in lire. Then, in a very British kind of way, they tidied their rooms, exchanged addresses with friends and drank hot chocolate in the courtyard, an end of term feeling in the air.

Suddenly, two German Junkers bombers swooped low over the camp, apparently aiming straight at the centre of the building before they jinked and roared directly overhead. The men scattered and dived to the ground. The holidays were already over.

Just before midday, a sentry came racing back into the camp on his bicycle with the news that a German convoy was drawn up on the main road about two miles outside Fontanellato. True to his word, Vicedomini gave the order for the bugler to blow three Gs as the alarm.

Within minutes, everyone was out of the building and formed up in companies on the playing field opposite the gap in the wire. Lieutenant Colonel Everett's Company was the first to be ready and marched in threes out through the gap, still wearing the red prisoner's patches on their backs and, by one report, smartly saluting the SBO as they passed him at the wire with, according to another report, Ronnie Noble, a wartime news cameraman, photographing the scene. Everett's company was quickly followed by the others, and then came Eric Newby, riding incongruously on a very small horse, having fallen down the marble main staircase two days earlier and broken his ankle. Vicedomini and about forty of his men remained behind.

Keeping up a smart pace in the baking midday sun, escorted by some of the Italian guards and hardly able to believe that they were free, the men headed north-west through open fields and small vineyards, to a lying-up area called Rovachia di Paroletta, their progress followed by gangs of small inquisitive boys and girls and, for a few heart-stopping minutes, a low-flying Junkers 52. This hiding place, which was about three miles from the camp, had been recce'd the day before by de Burgh's Chief of Staff, Mainwaring, and by the Italian second in command, Captain Camino. It was a deep, winding, dry riverbed, with a steep flood bank and overgrown with scrub, poplar and beech trees. It came to be known as the Bund. Here the companies dispersed into their own areas to hide, or to crawl under some vines nearby.

'Wonderful feeling to be free', writes Leslie. 'Hiding all day and night.'

A trickle of local people appeared at the Bund, bringing supplies from the camp, Red Cross parcels and contributions from their own homes. De Burgh sent two men back to see what was happening in the camp. When they returned, heavily disguised in Italian clothes, a couple of hours later, they had disturbing news: thirty German soldiers had arrived two hours after the prisoners had fled. They had fired over the heads of the villagers and then turned on Vicedomini, who was waiting in his office, having sent all the other guards home. This was all very disturbing news for the men, many of whom had convinced themselves that the chaos in Italy after the Armistice would be so great that the Germans would quickly be forced to withdraw northwards, in the face of a speedy Allied advance from coastal landing points in the south.

An Italian soldier had witnessed the scene.

'Where are the prisoners?' the Germans had demanded.

'I had an order to liberate them,' Vicedomini replied.

The German lieutenant then beat and kicked him savagely, and there was talk of immediate execution. Instead, they handcuffed him and dragged him out of his office and down the stairs to the courtyard, where they bundled him into a lorry. The Germans dined on the fish and potatoes prepared for the prisoners, polished off what was left in the bar, looted and vandalized the camp and then roared off, taking Vicedomini with them. He spent the remainder of the war in a labour camp in Poland and returned to Italy after the war, a broken man. He died soon afterwards.

De Burgh gave instructions to his company commanders that the best thing for the men to do was to remain where they were until the situation became clearer. At that point, no one had any idea how long it might be before the Germans returned in force to search for the prisoners, or whether the Eighth Army might arrive before that to rescue them. Already the rumble of lorries had been heard drawing ever closer to the Bund, and the likelihood of imminent discovery must have seemed very real.

The men in the Bund started to discuss their plans for getting away, forming up into small groups of friends and trying to decide (on the basis of little or no evidence either way) whether it would be better to travel north towards the Alps and Switzerland, west to the coast, or south towards the front lines of the opposing armies. Several chose to slip away that night, while the going was good, but the majority stayed where they were, in the company of clouds of mosquitoes and midges, and with the constant roar of traffic on the nearby Via Emilia trunk road. All night long, the sky was lit with a red glow, and the air reverberated with the sound of high explosive.

Tony Davies describes the scene:

> The night was beautifully clear and warm, and a greatcoat was all the covering we needed. Those not on sentry go were soon sleeping soundly. Michael [Gilbert] and I were on duty from 2am to 4am, and although it was rather chillier by this time, the atmosphere was delightfully clear and fresh, and the feeling of freedom was intoxicating. Lying there, peering over the darkened fields, we could hear the dull thud of explosions in the distance, and flashes lit up the night sky for seconds on end. In the direction of main road, the Via Emilia from Rimini to Milan, there were sounds of much traffic; and this tied in neatly with our pre-conceived ideas of German intentions. Explosions, we said, meant the destruction of sumps prior to a hasty withdrawal, and the sound of the traffic was the withdrawal itself. The possibility that the traffic was moving south instead of north never occurred to us. Comforted by our satisfactory delusions, we passed the night cheerfully, discussing the parties we should have when we returned to the regiment.

The following day, local farming folk in considerable numbers began arriving at the Bund with gifts of food and clothes, encouraged by Captain Camino, who had remained behind with the prisoners rather than hurrying home. The village baker appeared with several hundred loaves he had baked, and a farmer came who had milked his whole herd for the prisoners. Dozens of the men were taken off to billets in local farms, and some decided to disperse about the countryside in small groups. Leslie took himself off to a local farm for a wash and some wine.

It is extraordinary, and a real tribute to the spirit of the Italian people, that despite the massive personal risks they were running in shielding enemy soldiers or escaped prisoners, no one betrayed their whereabouts to the Germans, so recently their partners in war. Few, it seemed, had had either liking or respect for their erstwhile allies.

The locals also brought many and various snippets of news and rumour of Allied landings up and down the coast, and of German retreats, and these gave the prisoners encouragement in thinking that rescue might still be at hand. On the other hand, they also reported that the noise of explosions the previous night and the roar of traffic had been the result of a fierce seven-hour fight for Parma railway station, between Italian troops and a German Kommando.

In his own diary, Dougie Turner talks about the 'awful tangle of misleading rumours, which influenced all our future decisions'. The cautious de Burgh treated the good news stories with a certain amount of scepticism and sent an officer off to a nearby farm where there was known to be a radio, to listen in to the BBC. The officer returned with the sobering information that the Allied armies were still down in Calabria, the toe of Italy, and advancing only slowly. There was no Allied landing at all in the north – rescue for de Burgh's men was clearly not imminent.

De Burgh held a conference at 1300 hrs, the main points of which were recorded by Leslie in his notebook. He reported that the Germans were attacking Milan, but that the Italians were resisting and were said to have blocked the Brenner Pass. In the south, although the Germans were withdrawing, they were making life difficult for the Allies. De Burgh went on to say that company commanders were free to decide that their men could leave that night, although he and Camino both recommended staying put to await clearer information about the situation. In his view, for those who wanted to be on their way, the best route was south-west: 'Cross the railway and make for the hills.' Two companies of PoWs decided to leave that night to cross the Via Emilia and the railway line, still in their Army greatcoats and battledress tops.

Leslie stayed at the Bund and, on the following day, Saturday, 11 September, decided to move to one of the farms and get himself kitted out in Italian clothes. Colonel Richard Wheeler, with whom Leslie had for a time shared a room, had taken on the task of re-clothing the camp. Dressed incongruously in a suit and a bowler hat, he organized an orderly queue of 'customers', who then filed past a heap of donated Italian clothing, taking what they wanted, before changing amongst some bushes and burying their old uniforms. On emerging from the wood, resplendent in their new garb, the soldiers would be greeted by Italians waiting with more clothing to add to the pile – and some were invited back to individual farms to stay.

Having collected his clothes, Leslie decided to return to the prison camp to see what was happening, but found the Germans were in occupation and beat a hasty retreat. He returned to the farm in the nearby hamlet of Paroletta, where the kind owners had also taken in two other PoWs, Graham-Campbell and Briggs. An RAF officer called Reg Dickinson, who had been shot down over the Mediterranean and rescued from the water by an Italian naval vessel, joined them later.

On Sunday, Leslie was 'learning Italian hard, hiding in the fields by day and in a cottage by night'. The diary contains a page or two of Italian words – '*arrivederci*/goodbye; what is the time/*che ora e*; *coltello*/knife', plus lists of supplies and the names and addresses of his mates. But although he was keeping busy, the entries feel somehow tentative and full of doubt. When to go, and where?

The next day, his mind was made up for him. There is a note in the diary of the SBO's final briefing late that afternoon:

> People can go in small parties at any time. Tomorrow – very dangerous day. No smoking voices coughing.

The diary reflects de Burgh's briefing:

> Italians decidedly nervous. Shall have to move. Queries where – frontier? East coast? Saw Mainwaring – says Germans have released Mussolini. Brit advancing in south. SBO advises move because of fascist threat. Move to Bund – meet Dickinson and arrange to meet tomorrow.

All over Italy, men exactly like my father were faced with a similar decision and had very little by way of reliable information or advice to help them make it.

In the seventy or so PoW camps and sub-camps in Italy some 80,000 men had been held. After the Armistice, their Italian guards, to a greater or lesser extent, and in an extremely confused and confusing military and political situation, abandoned them to their fate. Most SBOs had received the Stay Put order from MI9, and many chose to obey it and told their men to obey it, even to the extent, in camps like Chieti and Macerata, of posting sentries to guard against men escaping, and threatening anyone who disobeyed with a court martial. Len Dann, who was in Macerata, describes in *Laughing We Ran*, how he escaped through a small gate just seconds before fellow prisoners closed it on the orders of their SBO. In a camp of 6,000 men he was one of only 1,000 who got away, nearly half of whom were recaptured by the Germans within hours and put in a train with the rest, heading for Germany and another eighteen months in prison.

In many camps, however, like the one at Fontanellato, the SBO judged that the Stay Put order was out of date and sooner or later advised or allowed his men to get away while they could. It is impossible to be precise about the numbers, but Roger Absalom (regarded as the leading authority on this Italian 'great escape') estimates that 'perhaps one third of the large camps and almost all of the small camps [were] open to escape for a substantial period of time' before the Germans swooped and took the remaining prisoners off to Germany.

But being free to escape and actually escaping are two different things. For some, particularly after months in captivity, the temptation to stay and wait to be rescued was strong. Many had little idea where, in fact, their camp was situated, and little knowledge even of the physical geography of Italy as a whole. The Italian authorities had carefully removed all maps from reading materials sent to prisoners and, though the RAF did drop maps printed on silk after the Armistice, few prisoners got one, so they did not know where the roads, rivers and railways ran. Speaking little Italian, and having no clue who, if anyone, they could trust, even a simple task such as asking the way was fraught with risk.

Socially, too, there were challenges for the escapers. As Absalom notes, in *Strange Alliance*:

> It was a crowded countryside in which a stranger could not move
> for a mile or two without being observed by many shrewd eyes . . .
> where townspeople of all classes habitually looked down upon
> farm-labourers and peasants . . . [in which] every rural area had its
> own distinctive social stratification . . . [and where] neighbouring

villages and households were often in permanent feuds over customary rights or festering ancient torts. Outside the towns few could speak standard Italian with confidence and some not at all, confined within their mutually incomprehensible dialects: illiteracy was still common, especially amongst women.

The military situation was similarly uncertain. The Allies were known to have invaded the far south of Italy, but no one knew for certain how fast, if at all, the invading troops were likely to be able to advance northwards, and there were constant rumours (completely unfounded), amongst both PoWs and locals, of further landings in the north. These rumours spread fast and 'with ever-greater exaggeration at each telling'. It was anticipated, meanwhile, that the Germans would overrun Italy as soon as they could; but, again, no one knew for sure how quickly that would happen, or whether scooping up prisoners would be high on their list of priorities.

Living as they did in a country with no functioning government and no reliable news outlets (apart from the BBC's Italian service), the local people themselves were in no position to give advice based on anything more than rumour, gossip and supposition. Much of the advice received by PoWs from Italians in these early days supported the idea of not moving on at all, but instead, of staying on a farm and awaiting events. It may not be a coincidence that, with their sons still in the Army, or prisoners themselves, it suited the farmers to have some free extra labour. 'Staying put' in a relatively comfortable billet suited some prisoners, too.

In fact, although the Allies landed in the toe of Italy in early September 1943, they were able to make only slow progress up the eastern coast, and no progress in the west north of Naples, because of the difficult mountain terrain and a stout, speedily-mounted German defence.

The question therefore of 'which route' was crucial, but fraught with difficulty and the unknown. To go north was a shorter distance, but it meant crossing the Alps, possible detention in neutral Switzerland and, of course, effectively marching straight into the hands of either a retreating or incoming German army – but nobody knew which it was likely to be. Going due west, in the hope perhaps of an early Allied landing in the north-west corner of Italy, was an even shorter distance, but the risk was that there would be no such landing. Planning on hiring or stealing a boat and making an escape by sea, in the rough waters of the autumn Mediterranean, was not attractive to many. So that left the southern route, favoured by most in the event, but a terribly long way, with winter coming on, for men with few clothes, little

Italian, and no idea of the best route down the spine of Italy, the Apennine Mountains.

Contemporary German records show that at least 24,000 prisoners of war held in Italy were transferred to Germany before mid-November 1943 and, by the end of December, British War Office records show that that number had grown to 50,000. This suggests that some 30,000 were still at large, in hiding or on the run, mostly still in Italy, three months after the Armistice.

Leslie would shortly be one of them. He went back to the farm and agreed with his three PoW friends that they would leave the next day, in two pairs – Graham-Campbell and Briggs, himself and Dickinson. That night, they returned to the Bund, ready for the off the next day.

Chapter 15

On the Run

Week 1 Miles walked 24

It was two hours before sunrise on Tuesday, 14 September. On the Bund, in the chill early autumn air, men were stirring under their blankets, shrouded in an assortment of ill-fitting overcoats and jumpers. Nothing much disturbed the taut, nervous silence apart from an occasional stifled cough, or the sounds of a man crawling out of his makeshift bed and heading off into the bushes to relieve himself.

As time slowly passed, there were low, muttered greetings as another day began, the fifth since the breakout from the camp. The optimism of the

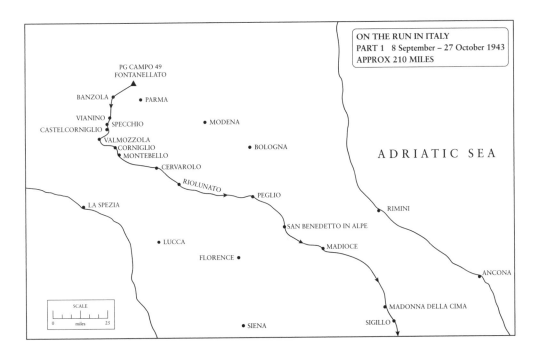

ON THE RUN IN ITALY
PART 1   8 September – 27 October 1943
APPROX 210 MILES

PG CAMPO 49
FONTANELLATO

BANZOLA   • PARMA

VIANINO
CASTELCORNIGLIO   SPECCHIO   • MODENA

VALMOZZOLA
CORNIGLIO   • BOLOGNA
MONTEBELLO

CERVAROLO   ADRIATIC SEA

RIOLUNATO

LA SPEZIA   • PEGLIO   • RIMINI

SAN BENEDETTO IN ALPE

• LUCCA   MADIOCE

FLORENCE •

ANCONA

SCALE   MADONNA DELLA CIMA

0   miles   25   SIGILLO

• SIENA

previous evening, fuelled by glasses of the rough, deep purple local wine, had already dissipated, as the men started once again to dwell on the dilemmas of the uncertain future ahead of them. Several of their comrades had already slipped away, north towards the Alps, west to the coast, or south over the mountains towards the advancing Allied armies. For those who remained, the questions were the same – where and when and how?

For Leslie, the time of waiting and wondering was over. He stretched, slipped out from under his blanket and, eager to be off, woke Reg Dickinson, his chosen travelling companion. Together they collected their few items of kit and looked each other over: Leslie in his Army boots and little cap made an unlikely Italian, but it was the best he could do. He checked his pocket – yes, the diary was still there, and he was ready to go. Impatiently, they waited for their Italian friends from the farm who had agreed to bring them some provisions for the start of their journey and see them on their way. Then, at 0530 hrs, they were ready.

Dougie Turner watched them go:

> The last I saw of Porky Young he was dressed in Italian civilian trousers which ended some two inches above his army boots, a shirt which barely reached down to his trousers and a small cap perched on top of his head. Looking exactly like an escaped PoW, he strode off into the vines.

They had decided to head across the plain, towards the ramparts of the Apennine mountain chain which runs south towards Rome. They whispered their goodbyes to friends and fellow officers, Leslie's chin came up, he squared his shoulders, and away they went, slipping off through the trees, keeping close to the banks of the dried-up stream bed as they made for their first challenge, the crossing of the railway line from Parma to Milan and the busy Via Emilia main road, already alive with supply convoys and German troops on the move.

The railway line was a formidable obstacle – built up on a steep embankment, with four strands of signal wire about a foot off the ground. As they crawled underneath it, the wire gave off a loud twang, which they were sure would be heard up the line. The road, too, was a struggle to get across, bounded as it was on either side by a high wire fence which had to be surmounted during the infrequent pauses between supply convoys grinding past. The Italians saw them safely across and then returned to Paroletta – and Leslie and Reg were on their own.

Once across, they began to relax as they stretched their legs and strode off towards the mountains shrouded in their morning haze. As they continued to follow the track of the dried up Parola creek they were walking through vineyards, the grapes ripening fast as they baked in the September sun, and they helped themselves greedily to quench their thirst. The maize harvest was nearly over, piles of cobs at the edges of the fields awaiting collection, the stalks of the plants left standing to be cut down and ploughed into the parched land.

Still on the plain, they hurried on, sticking to the narrow country roads for the sake of speed, but keeping a wary eye and ear cocked for the sounds of a German patrol. The lanes were busy, though, with locals at work on the farms, and the remnants of the Italian Army, deserters now, heading for home. For these two men in their ill-fitting peasant dress and poor to non-existent Italian, each encounter must have seemed fraught with danger and the fear of imminent exposure and capture. There were villages and hamlets on the way – Borghetto, Costa Pavesi, Pieve di Cusignano – but they gave them a wide berth.

By the time the sun went down that evening, around 1930, they were already dangerously tired. Their exhilaration had worn off and, as the plains gave way to the foothills of the Apennines, the sense of the long slog to safety ahead had become their hourly reality. They decided to press on, to make up the mileage in the cool of the evening and under cover of the rapidly darkening sky.

By 2200 they were finished, as they stumbled down a wooded hillside into the tiny village of Banzola.

*

Years later, at the foot of the hill, in a small clearing beside a farmhouse and within sight of the church, I sat in my car and waited for them. It was 2003, at the end of my sixtieth-anniversary visit to Fontanellato. The trip was almost over, and some had already returned home. I decided to spend my last evening trying to find the place where Leslie spent his first night on the run. Banzola wasn't easy to find – there are no place names in the diary, since to include them would have put generous Italian helpers at risk in the event of his capture, but Leslie subsequently compiled an itinerary with the names of the places he stayed in. Without this, his entire escape route would have been a mystery to me.

As soon as I drove into the village, the hair on the back of my neck started to rise. I parked the car in the small clearing near the church and settled down to wait. I won't ever forget those moments. The sun was going down, the shadows lengthening, the village already quiet and awaiting the night. To my left was a wooded hillside, the hillside down which, I was completely sure, I would soon see my father stealing, peering warily about him, his heart thumping as he assessed the chances of a friendly welcome, or of betrayal and capture. I waited, hardly daring to breathe, certain in my imagination he would appear, completely alive to the dangers he faced, willing him on, prepared almost to start knocking on doors on his behalf . . .

*

The task of identifying where to ask for hospitality was a tricky one. One PoW developed a scoring system using haystacks – five haystacks: too rich, might be a fascist; one haystack: too poor, nothing to spare; two haystacks: about right, just enough to spare, not rich enough to have too much to lose. Most of the time, it was just the luck of the draw, and the escapers soon became used to negative responses ('I have nothing', 'Ask down the road'), as well as more generous ones.

In Banzola, the first door Leslie and Reg banged on was opened at once. There was a party going on and, at first, they were probably taken to be expected guests. But when the truth was discovered, there must have been consternation. The house was occupied by two families, one with three children, all girls, and the other with four – and they must all have experienced moments of doubt and fear as they realized the risks they were running in even opening the door to these fugitive strangers. The men were quickly ushered into a barn, as the families worked out what to do.

The following day, any doubts their Italian hosts had appeared to have been resolved, at least for the time being, and the diary records that the men were put to work bringing in the last of the maize crop. Most of the farms were run on a medieval share-cropping system, whereby the landowner provided the farmhouse, outbuildings and equipment, whilst the sharecropper worked the land with his family and shared the harvest, and any income, equally with the landowner. The farms produced a mix of grain, vegetables and wine, with a few cows living indoors, usually underneath the family accommodation. There would have been no electricity, mains water, drainage or telephones. It was all very basic.

The Italians' fears must have come flooding back later as four more escapers from Fontanellato appeared (including their friends from Paroletta, Graham-Campbell and Briggs), all looking for shelter. 'Hostess gets windy', reports the diary, and plans were immediately made for the six to move on over the next two days. After a quiet day resting before their proposed departure, and a visit from two South African colleagues (which must have further alarmed their nervous hostess), Leslie and Reg moved off at 0300 hrs on Saturday morning, in 'lovely moonlight'.

The going was very hard, up and over steep wooded hillsides all morning, and before long it started to rain. Soon they were exhausted, having managed only ten miles. Looking around for somewhere to shelter, they came upon an isolated farmhouse near Vianino and decided to rest up in the nearby barn. Inside, they found four rather depressed comrades from the Duke of Cornwall's Light Infantry, all still in uniform. They had left the Bund four days earlier than Leslie and Reg, before the distribution of local clothing had been organized. Since then, they had been moving slightly hesitatingly from farm to farm, trying to find out how long it would be before the Allies reached them, and working out which way to go.

According to one of the men, Peter Watson, Leslie and Reg were 'cheery and full of optimism' and brought news that the British Government had broadcast an appeal to the Italian people that they should look after escapers – which they thought would be helpful, though it would take time for the word to get about, as few of the hill farmers appeared to have radios. After a lunch of bread and grapes the group sat around watching the rain and helping the farmer by stripping oak twigs for winter cattle feed. Hoping for a reasonable supper after this contribution to the work of the farm, Leslie and Reg decided to stay the night. The farmer, however, was clearly keen to see them leave, and declined to offer them any more food. So they set off hungry after the sky had cleared, watched by their DCLI friends, who were envious of their relative freedom of movement in civilian clothes.

By dawn they were crossing the Ceno River by a small plank bridge and heading on up the road for another three miles to Specchio. Here they found a prosperous-looking house next to the church, with an archway leading to a paved yard and barn beyond. They walked through and were amused to find Peter Watson again, and his colleague Peter Stericker, who had parted company with their other two friends in order to lighten the burden on their Italian hosts. After a good breakfast of bread and milk and ersatz coffee, Watson broached the topic of civilian clothes and, with Reg (who spoke some Italian) translating, they managed to persuade their hosts to give them some worn and patched up old clothes in return for Watson's

Army greatcoat. The farmer was chatty, and took them out for a tour of his fields and a look up the valley of the River Ceno towards Bardi where, apparently, a number of Allied ex-PoWs were being hidden. As they looked, four German trucks loaded with troops could be seen crawling slowly up the road towards the village.

The four of them decided to stay and enjoy the Sunday hospitality. 'Best day yet', says the diary, and Watson describes what happened next in *Mountain Highway*:

> Hardly had we finished breakfast when half the village arrived to see us. Girls – the room was full of them; girls round the walls, girls in the doorway, even girls on the stairs waiting to push their way in. Beautiful girls, all dressed in their Sunday best, with that wonderful taste for colour and design, which seems to be born in every Italian woman. Girls from Milan, from Piacenza and Parma, refugees to this remote corner of the mountains. We, who had not seen so many girls so close for two years or more were struck dumb. Only [Reg Dickinson] remained cool, with Air Force poise. He discussed film stars and dance music with a lovely young thing from Milan, and found common interests in Mickey Mouse and Ginger Rogers. The noise was terrific, everyone talked at once, squealed with laughter, giggled, screamed and sang. When the noise at last died away and the pressure relaxed, I was left limp and exhausted in my chair.

In the afternoon two Scots 'other ranks', on the run from the nearby Busetto work camp, passed through, and in the evening there was a visit to a wine shop in the village of Filippi, a mile down the road ('very good party in locked vino shop' says the diary), and a chance to hear the Italian news, which was full of reports from Russia but nothing about Allied armies in Italy. During supper, the girls from the village arrived again to see the English prisoners and, after a period of pandemonium and excited chatter, finally left with a chorus of '*buona seras*'. As silence descended, they could be heard sweetly singing Ave Maria in the darkness at a nearby shrine.

The men then began a debate about their situation. The farmer's advice was clear: 'To stay on a farm for more than one night is foolish and dangerous. If someone informs on you, you will be gone before anything can be done. You just want to walk around from house to house, staying one night in each, until your army comes.' This had its attractions, but there was no sign as yet of an Allied invasion in the north of Italy, and the nearest friendly troops were way down in the south, below Naples, 400 miles away and with the German army in between. If they stayed put, it could be weeks or months before they could be rescued. The fastest routes south, on the other hand, were along the roads and railways of the eastern or western coastal plains, and these would be busy with German troops being rushed south, with guards and patrols at every stage. Furthermore, the men had no papers, and no means of obtaining any, so a train journey would be fraught with additional risk of discovery.

The safest way south, therefore, was the high route along the Apennine mountain chain. It was bleak and bare, though, and both arduous and dangerous with winter coming on. The alternative was a slightly lower mountain route, where there would be more houses and farms for shelter and assistance, but where there was greater danger of being picked up by a German patrol, or of betrayal by the Italian fascist militia and its sympathisers.

Unattractive though the various options were, there was general agreement that continuing to move south was the best course of action and, early the next morning, Leslie and Reg slipped away, followed an hour so later by Watson and Stericker. After the decision-making and jollity of the previous day, what followed was a terrible anti-climax, as the men stumbled about on the hillsides all day, making little forward progress and eventually asking at several farms for food and shelter for the night, without success. Finally, an extremely poor family took pity on them and invited them in, but no sooner had the polenta been poured on to the wooden table, than a warning was received that four German soldiers were in the vicinity. The two men beat a hasty retreat out on to the hillside again and spent a bitterly cold and windy autumn night, their coldest yet, hiding amongst the rocks and scrub.

On the following day, their seventh on the run, they managed to find a good farm in a hidden valley near Castelcorniglio run by an elderly couple who allowed them to stay, along with six other British soldiers they had taken in. Leslie got his trousers repaired, had an Italian lesson with the couple and listened to the BBC again. Watson and Stericker appeared and gained the impression, before they walked on up the valley to the gloomy-looking hilltop 'castle' itself, that the other two had decided to stay and work on the farm for a few days.

Leslie didn't go in for lengthy descriptive passages in the diary, so there are no word pictures of the places he stayed. But it does not take much to imagine dark cave-like interiors, earthen floors, large open fireplaces with the pot suspended above the glowing embers, and curing hams and salamis suspended from the smoke-blackened ceilings. At mealtimes, the men would sit to eat first – a bowl of thin broth called *minestra*, with bread cut from a big flat loaf, or yellowy molten polenta poured on to the table and studded occasionally with a few lumps of meat or vegetable, washed down by rough local wine. Then cheese, maybe, or some nuts or grapes – and a last look at the cattle, followed by sleep, often all together in one room. Any visitors could usually expect to be banished to sleep with the oxen in the adjoining stable, on a bed of sacking or straw, the air thick with the sounds and smells of the animals' digestive systems working through the night. At dawn, the family would be up again and out into the fields, after a breakfast of bread and milk, whilst the escapers planned the next day's walking or set to as well to help about the farm.

Week 2 Miles walked 24

But whatever their intentions, everyone was scared, and the next day found the men hiding in the woods again, with a view to moving on the next day. Leslie started to feel poorly but, rather than rest, they had to leave quickly in the afternoon when a German patrol was spotted, obviously on the lookout for escapers. They found another household near Valmozolla that was prepared to help and, after a reasonable night in clean straw and a rest the next day, he was ready to continue. They returned to the elderly couple to say goodbye and to have a last listen to their radio, and then set off south again.

Leslie was already showing signs of becoming grumpy with Reg, who (not unreasonably) wanted to delay a decision about which route to follow until they were sure that the invasion force had landed and was on its way north: 'Great day this. Have at last got Dickinson to move south and today we made good progress.' As many of the escaping PoWs found, maintaining morale and confidence during the long and arduous trek south was extremely difficult, but incredibly important. Newby describes how, on his own after a period living with a family, he 'lost an essential part of whatever courage and willpower [he] possessed previously, and the capacity to make decisions, qualities which were essential if [he was] to survive.' Others were so affected by the hardships that they came to look upon recapture as a positive relief – though for others the pain of recapture brought on deep depression and a huge sense of disappointment, rage and frustration, coupled with a strong feeling of having failed.

The weather was still bad and, on Sunday, 26 September, a week after their party day in Specchio only ten miles or so away, a thunderstorm raged and crashed around them as they sheltered in a small farm near the prosperous village of Corniglio, watching the farmer's wife calmly suckling her baby in front of them. What with the weather, the need to move carefully to avoid German patrols, the rough tracks through a maze of hills and valleys, poor food and their weak physical condition after months in a prison camp, they were clearly finding the going very tough indeed.

But the next day, in spite of a disturbed night being bitten by fleas, they made good progress to the tiny hillside village of Montebello (which reminded Leslie of the picturesque village of Clovelly, which he and his Commando troop had visited on their bicycles almost exactly two years earlier) where they found an excellent farm – 'the best yet' – and enjoyed a fine meal of steak, rice and potatoes, followed by a night in a real bed. The generous farmer had been working his farm for sixty-four years, and had already played host to a string of escapers.

Week 3 Miles walked 36

For five days the rain fell from the sky and drenched the valleys, shrouding the encircling hills of the beautiful Alpe di Succiso in a heavy grey mist. Twice they set off early in the morning and progressed a few miles before 'rain stopped play'; twice they were forced to spend literally all day under cover. Shivering in dank barns, peering out at the heavy clouds and hoping for a break, their frustrations were magnified, and irritation dampened the sense of purpose and resolve that they had experienced after their encounters with Stericker and Watson and the partying at Specchio. A broken razor, a vital penknife lost in the hay; such trivial incidents became major events worthy of mention in the diary, as gloom became the order of the day. They met up with some Italian deserters, one of whom promised to guide them south to meet the advancing Allied troops – only to disappear early the next morning with their hostess's best pair of boots.

Despite this embarrassing debacle, the farmer's wife took pity on the men and showed them safely on their way; this was the start of two days hard walking in good weather, up and down the hills and through the extensive beech forests on the edge of what is today a national park running along the spine of the Apennines and embracing (at 6,000ft) some of its highest peaks. With the help of some good food and night-time accommodation, and an invigorating haircut, they managed another twenty miles on narrow tracks to Cervarolo and Gazzano, where they shared a cowshed with a South African, a Frenchman and a Russian, and heard on the farmer's radio the news that a force of Commandos had landed at Termoli, on the Adriatic coast, about

350 miles to the south, and had driven out the German defenders. In tiny Cervarolo, six months after the two escapers passed through, the Germans executed twenty-four local men aged from seventeen to seventy-six in reprisal for help allegedly given locally to escapers and partisans.

The weather held, and after a day resting in the cowshed they pushed on in bright sunshine to a small hamlet on the rocky mountainside of the 4,500ft peak of Sasso Tignoso, where they enjoyed the excitement of watching an aerial dogfight between American Liberator bombers and three German fighters, and had an argument about religion with the priest in the tiny church. They met some young Italians from Lucca, about forty miles away, who gave them 500 lire, two packets of cigarettes each and a shirt. Leslie lost one of his packets of cigarettes whilst crossing a stream later that day, but a warm bed that chilly autumn night made up for the loss.

On the following day, 6 October, as they followed a small river (the Scoltenna) north to get back on to what Leslie described as their 'old route', along the northern flanks of the Apennine chain and away from the more populous areas around Florence, the escape nearly ended in disaster. As they crossed the road in the small village of Riolunato, a German staff car appeared from nowhere and came racing down the street towards them. Trying to look unhurried, innocent and entirely Italian, they scuttled down a side street to avoid being stopped, and held their breath as the car roared past. That night they were back sleeping with the cows – and then it started raining again.

Week 4 Miles walked 48

For five more days it poured and, although they continued to make progress, it was depressingly slow. They travelled only forty-eight miles, in thin summer clothing, dependent entirely on the kindness of complete strangers, the *contadini* of the Italian mountains who themselves had little or nothing to offer beyond a bed for the night in a barn, a chance to dry off and a share in whatever meagre supplies they could spare. Leslie records so many small kindnesses here – 'met some very kind people'; 'priest helped us to get a map'; 'two new laid eggs each this morning'; 'carabiniere gives me a map for the next part of the journey'; 'boots repaired'; 'cup of tea on the way with refugees from Bologna'.

What is particularly extraordinary about this generousity is that, by this stage in their journey, the Germans were displaying posters in villages and towns warning people about the harsh consequences of sheltering escaped prisoners: farms burned to the ground, livestock slaughtered, harsh interrogations and torture, deportation to Germany and summary execution. In the village of Pietransieri, near Sulmona in the Maiella region, 122 villagers were massacred by the Germans in November for helping escapers. Only one small girl survived, by hiding under her mother's skirts. At Gattico, in the north, the Cervi family was suspected of helping escapers, so all seven sons were shot. There were so many cases like these.

At dusk, on the fourth day of rain, they crossed the main road and railway line from Bologna to Florence (and on to Rome), in the valley of the River Reno, 'one of our hardest obstacles'; and two days later, they crossed a second major road between the two cities, and another railway line, the Grande Galleria dell'Apennino. The roads and railways were packed with German troops moving south to counter the Allied invasion threat, so these crossings were moments of high drama and risk for the escapers. That night, they celebrated their success with chestnuts roasted over the fire after supper in a good billet in Peglio, with its square stone campanile poised dramatically overlooking the narrow valley.

Week 5 Miles walked 56

As the weather became colder, they continued to push east and south towards the Alpe di San Benedetto, another area of high mountain peaks and passes. Still trying to keep away from roads, they found the steep gradients hard, and frequently lost their way, but still they made good progress – seventeen miles on one day – and managed to find a good billet or two. Leslie particularly enjoyed the chicken broth in the gloomy secluded hamlet of Albero.

On Saturday, 16 October, on the way to the Alpine village of San Benedetto, the two men came upon a large group of Italian partisans (about 200 in all, they thought), who took them to their hideout high up in the mountains and accessible only via a precarious rough track.

Here they met a New Zealander called Gatenby, who had been staying with these partisans overnight. Captain Charles Gatenby was a fruit farmer from Nelson in the South Island. He had fought in North Africa and been captured at the battle of Sidi Razegh in Libya in November 1941. Imprisoned in Italy, he had managed to make a daring escape from the hospital for Modena prison camp soon after the Italian Armistice, hiding himself in a crate full of rubbish before it was wheeled out through the gate and poured on to the municipal tip after dark – whereupon, in his own laconic words, and looking like a tramp, he 'duly ambled south'.

Gatenby had enjoyed a good meal and a lively drinking session with the partisans, who had regaled him with the story of that day's raid on a nearby village to 'shoot up four Fascists who lived there'. They had returned from the raid loaded with clothing, food and other necessaries, having shot the Fascists and having also found two German soldiers, one of whom they had shot out of hand; the other they had stripped and then allowed to escape with his life, because he had produced a photo of his wife and two young children.

As the drinking continued, the singing began, with toasts to a large red flag emblazoned with a hammer and sickle, toasts which Gatenby felt constrained to echo with gusto. They all got on famously but, when dawn broke on cracking hangovers, Gatenby became nervous about his companions and thought that perhaps it was time to move on. He must have been pretty relieved when Leslie and Reg were shown into the hideout and presented as fellow potential recruits. After introductions all round, all three were invited to join the band, but they declined, and hurried on their way, keen to get on south.

Malcolm Tudor, in his book *Among the Italian Partisans*, estimates that in the autumn and winter of 1943 there were about 10,000 partisans – a number which by the beginning of 1945 had grown to about 130,000. The first bands emerged in the mountains 'as a spontaneous reaction to the German takeover, and they were mainly composed of traditional anti-fascists, disbanded Italian soldiers and escaped Allied PoWs'. Many of them were women. Their activities were often supported by the Allied military intelligence agencies such as the British Special Operations Executive (SOE), MI9 and the American Office of Strategic Services (OSS), but in no sense did these agencies control the partisans, nor were the activities of the partisan bands themselves in any way coordinated or controlled by a higher authority. Each did what it thought best in its own area.

Leslie was immediately taken with Charlie Gatenby – 'he is good' – and was evidently very happy to have the New Zealander join him and Reg. Charlie was a rugged, no-nonsense Kiwi countryman, chipper and self-confident, generous and affable, and a fund of good stories. He and Leslie hit it off at once, and when Charlie asked if he might tag along with them, Leslie at least had no hesitation in agreeing.

They had a poor night's sleep in San Benedetto, and a delayed start the next day. It was raining again, and for two days they blundered about in the mountains, thwarted by rain and poor visibility, losing their way on indistinct shepherds' tracks and in gloomy beech forests and sleeping badly in remote huts. Leslie was bitten by a dog and quarrelled with Reg.

Week 6 Miles walked 68

They struggled up long 3,000ft climbs, were forced to make detours around impossible drops and had 'many narrow shaves with Germans'. Somehow, Leslie became separated from the other two and had to spend a night on his own with a sharecropper and his young family, the Bragagnis, living in an isolated farmhouse at Madioce, near Verghereto.

*

I met Angiolina, one of the nine Bragagni children, in 2018. She was fifteen years old the day my father knocked on the door, wet and shivering with cold. 'The poor man, he was in a terrible state, so my parents offered him food and a bed for the night. He wanted to stay in a chair by the fire, because he was afraid the Germans might come in the night – they often turned up without warning, and took what they wanted. We gave bread and some warm milk for breakfast the next morning, and he went on his way. I remember it so well.'

*

The men were reunited quickly enough the next day, but by this time Leslie had developed a bad cold and, to cap it all, was blaming Reg for losing their map, a particularly good one issued by the Touring Club of Italy. Tensions were rising between the three men.

The main bone of contention, heightened since Charlie had joined them, was the question of how best to proceed. At this stage they were walking across country on mountain tracks, carefully avoiding roads. It was incredibly hard going, as the mountains were steep and, as Charlie put it, 'no sooner had you crossed one mountain than you had to drop a way down into a deep valley and start on another one.' Charlie was still bleeding from a leg wound, and this was giving him considerable pain. When travelling on his own he had been accustomed to having the dressings changed regularly in villages he passed through, but this was no longer possible when they followed a cross-country route. Leslie and Reg still had decent boots in fairly reasonable condition, but Charlie only had a pair of worn-out gym shoes which were no protection on rough tracks and broken rocks. It was therefore important, from his point of view at least, to minimize the time spent actually walking in rough terrain before they reached safety.

Leslie put forward the idea of making for the Adriatic coast to the east, in the hope of somehow acquiring a fishing boat and then sailing far enough south to meet up with the Allied forces. Charlie argued against him, contending that this would entail six or seven days walking off their chosen route south, with no guarantee of getting a boat when they arrived – they had no money to buy one, no weapons to help them take one by force, and stealing one would be risky. They had no reserves of food or water for a long sea journey and, once out of sight of land, they would be at risk of being caught in a storm at this time of year, or shot up or captured by a German patrol boat.

The best alternative was to keep heading south, as they had been doing, but to use the roads whenever they could, in order to make faster progress before winter set in properly. Reg was against this, however, on account of the risk of capture by the increasingly frequent German search parties, or of being spotted by Italian Fascist sympathisers and reported.

The argument came to a head on 28 October, 2,000ft up in a barn on the Madonna della Cima (the Madonna of the Summit), as they sheltered from yet more rain, having stolen a replacement map from a priest. Leslie and Charlie told Reg that, in their view, the best chance of escape lay in heading south as fast as they could, using roads wherever possible. Reg felt that this would be too risky. In this impasse, the three decided to split up: Leslie and Charlie would travel together; Reg would make his way alone. (He was eventually captured four months later, south of Rome, given away by a man whose family had been taken hostage).

Week 7 Miles walked 64

Leslie and Charlie said their goodbyes to Reg and set out together early the next morning. Their mood had lightened considerably, and they enjoyed what the diary describes as the 'best two days of trip – marvellous friends – all sorts of gifts'. Charlie comments that, whilst there was the ever-present danger of running into a German patrol, or the Fascist-leaning Forest Guards, or of knocking on the door of the wrong house, they were on the other hand walking through some of Europe's most beautiful mountain scenery, meeting new people who were interested in them and their story and willing to help them on their way, and seeing village life in close if poverty-stricken rural communities.

For three days they made good progress, walking at least thirty miles on mountain roads at heights of over 3,000ft, on the boundary between the

Umbria and Marche regions of Italy. They had decided to bear slightly to the east, in the direction of the Gran Sasso, at 7,500ft one of Italy's highest mountains, reasoning that if they were up high they would be less likely to bump into German patrols.

The early omens were good. In bustling Sigillo the family they stayed with wept to see them go; in Belvedere (destroyed by an earthquake in 1997) they were looked after in the church school; in Bagnara they were able to listen to the BBC; and in Acqua Pagana they got news of some of Leslie's friends from Fontanellato, from another PoW they met along the way. But then the going became more difficult again.

They were now approaching the Sibylline Mountains, an area of dizzying peaks up to 8,000ft, extensive beech forests and lush grasslands, with relatively few villages or roads showing on the map. Rather than walk round it, they decided to cut straight across, acknowledging the risk that they might find nowhere to sleep and no one to give them food. Stocking up as best they could with a little extra bread, and relying on mountain streams for refreshment, they set off into the wilderness. All day they climbed, up and down one bramble-filled gulley after another, to a height, Charlie reckoned, of nearly 5,000ft. There were no real tracks, and no possibility, when they were in the forests, of fixing on a distant point and navigating by it. They didn't pass a house or see another soul all day on a cross-country trek of nearly thirty miles. They slept out that night with some sheep, and Charlie 'slept like a log', even though 'conditions were incredibly filthy and the stench something awful'.

The next day, with all their food gone, they must have been close to panic. As they set out again they prepared themselves mentally for another night in the freezing cold and damp, but then they suddenly detected a faint smell of smoke on the wind and soon came upon a small group of *carbonari*, making their living by burning wood to make charcoal for the fires of nearby villagers.

Newby, in *Love and War in the Apennines*, describes the kind of scene that must have met their eyes:

> It was something I will never forget. A whole group of them, men, women and children, all living together in a *baracca* [shack] covered with turf and all of them as black as night with the burning of the charcoal, and their teeth shone in their faces with an unnatural whiteness, as if they were 'nigger minstrels' on some pre-war pier. Nearby the charcoal was burning, a huge wigwam of trees which

were being slowly carbonised by the fire, with earth and turf piled on them to prevent the wood from bursting into flame and being consumed. [They spoke . . .] in some strange dialect which [we] could scarcely understand, inviting us into their *baracca* and when we were all crowded into it one of the men produced a greasy-looking bottle of marvellous grappa and gave us all a swig. They had a fire going and we all sat round it, the men, women and children, one of them a baby at its mother's breast, as black as she was. No one spoke much. We were too tired; they were too dispirited.

The *carbonari* encountered by Leslie and Charlie were a bit livelier, and asked lots of questions of the '*Dove andare?*' '*Dove venire?*' '*Quanti bambini?*' variety (Where are you going? Where have you come from? How many children?), but Leslie at least must have been as exhausted as Newby, since his only comment in the diary is 'party of Italians, another poor night'.

As they emerged, eventually, from the forest, the Gran Sasso was visible in all its snow-covered majesty, 25 miles to the east. Daunted by its size, and by snippets of news to the effect that it was likely to be some time before the Allied armies reached anywhere close, the two decided to veer back on to their original course, slightly to the west, leaving the Gran Sasso still within sight to their left.

Week 8 Miles walked 44

But even this change of course did nothing to improve their luck, for after they left the 'good village' of Cesaproba they had their first experience of going into a village and 'not being able to raise a bite of food of any description'. They knew that there were Yugoslav PoWs staying in the area, but the villagers seemed to view English-speakers with suspicion and, to Charlie's disgust, neither the villagers nor even the priest would have anything to do with them at all. Even after hearing a tirade about 'British troops dying on their soil in an endeavour to liberate their country', the villagers refused even to show them a barn where they could sleep. Whether this attitude was really due to intransigence, or to understandable fear of German reprisals for helping Allied escapers, isn't clear, but the net result was that Leslie and Charlie trudged bitterly out of the village, down into a gulley, over a small river and up on to the facing mountainside, hoping perhaps to find another *carbonari* hut to sleep in.

By Charlie's account:

> The night was bound to be bitterly cold as we were at a considerable altitude. When it became too dark for us to travel any further, and too risky on account of the danger of falling over some unseen precipice, we finally just lay down under some trees. After lying there shivering for three or four hours, I finally dropped off into a fitful sleep of exhaustion. Later Leslie claimed he did not sleep a wink. We got up once or twice, stamped our feet and beat our hands against our sides to start the circulation moving more freely, and lay down again.
>
> Leslie was wearing a watch so at about 4 o'clock, an hour or so before dawn, we decided we could stand it no longer and started to move slowly forward in what we considered to be our direction. When dawn came the ground and the trees were covered with white frost so you can imagine how bitterly cold that night was. That morning was the only morning when Leslie and I had words. It really did not amount to much, just a matter of which direction we would take and both of us were quite sure that our direction was the right one. I remember saying to him 'you can go in whichever direction you like, in fact anywhere in Italy but this is the way I'm going' and walked angrily away on my own. He followed anyway and by the time the sun came up we were both laughing over our foolishness and I apologised for being so rude.
>
> Considering what we had to put up with and what we did put up with later, it is amazing that we did not fall out more often and except for this occasion even right to the finish we never disagreed whatsoever.

That day, as they moved south, they entered the Abruzzi region of Italy and, skirting L'Aquila (the epicentre of a terrible earthquake in 2009), they came to another dangerous crossing – the main road and rail link between Pescara on the east coast, Rieti and Rome. Charlie spoke to some people working in the fields as they approached the crossing who warned him that the bridge over the railway that they were heading for was well guarded by a platoon of German soldiers billeted in a house nearby. Rather than retrace their steps to another crossing point, they scrambled down on to the tracks themselves, under the cover of a scrubby hedge, and made their way along to a point where rails, road and hedge ran close together. Watching for a gap in the military traffic, they raced across the busy road and up the bare incline on the other side, expecting any moment to hear shots ringing out.

About a mile along the road, as they lay catching their breath in the warm sunshine, Charlie chatted to some passing Italians, who told him about a local factory which the Germans were using as a petrol processing and storage plant. Ever the professional soldiers, the two crept closer to have a good look and record the information, to pass on when they got home.

They spent that night near Lucoli (where the villagers have now planted an apple tree in Leslie's honour) – 'quite reasonable billet'. For some time now, Leslie had been suffering from a very sore heel and limping badly. He hadn't complained much about it, but whenever they stopped to cool their feet in a mountain stream, Charlie had noticed that it was very inflamed. It was now causing serious problems, and slowing them down. With Charlie stumbling painfully along on his sore leg and in his worn out gym shoes, and Leslie hobbling after him with his bad heel, they were a sorry pair – and putting themselves at ever greater risk of serious injury or worse with every day on the march.

The next day, Saturday, 6 November, was a brute. Edging west, apparently hoping for an Allied invasion on the west coast, they had to cross the densely-forested flanks of 6,000ft Monte Cava. This was some of the roughest going they had encountered. Late that afternoon, completely done in, the two men stumbled into the outskirts of a village called Corvaro, about 45 miles from Rome.

Charlie, in his no-nonsense New Zealand way, asked a passing Italian if there were 'any Fascists or Germans in the village', and then if it would be possible to get something to eat. The answer was promising, so they headed on into the village and found what looked like a small shop in the main street. In the gloom of the interior they could see very little for sale, but they got a warm welcome from the blowsy lady of the house, who was soon bustling about preparing a scratch meal of bread and raw bacon, washed down with a glass of wine and rounded off with a pack of cigarettes. They wolfed it all down.

While they were enjoying this hospitality, a well-dressed family came into the shop. They were Jewish and had recently fled from their home in Rome, in fear of what the Germans would do to Jews once they had completed their occupation of the country. They were also worried about the effects of Allied bombing raids on the city. They were hiding out in the area, were very friendly, and one of them spoke reasonable English, so a conversation developed, and the English-speaker mentioned that there were two other English officers living up in the mountains not far away. He was keen that Leslie and Charlie should go and see them, and offered to show them the way.

The two men debated this for a while. Although intent on reaching the Allied lines as soon as possible, the next day was in fact a Sunday, not a good day for anyone poorly disguised as an Italian to be wandering about in the Italian countryside, crowded as it often was on Sundays with real (and naturally curious) Italians with time to kill and questions to ask. They were dead beat as well, and Leslie's heel needed a rest from the punishing treatment it was getting. So they decided to accept the offer, provided the lady of the house was prepared to let them stay the night. She readily agreed to their bedding down with the horse in the semi-basement, and it was all settled.

As they were about to turn in, a stocky middle-aged man with a broad, good-humoured grin arrived and bade them a friendly welcome. He was Giuseppe de Michelis, 'Peppino' as he was known throughout the village, husband to their hostess Bernadina – whom he evidently adored, and to whom he regularly deferred. Peppino was a highly-respected member of the local community, a self-educated engineer and musician who played the organ in the local church and had built his own water-clock. These two generous people were to become friends to Leslie and Charlie in a way they could not have imagined as they settled themselves down for the night in the basement, next to the family horse.

Chapter 16

Christmas in Corvaro

Week 8 (*contd*)

With winter approaching, the Allied invasion of Italy had become a long attritional slog, in terrible weather and challenging mountain terrain and against determined and well-prepared German defensive positions. Although the whole of southern Italy was in Allied hands by the end of October 1943, further progress north was then virtually halted until early January 1944. By this time, the Allies had suffered 92,000 casualties, and the Axis 177,000. It is not known exactly how many of the

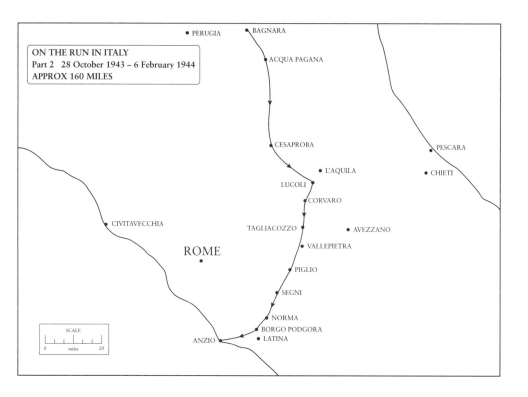

ON THE RUN IN ITALY
Part 2   28 October 1943 – 6 February 1944
APPROX 160 MILES

80,000 or so Allied PoWs held in Italy in September 1943 were at this stage still at liberty. According to Roger Absalom, the files show that, by late 1943 there were still about 30,000 men on the run, some 7,000 having already made it to Switzerland or to the Allied lines in the south.

When Leslie woke up in Corvaro on 8 November 1943 he knew that something was wrong. He had slept badly and felt hot, sweaty and out of sorts. Gatenby noted with concern that his partner's face was very flushed and immediately went off to consult their hostess, Bernadina, who quickly produced a thermometer. When this showed a reading of over 38°C she became worried and, after fussing around with hot drinks, decided that Leslie had better see a doctor. Influenza was the verdict, and the patient had to stay where he was for several days.

This was a serious setback to their plans, with heavy skies already promising snow. Leslie was all for Charlie 'pushing on alone', but the Kiwi wouldn't hear of it. They had been through so much together and, knowing that if their positions had been reversed Leslie would not have left him, Charlie had no hesitation in deciding to stay put. In this he was encouraged by the reaction of Peppino, who seemed quite happy to see them stay on and relished the opportunity of having someone new and exotic to chat to.

There was no improvement in Leslie's condition the next day, and that night brought a fierce storm and the anticipated heavy snowfall. The family moved the two into a small room above a nearby stable which they owned, and brought Leslie eggs, milk (both difficult to obtain) and warm broth each day until his condition started to improve. As he lay in bed, the two men began debating their predicament. They faced a frustrating dilemma: on the one hand, though desperate to move on, they realized that snow at 3,000ft could mean that any further trekking on foot might well be impossible until the following spring. On the other hand, remaining with the de Michelis family in Corvaro, with German soldiers all around, risked recapture for the PoWs and, thanks to a recent German proclamation, death for Peppino and a concentration camp for Bernadina, as well as possible reprisals for the whole village.

Furthermore, it was obvious that the family's resources and supply of food were already stretched, so feeding the two of them for even a short period would be a substantial extra burden. The couple had five children: Luigina, Marina aged fourteen, Rosina, twelve (very pretty, and the darling of the village), a boy of about five called Benedetto (or occasionally Peppino after his father), and a baby, Santina. Peppino's mother also lived with them, 'a fine old lady who seemed to do a lot of the housework'. The family had enough on their hands, but they would not hear of the men moving on. In fact, commented Charlie, 'They could not do enough for us.'

For Leslie and Charlie, and thousands like them, the sustained kindness to complete strangers of so many brave Italian people meant the difference between life and death, freedom and capture, safety and danger, shelter and exposure. It was a generosity that defies intellectual explanation and that stands, even today, as an outstanding example of mankind's occasional capacity to do good purely for the sake of it.

Weeks 9–17 Miles walked 0 Miles walked so far 364

It took Leslie more than two weeks to recover from his infection (which had developed into pneumonia), and it was some weeks after that before he felt at all fit again, so they had plenty of time to get to know Corvaro and the family they were living with. They became celebrities in the small village, their residency a cause of some pride to the friendly locals, who took to calling them 'Maggiore Giovane' and 'Capitano Carlos', in their hard-to-understand local dialect.

The men were quite shocked by conditions in the village. Corvaro was built on the side of a hill, its houses spreading down on to a flat plain. The original village was severely damaged by the massive earthquake which struck and destroyed the nearby town of Avezzano in January 1915, killing an estimated 30,000 people, including several hundred in Corvaro. The rebuilding operation after the quake had been quite haphazard and had left many houses still 'all tumbled down and some of them only shells of what they used to be', even in 1943, nearly thirty years later.

The houses were 'all jammed close together and the streets of cobble-stones and incredibly filthy everywhere'. Domestic animals and family livestock roamed the streets at will and, with no sanitation in the houses, animals and humans often relieved themselves wherever and whenever nature called, leaving other animals to clear up the mess; so wrote Charlie, who became the butt of local humour when he asked for some toilet paper, only to be told that 'everyone, right down to the smallest child, just used a stone'. None of the houses had running water, and fresh water had to be collected from the village pump.

The two men used to go to wash in a small stream about a mile from the village, where they quickly attracted a curious regular audience of village folk. Apparently, to get water on your back was thought to be 'absolutely fatal . . . and courting sudden death'. There was no soap of any kind available in Corvaro (the notion of using such a thing the villagers probably felt was as funny as Charlie's request for toilet paper), so they had to use 'a handful of soil to get a good scrub'. They never succeeded in ridding themselves of the lice which they had attracted during their travels.

Charlie was shocked by what he saw as a lack of formal education or knowledge of world affairs – 'no newspapers had ever come there and they were quite ignorant of what was happening in the outside world – had never heard of New Zealand'; nor did they know who 'was concerned in the war – not the foggiest idea'. He claimed 'there was not even a scrap of paper in the village other than a few bibles which the Italians treasured.'

On 19 December, after a hiatus of nearly six weeks while he recovered from his infection, Leslie resumed his diary. He and Charlie were moving to a 'mountain *casale*' (small homestead). By this time, the Germans had established a garrison in Corvaro, with a large vehicle park, as part of the nearby German winter defensive barrier called the Gustav Line, and there were Germans everywhere. The garrison was less than 100yds from the de Michelis shop, and it was obviously becoming too risky for the men to remain hidden in the village. There were frequent Allied bombing attacks in the area as well, including targeted attacks on the vehicles, which added to the dangers.

The *casale* was a small, very simple stone cottage at the head of a valley running up behind Corvaro, about three miles out of the village. This was known as the Valle del Malito (the valley of the brigand) and was under the control of a local band of partisans called the 'Gioda', after their leader, Giovanni de Agoutis. It is served now by a proper road, but in those days it was reachable only by a rough footpath. The *casale* had a sloping roof of red clay tiles, rough stone walls and one room with an earthen floor and a stone fireplace – which could be used only with caution, for fear of attracting the attention of the Germans. Behind the cottage was a small stone lean-to, where the men slept. In the severe winter of 1943/44, in 6ft of snow, it was perishing cold and dank. Charlie and Leslie lived there for six weeks, either relying on the family to bring food up to them or, later, borrowing the horse from the family once a week to fetch supplies from the village themselves. Water they drew from a small stream just up the road.

By this time they had met up with other escapers living in the vicinity, hiding in the hills around the village and waiting for better weather. These men were amongst the hundred or more escaped Allied prisoners who were being looked after by the brave people of Corvaro at this time, encouraged from his pulpit by an inspirational local priest, Don Filippo Ortenzi.

Three escapees came to join them in the *casale* for a while, and all five of the men trooped down to the village on Christmas Day for a party with the de Michelis family and some of their friends. Two of the newcomers left soon after Christmas, hoping to be able to escape in a boat from Civitavecchia, just north of Rome. Leslie and Charlie were then joined by Vivian Wilson Lloyd, David Laird (who had been in Fontanellato), a New Zealander called Jim Stone, and Barry Keyter, a South African airman who had been shot down a few days previously and was now evading capture.

Life in the *casale* was simple for the six men, though clearly crowded and uncomfortable. Beset by frequent snowstorms and blizzard conditions, they focussed on repairing the roof (which leaked constantly), keeping the snow from blowing through the rickety wooden door on to their bedding, maintaining their supply line from the village, collecting wood, playing bridge – and avoiding periodic German patrols and search parties. At one point their hut was robbed, which must have come as a shock after all the kindness they had received from the locals; and on another occasion they had to spend three days attempting to recover from the villagers a load of supplies which had been parachuted in by the RAF for the use of escapees hiding out in the area.

Week 18

On 15 January Leslie made the first of several visits to a small hamlet called Santo Stefano, a couple of miles from Corvaro, and stayed the night. This was not an idle piece of sightseeing but the start of the next and final stage of their escape: a stage that would bring them face to face with mortal danger, and tragic death.

Chapter 17

News of a Landing

On their first afternoon in Corvaro, as Charlie and Leslie were being warmly welcomed by Bernadina de Michelis, there came into her shop, as has been mentioned, an evidently well-to-do Jewish family from Rome. These were the Elfers.

Antonio Elfer was a fur trader from Trieste (then part of Austria) who had married Elisa, a highly-educated woman and a talented musician from Vienna, in 1919. The family lived in a beautiful villa in the affluent Prati district of Rome, close to the Vatican, and were part of Rome's liberal intellectual elite. They had two children, Eugenio, born in 1920, and Silvia, born in 1923. Eugenio was studying Political Sciences at the University of Rome. Like her brother, Silvia was intelligent and already a noted beauty, with a talent for music, art and dancing. The two children spent their summers on the beach near Anzio and their winters skiing in the Abruzzi, fifty miles or so from Rome – and not far from Corvaro.

The Elfers remained in Rome for the first part of the war. Life was not easy for Jews in wartime Italy. Although Mussolini resisted the racist policies implemented by the Nazis against the Jews in Germany, there is nevertheless evidence of systematic disenfranchisement of Jews in Italy from 1938 onwards. In September 1943, after the Italian Armistice, the outlook for Jews in Italy became very much more serious as the German occupation began, and the Elfers soon fled their comfortable life in Rome for the mountain town of Avezzano, about 15 miles from Corvaro, where they stayed with some friends, the Zaccarias.

By one account, Antonio had purchased a local timber business at the start of the war which he used as a cover; timber was a protected industry, and Elfer used the business to provide employment for local partisans and Jews so they could avoid being called up into the Italian Army. He made Zaccaria the works manager.

The Elfers' son Eugenio – Nino to his family, Doc to his friends – had become involved with the partisans and quickly began to attract the attention of the Gestapo. He was spotted distributing weapons in Rome, from a truck unwisely bearing the name of his father's fur trading company, whereupon the Gestapo paid a visit to the Elfer family home. Here they were stalled by Elisa, so the family story goes, just long enough for her son to escape out of the back door. It was shortly after this incident that the family took to the hills.

Accompanying the Elfers in Avezzano was a young man called Carlo Tevini. His mother, Beatrice, was living in Rome with Boggiano Pico, a prominent Catholic nobleman, lawyer and writer. It was Charlie's understanding that Carlo and Silvia were engaged, or at least 'courting'. Carlo presented himself as an Italian Army officer working as a British liaison agent to help escaping Allied PoWs, and now himself on the run from the Germans and their Italian Fascist helpers. He said that it was imperative that they get to the British lines as quickly as possible.

Elisa Elfer disapproved of Carlo and worried about the attention he was paying her daughter. She believed that his family had Fascist connections, and that his relationship with her daughter, a Jew, might put the girl and, indeed, all of them at risk from the German authorities. When Carlo accompanied the family to Corvaro he was expected to return to Rome immediately; but he stayed on and on, refusing to go back, even when his mother (herself concerned about her son's relationship with a Jew) sent a car to collect him, driven (to make matters worse) by a man claiming to be in the pay of the Germans. Small incidents like this worried Elisa.

Once in Avezzano, Nino continued with his resistance activities, helped by his sister Silvia. He was an idealist, not a fighter, and rather studious. Supported by MI9, he set about locating escaped Allied prisoners, making sure they were securely hidden and bringing them food, medicine, money and clothes whenever he could. He was supplied with a radio transmitter so that he could keep in contact with his MI9 handlers. He also started to guide PoWs towards the Allied lines, as many as a hundred by one account and including a General Thomson, who had been held in PG Camp 91 near Avezzano. Thomson's group was heading towards the British Eighth Army line near the Sangro River when they were picked up by a German searchlight and, in the ensuing firefight, lost two men. Nino led the other officers to safety and was highly praised for his bravery.

Nino's activities brought increased danger for his parents, who soon left Avezzano, helped again by the Zaccarias. They set off for a new hiding place, crossing the mountains by mule, and found their way to Corvaro, where the parents were installed in a small cottage without heating or running water.

The two children preferred to stay in the small nearby hamlet of Santo Stefano.

Nino was now on the Wanted list and, early in the morning of 16 November, a troop of more than a dozen heavily-armed Gestapo officers, some in uniform, some in plain clothes, arrived at the house in Corvaro where the Elfers were being sheltered, intent on arresting the whole family. Waving a gun in Zaccaria's face and threatening him with death, they demanded that he hand over the Elfers. For ten hours he prevaricated, seeking to convince them that the family had left for Avezzano. Late in the afternoon, an informer told the Gestapo that Nino was in fact hiding in the Corvaro house and that his parents were in Santo Stefano. The Gestapo put this to Zaccaria, but he called their bluff by offering to accompany them in a search of the two properties, and eventually they gave up, threatening to return the following day.

Elisa, in a moving account of the incident after the war, described how 'thanks to the fairness of Corvaro people, they did not find us. But the round ups became so frequent that we were obliged to go from one shelter to another, making the life of tracked savage beasts.' She even suspected that someone might have tipped off the Gestapo as to their whereabouts. In the end, Zaccaria moved them to L'Aquila province, and they stayed in hiding there until it was safe to return to Rome.

As Christmas approached, and with her children wanted by the Gestapo and living rough in the mountains with the partisans, Elisa must have felt lonely indeed. A few days after the move, Nino and Silvia came to visit their doting parents, arriving (according to the village doctor) 'late in the night and on horseback . . . furtive and cautious like robbers, aware of the capital punishment that weighed on everyone'. For Elisa, by now fully aware of the risks they were running, the visit must have been a torment.

After Christmas, on Friday, 7 January, Leslie recorded the following entry in his diary: 'Great news from D. Going next week'. 'D' was short for Doc – Nino's nickname, on account of his university studies. Leslie and Charlie had been in conversation with him for some time about the possibility of his guiding them to the Allied lines. But the snow was still falling hard and, whether for that reason or because of some other obstacle, they heard five days later, 'D not able to go on Friday'. The Allies launched a massive attack on the nearby Gustav defensive line on 12 January, and the heavy additional military activity may have made it too dangerous to proceed.

Nevertheless, the meetings with Nino continued. On 15 January the two escapers walked to Santo Stefano and stayed the night for a game of bridge and a listen to the BBC. For the next two days they were stuck in Corvaro because Germans were spotted scouring the hills. They chopped wood and played bridge – and then Nino became ill, so there was a further frustrating delay. A couple of days later, they were in Rosciolo, the next village to Santo Stefano, and noticed 'much air activity' – clearly a prelude to an Allied attack of some kind.

Week 19

On Sunday, 23 January they were back in Rosciolo, for a 'conference about leaving' with some of the other escapers in the area. There they received some momentous information, and it appears in the diary in capital letters: 'NEWS OF LANDING'. The Allies had landed at Anzio on the previous day, less than 100 miles away, on the west coast of Italy, just below Rome. Suddenly, the entries in Leslie's diary take on a new air of urgency and purpose – if they could get to Anzio, they could get home.

For two or three days there was a great deal of toing and froing between Corvaro and Santo Stefano, and it was decided that they would leave by the end of the week. It was clearly vital to get to Anzio as soon as possible, before the German defensive ring became impenetrable – but also because Giovanni de Agoutis, the head of the Gioda partisan group, their protectors in the valley, was concerned that if they stayed much longer they risked discovery by the increasingly frequent German patrols. In fact, four members of the group (David Laird, Vivian Wilson Lloyd, Barry Keyter and Jim Stone) set off in mid-week for Frascati on the outskirts of Rome, via Tivoli, evidently believing that Rome would be quickly captured and that that would be the best place to rejoin the advancing Allied forces.

Leslie and Charlie, with their guides (and possibly would-be fellow escapers) Nino, Silvia and Carlo Tevini, decided to wait a few days to see how fighting at the beachhead developed before setting off. They cleared the *casale* that had been their home for six weeks, had an uproarious, cognac-fuelled leaving party, said their goodbyes to the de Michelis family and other friends in the village and moved to Santo Stefano. The last stage of the long journey home was about to begin.

Chapter 18

Triumph and Tragedy

The Allied invasion of Italy was making only slow progress in the face of determined German defence and through difficult mountainous terrain.

Neither side was equipped or trained for mountain warfare, but the Germans used mines, booby traps, strategic demolition and a rearguard of well dug-in infantry, heavily armed with mortars, machine guns and light automatics, plus effective air support and canny choices about where to fight and where to run, to frustrate the Allies at every turn. In continual drenching rain or snow, endless seas of mud (which brought even the best tracked vehicles to a halt) and biting cold, conditions for the troops were miserable in the extreme – and Churchill's desperate impatience to 'get on with the job' made life miserable for his commanders, too.

At a conference of Allied leaders in Iran in late November 1943 it was eventually agreed, notwithstanding American concerns about possible delays or diversion of resources from the landings in northern Europe, that the invasion of Italy would be stepped up in the New Year by further landings just south of Rome, with the aim of capturing the capital quickly and weakening German forces, which would then be fighting on two fronts. The American landings, in what became known as Operation Shingle, were to take place at the seaside resorts of Nettuno and Anzio, with the British landing a little further north at the Lido di Lavinio.

Just before dawn on 21 January 1944, the Allied invasion fleet, over 370 vessels strong, sailed from its harbours around Naples and north towards Rome. It was cold and clear, the water was calm and visibility was good. From the deck of every ship a vast armada could be seen stretching to the horizon, with fighters patrolling overhead, and every gun manned.

By midnight the fleet was anchored three miles off Anzio, and all was quiet. Two hours later, with a sudden stunning and sustained roar, the big guns opened up, sending a wall of flame and destruction crashing into the buildings along the length of the invasion beaches. Waves of landing craft stormed ashore, unopposed by the German defenders, and by midnight that day, 36,000 soldiers and nearly 3,500 vehicles were on the beaches and heading inland.

But in what many see as one of the great missed opportunities of the war, the invaders didn't go very far. The American commander, Major General John Lucas, known for his caution, either misunderstanding or simply confounding his orders, chose to focus on building up his beachhead rather than attacking the initially bewildered Germans – and the momentum was lost. Over the coming days, as German forces were rushed to the area determined to hold the invaders on the beaches and then push them back into the sea, Churchill remarked, 'I had hoped we were hurling a wildcat into the shore, but all we got was a stranded whale.'

Week 20 Miles walked 24

By 29 January, as Leslie and Charlie set off with the two Elfers and Carlo Tevini from Santo Stefano, there were 69,000 Allied soldiers on the beachhead, opposed by 71,000 Germans and engaged in a vicious, bloody fight, often at close quarters and even hand-to-hand.

Leslie and Charlie knew nothing of all this as they left Santo Stefano before dawn that day in a farmer's cart and crossed the Avezzano road. Charlie had been given new boots and a coat by Nino and must have been feeling ready for anything. Leslie, on the other hand, had terrible diarrhoea and was probably wishing himself back in Corvaro with the de Michelis family. Snow several feet deep lay all around and, as the sun came up, they were able to admire a beautiful winter's day and the stunning mountain scenery all around them. But they were walking across the grain of a bleak, deserted almost lunar countryside, with few roads or even tracks, and as they came to the 4,000ft Monti di Nebbia (Foggy Mountains), their sense of dependence on their Italian guides must have been humbling. As they got closer to the front line they had to traverse a wide plain, criss-crossed with roads now filled with German military vehicles heading towards Anzio. With the sun setting early, they slipped between the convoys and on to the busy town of Tagliacozzo in the dark.

They spent the whole of the next day climbing, through thick, soft snow that dragged at their feet and soaked their thin clothes, the bitter cold stinging their faces, fingers and toes. Leslie's stomach was improving, but still he could eat nothing all day. By nightfall they were hopelessly lost and had to try to sleep in a cave, huddled together for warmth and for their lives.

Charlie said, years later, 'The cold was really intense; I suppose none of us slept more than in half hour patches, then we were all up beating our arms and stamping our feet. I thought, "Good life, I'm never going to get across to the other side".'

Setting off again early the next morning, they spent the day crossing the dense beech forests and 6,000ft peaks in the Simbruini range, popularly known as 'Rome's Alps', and down through the eerie Valley of the Stones, before finally staggering into the stunning hilltop town of Vallepietra. 'An excellent village – good bed – night disturbed 12.30 by German scare', reported Leslie in his diary. At last he was able to obtain some medicine for his stomach, and they met up with two Americans, though who they were and what they were doing, the diary doesn't say.

Week 21 Miles walked 32

On Tuesday, 1 February, the five had a well-deserved lie-in and a late start, then made good progress south along the valley of the Simbrivio River. They passed some German soldiers on the path, and one of them ordered Leslie to help move a lorry that had become stuck – he did, but his heart must have been pounding. They decided to stop for the night at the ochre-painted Convent of San Lorenzo, overlooking the town of Piglio. Leslie was exasperated by one of the priests, who wouldn't stop talking as they were trying to get to sleep, and their tempers must have been frayed by the sound of loud gunfire from the terrible fighting on the front line at Campoleone, by now only 30 miles away.

After a hearty breakfast they left the Convent early the next morning and continued moving south. As they neared Rome, the volume of German military traffic became ever greater, with columns of troops moving towards the front line at Anzio or preparing the defences further back. They had to move cautiously and slowly through the snowy lowland hills, the sound of gunfire constantly in their ears.

They spent a restless night in a shepherd's hut near Anagni, and the following morning, crossed the main road from Chieti and Pescara on the east coast to Rome, followed by the mainline railway. As they travelled they heard news of the fierce battle for Cisterna the previous day, when two US Ranger battalions totalling 767 men were virtually wiped out, 700 men being either killed or captured. The town remained in enemy hands, news which must have given the escapers an inkling of the fierce struggle around the beachhead at Anzio, for which they were now heading. They skirted the busy walled town of Segni overlooking the valley of the Sacco River and found shelter again for the night in a shepherd's hut. They got little sleep, kept awake by the sound of British guns pounding German positions.

Friday, 4 February was described by Leslie as the 'worst day of the trip'. For twelve hours they struggled over the forested slopes between Segni and Norma, climbing around the 4,500ft peak of Monte Lupone in torrential rain and appalling visibility. By nightfall, as they stumbled into the small scruffy town of Norma, perched high on a sheer rocky cliff overlooking the Pontine Marshes and on west to the sea, they were done in. The burning ruins of Cisterna were just six miles away. They collapsed, four in a bed, to await the dawn.

The night brought them little comfort. The weather was foul. Heavy rain, driving sleet and a freezing wind meant that the fields were waterlogged, the ditches were filled with water and the roads were sheet ice. Both sides were pounding each other's lines with massive and sustained heavy artillery and bombing attacks, and the constant distant crump of high explosive that morning must have played on the group's jangling nerves.

The obvious next step was to conduct a recce, but Norma was crawling with German troops, and going out at all was a risk for the two non-Italian escapers. Nino slipped out early on his own to recce a route through to the front lines, while his sister and Tevini talked to local people and managed to obtain a sketch map of the German and American dispositions in front of them. They knew there would be great lengths of barbed wire, extensive minefields, lookout posts, searchlights and snipers, sentries and constant patrols. All of this they would have to navigate in inky winter darkness, across a billiard-table flat plain, lit only by the nightmare flash of bombardment, probing searchlights and hanging flares.

As they ventured out in the late morning and looked west from the town high above the marshes they would have seen in the distance, had the weather been kinder, the Tyrrhenian Sea, with Allied warships anchored offshore maintaining a heavy bombardment on the German positions, and landing craft still plying to and fro bringing fresh supplies and reinforcements for the troops ashore. Closer at hand, and snaking back towards them from the sea, through a spider's web of small roads and patchwork fields, was the huge Mussolini Canal, 20yds wide, with banks 30ft high. This provided some definition for the shifting line between the German Tenth Army and the American VI Army Corps on the southern side of the beachhead. Running left to right in front, and separating them from the front line was a railway and the ancient Roman road, the Via Appia.

As they thought about all this that afternoon, their hearts initially failed them. Their situation looked hopeless, even suicidal. Had they known that, at that moment, the very future of Operation Shingle itself hung in the balance, they would have felt even worse. But they had really no alternative, short of a gruelling and ignominious return to Corvaro, with no certainty of eventual rescue once they got there. They knew their lives were on the line and that the chances of survival, let alone escape, on the furious battlefield in front of them were small, but they determined to try. The three young Italians knew the area well from their summers on the beach, and Charlie and Leslie, with their military experience, knew enough about how minefields were laid to believe that, in Charlie's words, 'With any luck . . . we may have a slight chance. It was a ridiculous statement of course, but it was the only hope there was left.'

That evening, as darkness fell, and with Leslie's stomach once more causing him pain and problems, they slipped out of Norma and stepped on to the battlefield. It was Charlie's birthday.

The Pontine Marshes, at the foot of the Norma cliff, are 330 square miles of ancient wetland, created by the failure of streams draining the Alban Hills and the mountains beyond to find a clear route to the sea through the barrier of sand dunes at the edge of the marsh. From Roman times, successive attempts had been made to drain them, but until Mussolini's work in the 1930s, these were only partially successful. The Roman Appian Way, which ran from the Forum in Rome to Brindisi in the far south, had to be built up on a stone causeway twenty miles long across stagnant and foul-smelling malarial pools in order to traverse the marsh, and the causeway and its bridges needed constant repair.

Mussolini's visionary solution in 1930 was to create a network of canals and trenches draining into the massive canal that bears his name. Using 120,000 forced labourers, rivers were dredged and banks were raised, whilst the existing population of smallholders was moved out to make way for the work. Upon completion, the families of 2,000 Great War veterans from the north of Italy were moved into standardized two-storey houses on small farming plots, and five new towns were built to service the area.

When the Germans started constructing their Winter Line, they partially flooded the marsh in order to impede the post-invasion movement by the Allies of heavy equipment through the area, creating a massive mosquito-infested swamp as a battlefield and using Mussolini's small farmhouses as refuges for infantry and cover for tanks.

After their months in the mountains, this was the desolate, exposed, boggy plain that Leslie, Charlie, Nino, Silvia and Carlo now had to cross.

Moving in single file along muddy, snow-filled ditches, avoiding the raised roads wherever they could and steering well clear of any form of habitation, they started quite literally to crawl in the direction of the new town of Latina eight miles away to the south-west. It was pitch dark, overcast, drizzling and freezing cold, They must have felt like small bugs inching their way across the smooth surface of a slide under a microscope, moving as they were behind the German lines, completely certain that they would be summarily shot if spotted. Ahead of them lay minefields and then no-man's-land, lit up occasionally by the flash of a big gun or the nightmarishly bright light of a flare. Machine gun tracer bullets criss-crossed the area at head height.

The Appian Way, which they had to cross to get to the American lines and which was heavily used by German transport, is four miles from Norma. At a painfully slow crawl, often on their hands and knees, pausing every few moments to peer nervously about, straining against the distant bombardment to hear the chink of a German machine gun or the cautious, watchful step of a German patrol, it would have taken them hours that night to reach the road.

Having clambered up on to the exposed causeway, they crossed about half-way between the Mussolini Canal and the incongruously-named Via Epitaffio (Epitaph Road). As they entered the marsh proper, Charlie spotted the tell-tale signs of a hurriedly-laid minefield across their path. They stopped and then, with Charlie in the lead, started to creep between the bumps, holding on to each other's ankles, one behind the other, hardly daring to breathe.

They still had several miles to go to the Allied line and began to fear that dawn would find them stranded in no-man's-land, beyond hope of rescue or concealment. After a whispered confab, they decided they had to risk walking, as and when they could reasonably risk it; in reality they had no choice, as time was running out fast.

Suddenly, on a small road beside a stand of pine trees, a machine gun opened up in a shattering clatter of noise in front of them and to their right. Nino and Carlo were out in front, a few yards ahead of Leslie, then came the other two. The two in front went down, whilst Charlie and Silvia hurled themselves into a ditch. Rolling over, Leslie desperately scrambled back across the road with his head down, joining Charlie in the ditch and expecting the two Italian men to follow. They waited long tense minutes, but there was neither sound nor sign of movement from the road. They called out, but the only reply they got was a burst of gunfire. After a while, Charlie crawled back along the ditch and found Carlo bleeding badly from the chest and struggling to speak. Charlie 'thought for certain he would die', and they had no choice but to leave him. Of Nino there was no sign.

Their nerves shattered, they now faced an impossible and heart-breaking dilemma. Their two Italian guides, they assumed, were dead; they had with them a vulnerable 20-year-old girl, the sister of one, girlfriend of the other; and they were pinned down by machine-gun fire, unarmed themselves and caught between the two armies. Dawn was approaching and, if they did not move almost immediately, the likelihood was that they would all be captured or, more likely (disguised as Italians as they were and without papers), killed as spies.

Silvia was distraught, determined to stay with her two compatriots. By this time, however, by Charlie's account, the Germans were throwing stick grenades in their direction. Charlie pulled her to her feet and, amidst a hail of bullets, the three ran across a field away from the road and fell, after a few yards, into an irrigation ditch, where they hid for a while and tried to comfort the sobbing girl. After some time they persuaded her that they had to go on or be killed themselves.

They decided to wait for the moon to set but, as soon as it did, another bombardment opened up. They waited again, then began to crawl painfully forward. Twice they were fired on, twice they lay motionless in the ditch until they judged it was safe to move again. Leslie thought the position was hopeless, and that they would have to give themselves up.

They came upon another minefield, which again they navigated on their hands and knees. They felt now as if they had nothing left to lose. They had no idea how far away they were from American help, or what further obstacles and dangers might lie in their path. They started to run towards the Canal.

Another machine gun opened up, 50yds back and to their right – more Germans. Then more firing, this time from the left, towards the American line. The firing began in earnest now, the three fugitives pressing themselves into the sodden ground and worming their way forwards.

A small mound appeared ahead of them, probably a spoil heap along the edge of the canal. They inched their way to the top. A machine gun clattered out. Charlie 'could see it traversing because it had tracer as well as ammunition. I think I'm quite safe, when suddenly I'm turned on my back, a bullet caught me in the right arm and turned me over.'

Behind them, Silvia moaned and fell back. She had been hit in the throat. Leslie yelled at their attackers: 'Stop shooting! Stop shooting! British!'

Finally, finally the shooting stopped. An American voice called out, 'Advance with your hands up', and they stumbled forwards into the arms of an American patrol. Filthy, lousy, dressed like Italian peasants, covered in mud and blood, and shaking, it took a while before the Americans would believe that they were escaped PoWs. The patrol leader radioed back to his headquarters for instructions.

When eventually he got the all clear, they hurried back to Silvia, and got her transported to the American Field Hospital at Anzio, where she and Charlie received emergency surgery.

Silvia died the next day.

Chapter 19

Going Home

For Leslie, the end of an extraordinarily intense eleven-month adventure in Italy came very quickly. While Silvia was undergoing emergency surgery in the Field Hospital at the beachhead, and Charlie was on his way to a hospital ship out in the bay, Leslie was fitted up with some new clothes and plied with cigarettes and 'tons of good food'.

But his undoubted happiness and relief at being no longer on the run was tempered by no fewer than seven German air raids and two artillery bombardments on his first morning with the Americans. He also had to cope with the news of Silvia's tragic death. This must have come as a hammer blow after their gruelling few days together approaching Anzio, and it is not hard to imagine the turmoil of mixed emotions that must have been flooding his every waking thought during these days. It fell to him to organize her funeral, which took place the next day, Tuesday, 8 February, in the early afternoon. In the temporary American war cemetery at Nettuno a small group of men huddled briefly around her grave in the grey, cold winter light and under a flurry of snow.

Her death must have affected Leslie deeply, with a sense of guilt and even shame, for the rest of his life.

But he had little time to reflect – forty-five minutes after the funeral, he was boarding a ship bound for Naples, where he was lodged in a transit hotel to await transport back to England. On 11 February he was debriefed in Naples (or 'interrogated', as the faded paper copy of his typed statement puts it), and a letter was sent by the War Office in London to tell his parents that he was safe in Allied hands. This was the first time they had heard from him since September 1943, despite several appeals they had made in national newspapers for news of him. After a couple of weeks waiting for a ship in Naples, he finally embarked on 4 March. It was time to go home.

The war in Italy dragged on until Germany surrendered on 29 April 1945, and hostilities ceased on 2 May. The campaign is estimated to have cost the lives of 60,000–70,000 Allied soldiers, and 40,000–150,000 Germans.

Over 150,000 Italian civilians lost their lives, as did 15,000 partisans, in the brutal German post-Armistice occupation. In that time, Malcolm Tudor estimates that, out of over 70,000 British and Commonwealth PoWs in Italian camps in September 1943, 16,628 escaped and made it back home, 4,852 via Switzerland and 11,776 through the Allied Lines in Italy. Leslie and Charlie were two of the lucky ones.

Not long after the war, Leslie received a letter from Peppino de Michelis, thanking him for the money (25,000 lire) that he had sent and recounting what had happened in Corvaro after Leslie and Charlie left. He, too, had a sad tale to tell. On 30 January, the day after their departure from Santo Stefano, the Germans surrounded the village, and a remaining PoW, a South African, was foolish enough to kill one of the soldiers. The Germans then took several villagers away for punishment in local prisons. Peppino himself managed to get away with his family, but the Germans ransacked his house and shop and kept up the hunt for him until they were forced to retreat following the fall of Rome.

In the meantime, Peppino and his family crept back in – only to be forced out again by Allied bombing raids on the village and its German garrison. The raids killed several villagers, and the de Michelis family spent a month living rough. Peppino told Leslie that his two daughters, Rosina and Luigina, 'in the hardest moments used to call your names for help. Often Rosina said, "We have helped them when Germans might have made them *kaput*, and now they are bombing us." But I assure her it was not you.'

Charlie Gatenby spent time recovering from his wound in Naples and remained in Italy pending the breakout from the beachhead and the capture of Rome on 4 June 1944. He was then invited to set up a club for New Zealand forces in the capital, and he set about this task with his usual gusto. Once there, he wasted no time in visiting Antonio and Elisa Elfer, to talk to them about the death of their daughter and the probability that Nino, too, had perished. Antonio was a really sick man by this time, and he died two months later, in August of that year, 'of a broken heart' as Elisa put it in a letter to Charlie in 1946. The Elfers' villa in Via Scipione had been commandeered by the Germans and then looted by the caretaker as soon as the soldiers moved out, and Charlie must have found his visit painful in the extreme.

Charlie's next meeting was completely stunning. Strolling past the Spanish Steps one day, he pulled up short, sure he had seen a ghost. For there, striding along in a tailored Italian Army uniform, was Carlo Tevini – left for dead, thought Charlie, in no-man's-land near Anzio, killed by a German bullet.

Carlo had a devastating tale to tell. When the Germans opened fire, he had been hit in the chest and the leg and did indeed think his last hour had come. He was picked up, however, by the German patrol that had shot him, and nursed carefully back to life; as a known partisan, he told Charlie, they thought he would have information that would be of significant use. Once he had recovered, he said, he was handed over to the Gestapo, who beat him and tortured him continuously, smashing his teeth, searing his chest with hot irons, and pulling out his fingernails, before putting him in front of a tribunal and sentencing him to death. Somehow, he related, the Vatican intervened and, before the Germans could carry out the sentence, the Allies broke out of the beachhead, and Rome was liberated.

Carlo and Charlie became good friends, and Charlie enjoyed some generous hospitality in Rome from Carlo's mother Beatrice and her partner, Boggiano Pico. They kept in touch for a while after the war, Charlie receiving news of Carlo's marriage in 1947 and the birth of a son, and then a move to Dubai in 1977. Then he heard no more.

Once the fighting was over, Elisa, now a widow and struggling to wind up her late husband's failed fur business, embarked upon a dogged and determined campaign to recover the remains of her two children and bring them home to Rome. Silvia's body, which had been buried with due ceremony in the American cemetery at Nettuno, near Anzio, was relatively easy to find and to have returned to her mother, together with a death certificate. On 7 February 1946, the anniversary of Silvia's death, Elisa was finally able to lay to rest the body of her beloved daughter, buried with her father Antonio in Rome.

Nino's body was a different matter, since nobody knew exactly where or when he had died.

For help, Elisa turned to the Allied Screening Commission (ASC), a body set up in Italy a few weeks after the liberation of Rome to deal with claims for compensation from Italian citizens who had been of assistance to the Allies, including helping PoWs escape. In its relatively short lifespan it dealt with over 100,000 claims for compensation and issued 75,000 'Alexander Certificates' of thanks, one for the head of each eligible household (such as Peppino de Michelis). The ASC was commanded, coincidentally, by Lieutenant Colonel Hugo de Burgh, former Senior British Officer at the PoW Camp in Fontanellato, whose successful escape in a silk shirt and summer suit over Monte Rosa, the second highest mountain in the Alps, included a fall into a deep crevasse where he found the frozen bodies of three less lucky fugitives.

The original files of the ASC are now held in Washington DC and, with the help of a colleague, I managed to obtain a copy of the Elfer file. It is an extraordinary and deeply moving testimony to the heroism of one family in Italy after the German occupation of the country post-September 1943 – one family amongst so many.

On the summary sheet, in red ink, are written the words 'Recommendations for posthumous COMMENDATION for ELFER Eugenio and ELFER Silvia sent to WO [War Office] ref ASC(1)/AW/3/35 on 19 September 1946'. This would have taken the form of a certificate for a 'King's Commendation for Brave Conduct', awarded posthumously to Elisa on behalf of her children. The award was never made, a victim presumably of post-war nervousness about giving medals to the nationals of former enemy countries.

The file contained Elisa's correspondence with the Commission and cables from Charlie and Leslie, including a reply from Leslie to a telegram that he received from Elisa in the summer of 1946 – which I found amongst his papers after his death and which had puzzled me for thirty years. The message from Elisa read:

> Received only now your letter. God bless you for assistance poor Silvia. Her father died. Carlo safe. Eugenio not returned. Please wire what kind of documents had Eugenio crossing Anzio line. Deep thanks.

The telegram shows that, nearly two years after Nino disappeared on that fearful night in February 1944, Elisa still had no idea what had happened to him.

Through the Commission, and accompanied by an ASC officer, Elisa visited the area of the Pontine Marshes where the Germans opened fire on the five escapers, near the settlement of Borgo Podgora. They talked to a farmer, the owner of Podere (Farm) 355, who remembered meeting a young man who spoke with a 'French r' and had a limp, as did Nino; he also mentioned several other characteristics of the young man that reminded Elisa of her son. It was the same young man, the farmer said, whose body he had seen in a ditch 500yds from his farm, around the time that Nino disappeared.

Elisa clearly became convinced that the body in the ditch was her son's and, on 27 July 1946, following up on this visit, Elisa wrote formally to the local mayor asking for his help in finding it. She repeated the evidence given by the owner of Farm 355 and went on to give a heartbreakingly detailed description of the boy:

Height: 1.75m. Hair dark brown and wavy. One incisor in the upper jaw is slightly outstanding, the other one has a broken corner.

Age: 23 years. Hip dislocation.

Outfit: velvet knickerbocker trousers, turtle colour. Brown jumper. Wind jacket with leather shoulders. Goat hair shoe covers.

She also sent information about the papers that Nino had on him at the time of his supposed death, as evidenced by the telegrams she had received from Leslie and Charlie. Leslie had written: 'Eugenio had information valuable to British forces and identity card. Hope you have news soon. Do write Charles. Young.'

Charlie also responded: 'Eugenio carried my military identity card. Also information valuable to Allies. Refused to destroy same. Courageous friend. Please write. Regards Gatenby.'

Offering to pay the costs of reburial in a local graveyard if the body turned out not to be that of her son, Elisa asked the Mayor to conduct an exhumation and autopsy.

Five months later, in December 1946, the Medical Officer of the Commune di Latina sent Elisa a certificate to the effect that Eugenio's body had been recovered and identified near Farm 355 in the village of Borgo Podgora near Latina, just as she had indicated in her application. Finally, a year after she buried her daughter, she was able to bury her son.

The Elfer file at the ASC also contains details of Elisa's heartrending claim for compensation for the death of her children, which included a schedule detailing some of the hundred or more individuals whose escapes the two were said to have helped. The compensation assessed as being payable for each of the Elfer children was £1,200 0s.0d – Lire 480,000 – (approximately £32,000 today), countersigned by Major R. M. Jones recommending, 'Pay half rate'.

The 'half rate' recommendation seems to have stemmed from the report of an outside assessor (a Lieutenant Jannicelli), who recounted briefly the story of the two deaths and said that this was 'the most genuine and deserving case I have come across'. Nevertheless, although the claimant was now on her own following the death of her husband, he commented that 'she is rather well off and she had previously refused verbally to take any payment but appears to have changed her mind, it is suggested that only one loss of life should be paid.'

Eventually, 45,000 lire was paid to Elisa on 11 February 1947, whereupon she wrote to Lieutenant Jannicelli as follows:

Dear Lieut,

I ask you, who stayed at my side in the most tragic period of my life, to convey the feelings of my deep gratitude to our friends, the Allies.

In memory of my holy martyrs, I have decided to pass over to the War Orphans the sum that the ASC has so generously given to the mother of Nino and Silvia Elfer,

Deeply moved, I remain

Yours truly

Elisa Elfer Deutsch [her maiden name]

Possibly somewhat shamed by the ASC's decidedly ungenerous compensation offer, Major Hewitt of the ASC replied:

With reference to your letter to Lieut. Jannicelli. The members of this Commission wish to extend their heartfelt sympathy in your grievous loss, and to add their appreciation of your generous bequest to the War Orphans.

If there was more of this type of Christianity in the world, there would be less wars and trouble. Your family's glorious example is one which will live for ever.

Elisa lived on, working as a teacher and translator in Rome. She never remarried, and died in 1995, aged 105, in a flat in Via Germanico, not far from the Vatican. Her mind remained sharp to the end, and she loved to reminisce about her happy and music-filled childhood in Vienna, and the glittering parties there had been in the family villa in the Via Scipione. 'My precious friends try to make my solitude less painful,' she once wrote, 'but there are many hours filled with nostalgic visions.'

But the loss of her two children was a lifelong burden that she could not lay down, or bury with fond memories. In February 1946 she had written in

flowing copperplate script and in perfect English to Charlie, to thank him
for his telegram:

> You have known them, their golden heart and their noble characters,
> and therefore I call you, my dear friend . . . will you tell me, what
> she said? A word is a gift for me. My little saint, so courageous, so
> sincere, so pure . . . I pray that the Lord takes me away, so that I may
> join my three beloveds.

Leslie and Charlie (who was awarded the MBE for his wartime exploits)
kept in contact with each other after the war, and seem to have kept up a
sporadic correspondence with both the de Michelis family and the Elfers.
Leslie received other letters from Italians who had helped them, but 'as we
made no notes of any names I can't remember who they were'. His sister
Mary recalled a letter from the de Michelis family after the war, urging his
parents to look after '*caro* Leslie' (dear Leslie).

*

*Unlike Charlie, who visited Corvaro in 1977, my father never went back.
After his death, as I slowly started to research and read up about his wartime
experiences, I was at first both puzzled and slightly disappointed that he hadn't
returned. But the story of Nino and Silvia, as it has unfolded, helped me make
sense of his reluctance.*

*Although his account in the diary reads at times like a Boys' Own adventure,
his months on the run, culminating in the violent and deeply shocking deaths of
two brave, idealistic, committed and very young partisans, must have seemed to
him in retrospect both traumatic and, perhaps, shaming. Dunkirk, the fight for
Hill 583 and now Anzio had all ended for him in escape and survival, but for
others, people he loved or liked or who he fought with or was responsible for, they
all ended in violent death. My father as I knew him was a quiet, inward-looking
man, not at all the 'Mad Major' of his days in the Commandos, and I have now
a strong sense that, for him, a return to Italy and a confrontation with his worst
nightmares would have been almost impossible to bear. I will never know.*

But I did go back myself.

*I visited the small stone casale in the Valle del Malito in 2003 with Benedetto
de Michelis, the son of Peppino and Bernardina. He was still living in Corvaro
with his wife and family, his parents having died in 1991 and 1999 respectively.
Although they had moved to a modern house, they still owned his parents' former
home, where Leslie and Charlie had stayed, and his wife Lilia continued to run*

the old family shop there. They took me down into the cellar and showed me the grain cupboard in which the fugitives were to hide if the Germans paid a visit. Benedetto remembered sitting on my father's knee there during an air raid and being fed comforting peppermints.

Benedetto also showed me the 'Alexander Certificate' which his father had been given, on the recommendation of my father, as a token of gratitude for helping prisoners escape – to this day, these certificates are prized possessions in Italian families.

I went back again in 2017, visiting virtually every single one of the forty or so villages my father passed through and leaving in each place a photo of my father pinned to a tree or to a church door, with a letter in Italian offering thanks for the help local people had given him. We received many warm responses to these letters, including one from the delightful Angiolina, whose family, the Bragagnis, took my father in for a night in October 1943 – she had seen my thank you letter pinned to a tree and instantly recognized my father. We had several messages from young people, offering reminiscences about the war that they had heard from their grandparents. During the course of our travels in the Apennines we were often able to identify exactly the barn my father must have slept in, or the path he must have taken, and we enjoyed again the wonderful hospitality of the de Michelis family in Corvaro.

On another visit I met up with Piero Tevini, an artist and first son of Carlo, Silvia's boyfriend. Piero told me that, after his father had been released by the Germans in the summer of 1944 (possibly thanks to the intervention of his well-connected mother, Countess Beatrice), he returned to the Italian Army and worked in Rome, as a liaison officer to the New Zealand forces. It was in this role that he must have met up again with Charlie Gatenby (who was then running the New Zealand Forces Club in Rome). In 1945, working in Florence, Carlo met and fell in love with a beautiful professional violinist, Anna Tornai. They were married the next year (to the horror of his mother, the Countess, who called her 'that gypsy') and, in 1947 had a son – Piero. A second son was born a year or so later, but Carlo then left Anna for another woman. Thirty years later, he turned up again, with two more sons and saying that he wanted them all to be one family – but within two months he was dead.

I have also been able to establish a link with the Elfer family. In 2010, idly leafing through papers one Sunday afternoon, something prompted me to 'google' the name Silvia Elfer. Expecting nothing at all to appear, I was astonished to find a letter dated ten years previously from an American, Don Lee, to the National Association of Italian Partisans (NAIP) asking for information about his two cousins Eugenio and Silvia Elfer who, he believed, had died at Anzio in 1944.

I sat back at my computer, completely dumbfounded. After years when the name of Elfer was to me little more than a name on a piece of paper, it suddenly sprang to life. I wrote immediately to Don Lee with the full story of how his cousins died helping my own father escape. It was a painful letter, as I came to grips properly, for the first time, with the horror of what had happened to them. Don responded immediately, and generously, with a full album of family history and photographs, the beginning of a correspondence spanning nearly ten years as we have together worked to understand the full story.

Five years later, I received another extraordinary communication, from Tony and Peter Elfer, two more cousins living in London, who had seen my piece about my father's escape on the Monte San Martino Trust's website. When we met, a few weeks later, I mentioned that I was also in touch with Don Lee. They looked puzzled.

'Don Lee? Who's that?' they asked.

'Why – he's your cousin!' I said.

They had never heard of him, and it took a while to work out that, whilst Don was the grandson of Elisa's brother Alexander Deutsch, Tony and Peter were the grandsons of Antonio's brother Maurizio Elfer. Their father Walter Elfer had emigrated to England in 1939 (where he married an English girl) to escape Hitler's persecution of Jewish people, whereas Don's mother, Marietta Deutsch, emigrated to the US in 1940 (for the same reason) and married an American, James Lee – one small example of the impact that Hitler had on Jewish families.

Tony and Peter Elfer held one other piece of information: the precise location of the Elfer family grave, in the Jewish section of the Verano Monumental Cemetery in Rome. A year later, my wife and I spent a morning sitting under the trees in dappled sunlight at the graveside of Antonio and his family. The headstone reads (in Italian):

Antonio Elfer 1879–1944

Received in heaven by my very young children

Eugenio Trieste 1920 Latina 1944 and Silvia Trieste 1923 Anzio 1944

Who fighting heroically sacrificed themselves on the altar of freedom.

Beneath the inscription lies a small simple stone:

Elisa Deutsch Elfer
Vienna 1890 Rome 1995

A woman strong and wise
Mother of heroes

On the grave as we arrived was a single fresh white flower. We puzzled over this and wondered who might have left it. Placing a note on the grave before we went, but not really expecting a response, we received in fact two weeks later a letter from Sandro Sonnino, whose mother is buried nearby. He had been so moved by the inscription on the Elfer grave that he had resolved to keep the grave clean and tidy and to leave a white daisy there every week when he comes to visit his own mother.

At the going down of the sun and in the morning
We will remember them.

*

Chapter 20

Preparing to Invade

When Leslie returned to the UK in March 1944 he might have been forgiven for seeking an easy posting, after his trials and tribulations in Italy. But in fact he pressed for another posting overseas and, on 16 March 1944 (only twelve days after he had boarded ship in Naples, homeward bound), he was posted to 3rd Infantry Division, based at Fulford in Wiltshire. His original military home, the Bedfords' 2 Battalion, was by this time fighting its way up through Italy, having landed in Naples from Egypt on 21 February. The Battalion was still under the command of Colonel Bill Whittaker, one of the heroes of Dunkirk and the man who took over after the death of Colonel Johnson at Djebel Aoud.

In the UK, planning for what would become the greatest seaborne invasion in military history was already far advanced: the American General Dwight D. Eisenhower had been appointed Supreme Allied Commander, with four Brits reporting to him; and the coast of Normandy had been chosen for the landings, partly because the more obvious (and closer) choice – the Pas de Calais – was already strongly fortified, and offered fewer opportunities for eventual expansion of the beachhead, being bounded by numerous rivers and canals. The date of 5 June 1944 would soon be chosen as 'D-Day' for 'Operation Overlord'.

As Major Leslie Young reported for duty at Fulford, a huge low-level photo-reconnaissance effort, covering the entire European coastline (in order to avoid alerting the Germans as to the location of the invasion), was in full swing, and an appeal went out for holiday snaps and postcards of the mainland – which produced ten million items. The French Resistance started providing details of German troop movements and defensive installations, and a special unit was set up at Bletchley Park using captured Enigma machines (like the one brought back from the commando raid on the Lofoten Islands) to break encoded German radio messages and provide speedy information on plans and troop movements.

Training exercises for Overlord had begun in 1943 and were now in full swing. The habitual peace and relative tranquillity of rural England was rudely disturbed, particularly in the south, on a daily basis and for months on end by the movement of regiments and battalions from one part of the landscape to another, to and from military encampments in fields and on the outskirts of towns and villages the length and breadth of southern and eastern England. Along every road, it seemed, piles of ammunition, mines, stores and stocks of every description lay roughly protected under canvas or corrugated sheeting. For mile upon mile, parks for tanks and trucks and artillery pieces stretched as far as the eye could see. And everywhere there were soldiers to be fed and watered and supplied, and camouflaged as far as possible – Americans, Canadians, Poles, French, troops from all over the Empire and of course Brits from every part of the country – crammed into huts and tents and requisitioned country houses, and impatient for the invasion to begin. As an exercise in logistics alone, Overlord has no equal in history.

The training schedule was on a similarly epic scale, and Leslie came in on the last two frenzied months of it. A succession of formal rehearsals for every phase of the invasion, involving thousands of men and vehicles and hundreds of ships, was undertaken under code names such as Duck, Fox, Beaver and the like. The entire civilian population of a large chunk of west Devon was evacuated to enable rehearsals with live ammunition. Slapton Sands was taken over for training in the use of landing craft and the management of beach obstacles. There were exercises for landing and live ammunition in Scotland; naval exercises in Northern Ireland; casualty handling exercises in London; defensive and offensive operations involving gas; entire airborne divisions were dropped by parachute or glider by day and by night; replicas of known German defensive positions were constructed and routinely attacked; and there were thousands of briefings for men at all levels on what they would face on D-Day and thereafter, with every detail on the briefing maps complete – except for the place names.

Leslie was assigned to 102 Beach Group (based initially at Bournemouth, then at Hambledon and finally at Netley Hill, near Southampton), which had responsibility for controlling and facilitating the landing, assembly and onward dispatch of 20,000 men, stores and equipment for the Canadians' Juno Beach (which stretched ten miles from Courseuilles to Saint-Aubin-sur-Mer) on D-Day itself, and then as shipping allowed thereafter – including the return of casualties and PoWs to the UK, and the mopping up of enemy units around the beach.

In this capacity, Leslie took part in Exercise Goldbraid at Bracklesham Bay in West Sussex in late March, and in Exercise Trousers at Slapton Sands in April 1944, one of the first full-scale dress rehearsals for the D-Day landings. It modelled the landings on Juno beach and involved nearly 20,000 personnel and over 100 landing craft, with live rounds thumping into the surrounding hills and damaging the deserted houses. Then 102 Group took part in the much larger exercise in May called Fabius, the final dress rehearsal for the full invasion itself.

Soon after Fabius ended, a news blackout was imposed, and the two million men of the invasion force were sealed into their marshalling areas, with no further communications allowed with the outside world – most didn't even discover their actual destination until they were at sea.

Leslie kept his copy of the letter from Eisenhower, issued to all Allied soldiers, sailors and airmen on the eve of D-Day:

> You are about to embark upon the Great Crusade, toward which we have striven these many months. The eyes of the world are upon you. The hopes and prayers of liberty-loving people everywhere march with you . . . Your task will not be an easy one. Your enemy is well trained, well equipped and battle-hardened. He will fight savagely . . . I have full confidence in your courage, devotion to duty and skill in battle. We will accept nothing less than full Victory! Good luck! And let us all beseech the blessing of Almighty God upon this great and noble undertaking.

Operation Overlord was about to begin.

Chapter 21

Operation Overlord

By the end of D-Day, all five of the landing beaches had been taken by the Allies, but connecting them up took another six days, and none of four towns that were to have been captured on D-Day itself (Carentan, St Lo, Caen and Bayeux) had been taken. Although the German defensive line along the Channel coast was incomplete, and the Allied deception plan had been successful in causing confusion about the timing and location of the invasion, the Allies themselves faced difficulties in coping with the narrow roads and *bocage* countryside of Normandy, with its landscape of small fields enclosed by high banks, deep ditches and thorny

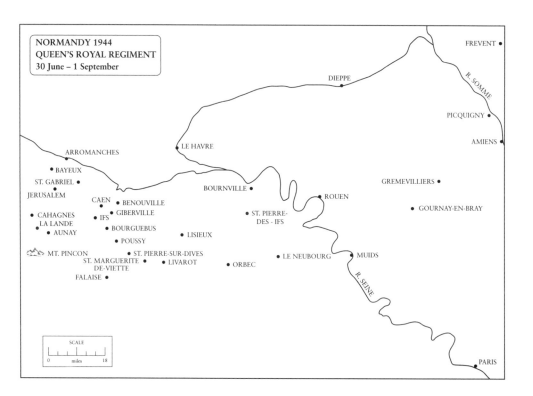

NORMANDY 1944
QUEEN'S ROYAL REGIMENT
30 June – 1 September

hedges. Furthermore, Caen itself, which was a key road and rail junction, was strongly defended, and Montgomery's chosen tactic of encircling it to the west, rather than risk a direct assault, was criticized as allowing the Germans vital time to build up their defences.

Within a week, all hope of the swift capture of further ground in northern France disappeared, and what remained was weeks of grim attrition, as the Allies fought to wear down the defending forces in a series of tactical manoeuvrings over small meadows and copses and through a succession of ruined villages.

Leslie, meanwhile, was somewhere in England, being held in reserve and probably chafing at the bit to get back into the fight. On 30 June, D+23, his name was finally called, and he boarded a requisitioned ferry and crossed the Channel, escorted by a small protective naval convoy and preceded by a minesweeper. They were heading for the Mulberry Harbour at Arromanches, newly-constructed from concrete prefabricated sections towed across the Channel in the wake of the invasion fleet, and he went ashore there the following day, to join a million Allied troops already fighting in France.

The scene as he landed was awe-inspiring. At sea, dozens of warships patrolled the Channel and the Normandy coast and approach routes, maintaining a regular bombardment on enemy positions inland; closer in, dozens of block ships had been sunk, their funnels and masts protruding from the sea, whilst scores of cargo ships lay offshore, protected by barrage balloons, awaiting their turn to tie up and unload at the encircling concrete arms of the Mulberry Harbour, or to disgorge their cargo of supplies, weapons, tanks and ammunition on to the countless landing craft that scuttled to and from the beaches. The rapidly-growing Allied army required more than 20,000 tons per day just to keep it in action, and the pace could not be allowed to flag. From troopships, mostly commandeered ferries, more landing craft brought hundreds of men ashore by the hour, day and night, returning to the UK filled with wounded soldiers by the score, or with file upon file of dejected German prisoners.

On land, hundreds of lorries rattled gingerly along the piers or across the beaches, following directions to one of the massive dumps of fuel, supplies or ammunition; new tanks, troop carriers or field guns lumbered along to find space to park amongst the massed ranks of fighting equipment awaiting deployment to the battle front. The pretty Normandy countryside near the coast became a chaotic mess of tank tracks, cables and wires, Army signposts, crashed aircraft and broken-down vehicles – interspersed with idyllic scenes of normal country life as French farmers continued to work their fields.

Leslie was posted to join the 842 men and 38 officers of the 1/6th Battalion, Queen's Royal Regiment, which formed part the 131st Queen's Infantry Brigade under Brigadier E. C. ('Peter') Pepper, his commander in the Bedfords when he rejoined in 1941 after his time with the Commandos. The Queen's Brigade formed part of the 7th Armoured Division (the Desert Rats), who had fought so hard in North Africa. His job, as an infantryman, was to support the tanks as they pushed and probed forward at the tip of the advance, clearing anti-tank guns or ditches in the way of the advance, spotting and removing snipers, mopping up enemy formations as the tanks rumbled ahead, and maintaining an all-round defence at night.

By this stage, having landed on the beaches at 0630 hrs on 9 June, the Desert Rats were being held in reserve, resting and training (particularly in the art of fighting in the *bocage*) near the tiny ruined crossroads hamlet of Jerusalem, near Bayeux. They had taken part in Operation Epsom and, at the end of June, had found themselves forming part of the defensive line around Livry, two miles west of Villers-Bocage. As the Regimental History relates:

> [This was] a trying period, living in slit trenches mostly in the rain in the very close and woody *bocage* country. The enemy held a series of outposts, frequently altering his positions, and there was constant patrolling by both sides. Regular shelling, mortaring and sniping brought a trickle of casualties . . . the trees and tall hedges caused many airbursts against which the slit trenches were ineffective and three inches of head cover had to be provided.

They were ready for a rest, and the opportunity was taken to make some changes at the senior level of command. Reinforcements from England, Leslie being one of them, had the chance to settle in to their new duties and, in his case, a new regiment. He was placed in command of A Company under the new Battalion commanding officer, Lieutenant Colonel John H. Mason, a fine athlete who had been with the Battalion since 1939.

They established their camp amongst the orchards around Jerusalem, a hamlet comprising little more than a farm, a handful of cottages and a couple of old manor houses. All the men lived in the open, plagued by clouds of mosquitoes, dysentery and lice, with the houses and barns used for recreation purposes. This was fine in warm weather, but in the rain bivouacs had to be improvised out of ground sheets and gas capes – the bedding was never dry, and the mud was inches deep. Food was mainly 'compo' packs containing tinned, ready-cooked rations for fourteen men for a day – though occasionally there was fresh meat, bread and tea, when the supply chain from the beaches allowed. The cigarette ration was fifteen 'fags' a day and, such was the efficiency of the cross-Channel supply route, mail from home came regularly.

Life revolved around the unit, the men having little interest in (or indeed time for) fraternizing with the locals or enjoying the scenery. There was in reality little to do, in between battles, except stroll nervously in nearby fields, play cards, drink the potent local Calvados – or talk. Companies went regularly by turns to Bayeux for the cinema, or a bath. For some, religion became a vital solace; for others, it was women, with enterprising but overworked Norman prostitutes plying their trade anywhere the opportunity arose – even, in one case, inside a burnt-out tank. As July wore on, facilities for behind the lines entertainment improved, but few men were out of the line long enough to enjoy them.

For most, fear was never far away – every convoy trundling past threw up clouds of dust for German artillery to aim at; careless talk by signallers, overheard by German radio locators, brought fire down upon their heads; everywhere the Germans had laid charges with tripwires between hedges or booby traps in abandoned farmhouses; and snipers were posted amongst the trees. Leslie had an early taste of the need for constant vigilance when his Battalion was strafed, without warning, just after lunch on 3 July, suffering one casualty; then a few days later, the area occupied by his new Company was shelled at dusk, with one casualty again.

The Division remained in the orchards around Jerusalem until 17 July. Brigadier Pepper visited for an afternoon; the Companies practised infantry and tank cooperation and *bocage* drill; Leslie and the other company commanders went on recces with their CO and underwent training in the vital task of establishing an anti-tank screen in open country and its subsequent development into a firm battalion base.

Then, on 16 July in the early evening, the relative peace of the orchards was broken with the news that the Battalion was to move back towards the coast, to St Gabriel, nine miles north.

The summer had produced something of a stalemate in the battle for Normandy. The American's much-delayed capture of Cherbourg and the Cotentin Peninsula had been followed by a sticky advance southwards to link up with Montgomery's forces for the drive east. Rain, mist and low cloud, coupled with offensive errors and stubborn defence by the Germans, slowed the advance to a weary crawl. In the east, a controversial massive and ill-directed airborne attack on German forces around Caen by 450 bombers (dropping over 2,000 tons of bombs) pulverized the city and killed 2,000 of its citizens, but failed in its attempt to destroy the Germans' capacity to resist. Operation Charnwood, which began the next day, resulted in the capture by Anglo-Canadian forces of the northern part of the city up to the River Orne, but the bridges across the river were either strongly defended or impassable, and the attackers were forced to withdraw.

Monty, under mounting criticism for the perceived slow pace of the advance and the failure to capture Caen (which had been an objective for D-Day itself), now came forward with a plan (Operation Goodwood) to capture the remainder of the city and the Bourguebus Ridge to the south-east, followed by a race south to Falaise. The attack was to feature a massive preliminary bombardment and, because the pool of infantry reinforcements was by now nearly exhausted, a force of over 1,000 tanks. Three armoured divisions, including the Desert Rats, were to come round to the north of Caen, attack southwards from the Orne bridgehead, move round to the east and then push on south, effectively encircling the German divisions still holding the southern part of the city and breaking the German line.

By 0800 hrs on 17 July the Battalion was already in position at St Gabriel for its march eastwards, and the company commanders went off during the morning to be briefed by Brigadier Pepper on their role in the forthcoming operation, followed in the afternoon by a briefing from Desert Rats' commander, Major General 'Bobby' Erskine. He was already the subject of criticism for what was seen as an over-cautious and lacklustre performance by the Desert Rats at Villers-Bocage the previous month, and must have felt under enormous pressure to do well in the attack on Caen. Later that afternoon, it was the job of the company commanders to explain the Division's role to all ranks. At 1800 hrs they received their orders for the next day.

As the 1/6th Battalion marched on foot out of its leaguer area the following morning, B Company in the lead and Leslie's A Company bringing up the rear, they were able to watch as thousands of bombers flew over on their way to pound the villages around Caen that stood in the path of the Allied advance, reducing many of them to rubble, and to drop hundreds of tons of fragmentation bombs on the German positions. As the British tanks rumbled south, a creeping artillery barrage opened up ahead of them.

But it was a frustrating day for the Battalion as they marched slowly east along roads jammed with troops and equipment on the move, creating clouds of blinding dust. One member of the Carrier platoon wrote later: 'All I can remember of Goodwood is sitting for most of one night in a traffic jam waiting to cross a bridge and the "non-existent" Luftwaffe being very existent. When we did cross, tanks and trucks were on fire all over the place. The dust was absolutely choking.'

By evening time they had marched about fifteen miles to Benouville on the Orne, which they crossed at 'Pegasus' Bridge, captured by glider-borne troops in the early hours of D-Day, and then paused for the night. Meanwhile, the massed tanks of the Desert Rats had been held up by (or been unable to find a way round) the same traffic jam and had thus failed to link up with the other two armoured divisions until late in the afternoon, thereby frustrating the proposed capture of the Bourguebus Ridge and the race to Falaise.

On 19 July the Battalion moved south until it reached the village of Giberville, on the eastern side of Caen, about three miles from the centre. There, in the late morning, they took up a defensive position straddling the main road and rail line from Caen to Paris, and started work establishing a base for the whole Division. The 1/5th Battalion paused in Giberville to help with the initial work of digging in, and then moved on south, discovering an abandoned battery of Nebelwerfers, used by the Germans to great effect to deliver high explosive poison gas and smoke shells accompanied by a loud, high-pitched howling noise that had earned the weapon the nickname 'Moaning Minnie'. 1/7th Battalion dug in nearby. The villages they occupied were little more than heaps of rubble, having been brutally cleared the day before by 11th Armoured Division, and many German dead were still lying around.

As the Battalions collected survivors as prisoners, the Germans in their turn started shelling, dropping butterfly anti-personnel bombs on the villages at night. One Battalion member recalled:

[There was] a long and continuous stream of casualties coming in [to the dressing station]. I remember saying there would be nothing left of the Battalion if this went on much longer. Worse still, there was a poor lad who had most of the bottom of his back blown away. There was nothing to be done for him so we just put him outside on a stretcher. The poor devil screamed for two hours. Morphine seemed to have no effect. He was pleading for someone to finish him off. Our sergeant had been in the war from the start and even he was white and shaken.

The 1/6th was ordered to stay put that evening and continue to consolidate the position, although patrols had established that the land to the south of Giberville was clear. That night, as they slept by the roadside, the Battalion was attacked by twelve enemy fighter-bombers, and one tank was 'brewed up' (caught fire, with its live ammunition exploding), but there were no casualties.

As dawn broke on 20 July the Battalion readied itself for a move south, but it was not until early afternoon that Leslie and the other company commanders were called forward to recce new positions close to Bourguebus Ridge. After a short journey by troop-carrying vehicle (TCV), the men set out on foot, described thus by one officer:

> Marching solidly through the village . . . slow obvious steps, no hurry, no eagerness, no fear. A bevy of shells fell and with them one man, now with one leg. His comrade behind stopped and bent over him and then straightening up, undid his gas cape from off his pack and spread it over the peaceful figure. Quietly and with barely any disturbance to their movement, they had passed through the village.

The whole area was flat, open and in full view of the enemy on the higher ground by Bourguebus, but the clouds of dust and smoke made such a dense haze that the Battalion felt able to continue to move cautiously forwards. That evening, Leslie's patrols made contact with a Canadian position on the Company's right, and they all survived another night of enemy shelling and mortaring.

The next day, the CO announced that the Battalion was to be relieved by the Canadians at 1800 hrs and would then return to Giberville. As they waited, a sniper was spotted in a haystack and promptly dealt with. A patrol was sent out to set fire to all the haystacks in order to deter other snipers, but the idea was scotched when it was realized that the resulting smoke would obscure their view of possible attacks – this was just as well because, three hours later, a German tank with accompanying infantry support was spotted moving towards them. A quick call to Brigade HQ brought a thunderous artillery barrage down on the heads of the attackers, and they dispersed.

An hour later, just as they were preparing to board their TCVs and looking forward to some rest, the Germans replied in kind with a crashing artillery bombardment along the road, causing havoc and casualties amongst those companies which had already left to march back to Giberville. Torrential rain, which turned the deep dust into thick glutinous mud, completed the misery for the exhausted men as they struggled back to their leaguer area.

Goodwood had run out of steam, and Monty's attempt at a massive rolling tank attack, in the style that had been so successful in North Africa, had failed to break through the enemy's defences. Over 5,000 men were dead or wounded. Many believed that Monty's planning and preparation was seriously at fault; whatever the reason, as Patrick Delaforce put it in *Churchill's Desert Rats in North-West Europe*, 'Thirty square miles of rolling Normandy countryside had been won – at a dreadful cost. The 493 blackened Sherman and Cromwell tanks were replaced more or less overnight, but the hundreds of young leaders were not so easily replaced.' On the other hand, Caen had at last been taken (by the Canadians), and the Germans who, as so often before, had put up an incredible fight, had been forced to move key divisions away from the American front in the west.

But the Germans too had suffered grievous losses, losses which they would find harder to replace than the Allies – and worse than the loss of men and equipment was the loss of morale and confidence amongst their senior generals, both in themselves and in their increasingly isolated and irrational Führer. After an attempt to kill him with a bomb under a conference room table failed, Hitler's distrust of his generals, and his frequent refusal (particularly in Normandy) to take their advice, now became chronic. His determination to drive the Allies back into the sea, rather than retreat in an orderly fashion, forces intact, to fight another day, became unstoppable. At the same time, distrust of one another amongst his senior officers became endemic, with some remaining loyal to the end, whilst others despaired.

For the next few days the Battalion had little direct contact with the enemy, but the whole area where they were camping was very crowded and under constant enemy observation from the Bourguebus Ridge, which the Germans still held. 'Luckily,' as the Regimental History puts it, 'the Germans did not seem to have much artillery ammunition and there were so many targets for him to aim at that the shelling was not usually severe.' The Battalion position was strafed by Messerschmitt 109F fighters, but there were no casualties, apart from another 'brewed-up' tank. Their sister battalion, the 1/7th, was not so lucky and lost three of its officers in shelling the same afternoon. The weather was still muggy and very wet, and clouds of mosquitoes rising from the cornfields in the evenings made sleep almost impossible, especially for those sensitive to bites who 'swelled up like balloons'.

By now there were over a million Allied troops ashore in Normandy – 591,000 British and Canadians and 770,000 Americans. Of these, perhaps 140,000 were the 'PBI' (poor bloody infantry), on the front line and losing lives on a daily basis. Allied casualties by this stage were running at 120,000, whilst the Germans had lost 113,000 men – and of these, on both sides, almost one fifth were attributed to 'battle fatigue', a condition which reached near epidemic proportions and was fully expressive of the grim nature of the conflict.

Nevertheless, despite the sense of growing frustration back home, by the end of July the Allies' use of overwhelming force was beginning to pay dividends.

On 24 July, as the weather at last lifted, the Battalion's officers were gathered together and given their orders for a new operation – 'Spring', a continuation of the proposed Goodwood advance, using combined infantry and tanks, down the main road from Caen to Falaise. This was part of a much bigger plan – Operation Cobra, the attempt by the American First Army under General Bradley to break out from the Cotentin Peninsula in the west, sweep south and into Brittany and link up with their British and Canadian counterparts in the east. That very day, in fact, 1,600 Allied aircraft had taken off for Normandy to pound the German defences in front of the American advance, only to be forced back by the awful weather – though not, sadly, before bombing part of their own forces, killing 25 soldiers and wounding 130 more. Not for the first time in Normandy, infuriated soldiers opened fire on their own aircraft in futile and frustrated retaliation.

At first light the next day the Battalion's column marched purposefully south towards Falaise with the Carriers and Leslie's A Company in the lead, their aim being to distract and draw off as many German units as they could from the American advance fifty miles west around St Lo. The failed bombing attack of the previous day had, of course, alerted the Germans to the possibility of an American advance; nevertheless, they remained convinced that the Canadian-led advance towards Falaise was the main threat.

The barrier to the Anglo-Canadian advance on Falaise was the Verrières Ridge, which the Germans had turned into their main defensive position south of Caen, with two powerful formations of SS infantry and Panzers, more troops in reserve and supported by artillery, dug-in Tiger tanks and mortar emplacements. Although not particularly high, the topography of the Ridge meant that the Allies would be exposed to fire from the Ridge itself and the heavily-fortified German-held industrial area to the south.

The Canadian Black Watch was to launch the first attack on the Ridge at 0530 hrs, supported by the 2nd Canadian Division, which met with heavy resistance and was delayed in reaching their assembly area for the attack, as were their tanks. The Black Watch nevertheless decided to press ahead and were tragically cut to ribbons by the well-entrenched Germans on the Ridge. Of the 325 Canadians who took part in the attack, 315 were killed, wounded or captured – the costliest day for a Canadian battalion since the disastrous Dieppe raid in 1942.

A mile back up the road towards Caen, 1/6th's forward advance came to a halt at Ifs, and the men were forced to dig in for the night and form a strong defensive base in front of the village.

The next day (26 July), they remained in position initially, a few hundred yards behind the Canadian forward troops, with 1/7th Queens on the line of the Caen–Falaise road, 1/6th to their right and 1/5th in the middle. They were under constant heavy artillery, mortar and Nebelwerfer fire, and casualties were inevitable.

Later that morning, the Battalion moved cautiously forward to support the men of the 1/5th Battalion, who were in an exposed position under heavy and constant shelling, much of it from heavy calibre guns, interspersed with bursts of Nebelwerfer fire, thirty-six rockets at a time. The Regimental History records: 'All who possibly could remained in their slit trenches, but casualties were considerable, including a number of cases of sheer exhaustion.'

That night, Leslie sent out two patrols, one to make contact with 1/5th on their left, the other to go forward and recce the ground towards Ifs. A blast of machine gun fire from 200yds away sent them scurrying back.

Rex Wingfield, an undergraduate turned infantryman, in the same battalion as Leslie, describes the relief of returning to base after a similar patrol in his book *The Only Way Out*, shivering, shaking and bathed in sweat, often close to vomiting. He felt that anyone who denied being afraid was probably a liar or an idiot, whilst noting how, once in action, there was often little or no time to be scared; it was only later that you had time to think about what you had seen and done.

On the following day, 27 July, the 1/6th was ordered to advance south again, under constant attack from German artillery and fighter-bombers; but then, in the evening, A and B Companies were told to move back under cover of darkness towards Ifs, where they dug in once again against a continuing German bombardment. The Regimental History describes the support they enjoyed from RAF Typhoons, whose 'attacks were not only most effective against the enemy, but most inspiring to our troops'. One soldier described 'another sunny warm day and the sky seemed to be full of Typhoons strafing the enemy positions. It was a fantastic sight to see them suddenly dip their noses and power down towards an unseen enemy. When they were some 2,000 feet up they released their rockets, continuing on down, firing their cannons as they went, before swooping up again [for another attack].'

Meanwhile, the 1/5th and 1/7th Battalions held firm against several enemy counter-attacks and constant shelling, until they were relieved by the Canadians on 28 July, having endured a pounding from 1,500 shells and 30 Nebelwerfer 'stonks', and having suffered numerous casualties.

By the end of July the American advance south from Cotentin in Operation Cobra was in full swing, and German resistance appeared, at last, to be crumbling. Montgomery came to the view that the objectives set for Operation Goodwood, of distracting the attention of the Germans in the east whilst the Americans made their dash south, had been achieved, so he decided to regroup his forces quickly, to keep up the pressure on the Germans and to harry them in their attempts to prevent an American link-up from the west with the Anglo-Canadian forces in the east.

On 29 July the Queen's Brigade was told to prepare to move westwards to Trungy, six miles south of Bayeux and not far from the orchards around Jerusalem, where they had camped a few days earlier. No sooner had they assembled for this march than the Battalion's area was shelled, and two men were killed. In sombre mood, Leslie's A Company followed the long column of troops as they wound their way west towards Caen, where they boarded their transport. The city was a sea of rubble, mud and dust, punctuated occasionally by a lone chimney or crazily-leaning sliver of wall. Trungy, with its large church dominating the village, seemed fresh and pleasant by comparison but, as the Regimental History notes, 'There was only time for a clean-up and one good sleep before [we were] on the move again.'

The strategy for the next stage of the campaign was to maintain relentless pressure on the Germans, with bombing attacks all night and a rolling series of infantry pushes along the length of the front line. The German line gave and then re-formed a dozen times, with villages sometimes changing hands daily – but still it held.

Operation Bluecoat, a massive attack by virtually the whole of the British Second Army, pushing south towards Aunay-sur-Odon in the east along a front nearly thirty miles wide, was launched on 29 July. The Desert Rats were in the centre of the line, tasked with the capture of Aunay itself and the imposing 1,200ft heights of Mont Pinçon, five miles south.

On 31 July they set off to march south at 2200 hrs through a patchwork of small fields and hamlets, pausing only for a brief rest before moving off again after breakfast the next morning, with Leslie's A Company bringing up the rear of the column. A tangle of troops and tanks on the narrow country lanes added to the sense of claustrophobic chaos, and it took the Desert Rats twelve hours to progress twelve miles.

1/5th Battalion was ordered to take the high ground at Le Breuil (to the north-west of Aunay), which it managed to do under heavy shelling and mortaring and after a final advance over a high ridge in full view of the enemy, despite heavy casualties. 1/6th Battalion moved through Cahagnes and was ordered to form a firm base a mile further on. There was a thick morning mist and German minefields all around, well covered by small arms fire. They chased off an attack by three German Panther tanks, captured some Germans and then took up their defensive positions on high ground to the east, overlooking the important 'Robin' crossroads on the way to Aunay.

On 2 August the Queen's Brigade continued its push southwards, with 1/6th Battalion engaged in a battle with some German tanks before pausing to make preparations for an attack that night on the west ridge beyond Le Breuil, where its sister battalion the 1/5th had spent the day clearing the woods. Meanwhile, 1/7th attacked the tiny hamlet of La Rivière (where ninety Germans were reported to be hiding) with mortar and tank support and succeeded in capturing thirty-four prisoners.

At midnight that night, Leslie's 1/6th Battalion attacked the ridge about one mile east of Le Breuil, where the enemy had gathered to prevent the Desert Rats' armour advancing towards Aunay. Protected by a creeping artillery barrage, Leslie led A Company forward on the left (with D Company on his right) but met only slight infantry opposition from the flanks, captured twenty-three prisoners and succeeded in taking their objective before first light. They sustained a small number of casualties, including some as a result of the artillery barrage falling short at the start of the attack.

By dawn on 3 August A Company was in position north of the road near La Lande, about two miles from Aunay, with B Company astride the road and D Company to the south. 1/7th was ordered to attack on A Company's left at 0830 hrs and soon established themselves to the rear of A Company, in the idyllic hamlet of Le Monde Ancien, hidden in a lush green dell, where they were heavily shelled.

Recce tanks from 8ᵗʰ Hussars passed through that morning on their way to La Lande, and three soft-skinned enemy vehicles tried to use the open road running north to south, but Leslie's A Company shot them up, killed or captured the occupants and then completed a busy morning by catching a German despatch rider carrying useful information about enemy dispositions.

In mid-afternoon the Germans counter-attacked savagely with tanks and infantry and strong covering fire, chiefly from light anti-aircraft guns sited on a higher ridge to the right. 'The German infantry, mostly SS, came on shouting and screaming,' reports the Regimental History, 'many stripped to the waist, but the medium machine guns caused havoc among them.' They dispersed quickly when a Mark IV Panzer tank was 'brewed up' by B Company, and one of the large German 'Elephant' self-propelled anti-tank guns was captured.

Forty minutes later, the Germans tried again, in greater force and under cover of a smokescreen from the east, their leading tanks quickly advancing through the standing corn to within 50yds of the three Companies' positions. One of the company commanders called up artillery support, which held them back for a bit, but within minutes B Company on the road was overrun by tanks and infantry, as was D Company to the right. At 1620 hrs Leslie's Company fell back slightly to defend them, but the Germans kept on coming with twelve of the feared Panther tanks, widely regarded as the best tanks on the battlefield, pounding the Battalion's positions as the German infantry probed and pushed forwards to gain the advantage.

By 1700 hrs, the Queen's War Diary reported, three enemy tanks had been 'KO'd', but several of the Battalion's 17-pounder anti-tank guns were out of action and, although the Germans were being held, reinforcements were desperately needed. A platoon of assault troops moved up from the rear, and the 8ᵗʰ Hussars arrived at 1715 hrs to assist the tanks on both flanks. The Battalion's defensive fire was strong, despite the setbacks, and by early evening the War Diary was reporting that the enemy attack had been halted: the German tanks had withdrawn, and there were fewer soldiers visible in front of the Battalion's positions.

The Germans had sustained heavy casualties and many dead. Leslie's Company had lost an officer and nine men wounded; B Company had lost two men killed and had an officer and eleven men missing: D Company had lost two officers and nineteen men killed, with six more wounded and two officers and fourteen men missing. The survivors of D Company were amalgamated with B Company, and the two remaining companies took up new defensive positions near La Lande and astride the road to Aunay. But the day's destruction was not over yet: at 2100 hrs, 1/7th Queens moved up to protect the 1/6th position, only to be caught in a disastrous Nebelwerfer concentration, sustaining another thirty-four casualties.

The Desert Rats were still two miles short of their objective, the ruined town of Aunay-sur-Odon, despite the fact that Lieutenant General Bucknall, the overall commander of their Army Corps, had been warned from the start of the need to 'push on' and take it by the end of July. He was sacked by Montgomery that night and, over the next two days, the Desert Rats' CO, Major General Erskine, was also replaced – to the dismay of his Division, many of whom felt that 'it didn't seem to be the way to treat the captor of Tripoli'. Critics of the Desert Rats' performance during the Normandy campaign, on the other hand, felt that he should have been dismissed earlier, after what was seen as a fiasco at Villers-Bocage.

On 4 August the three battalions in Queen's Brigade were still being shelled, and enemy tanks were seen and engaged in Saint-Georges-d'Aunay, just over a mile north of La Lande. By evening, however, all enemy action had died down, and when patrols were mounted to explore the hamlets between La Lande and Aunay, they found them to be deserted. The Germans had gone; their counter-attack had failed. The road to Aunay, however, was heavily mined and blocked by extensive shell damage, so it was decided that, in order to threaten the commanding 1,000ft heights of Mt Pinçon, the Desert Rats should move around Aunay to the north and east, via a network of narrow country lanes, themselves congested with troops on the move and collapsed buildings.

Leslie's 1/6th Battalion was the last to move, just before 2300 hrs on 5 August, its numbers seriously depleted and the men exhausted, having been in almost continuous action since mid-July. They had a day to rest and clean up, but then set off again at midday on 7 August through the ravaged countryside, past ruined farmhouses and deserted livestock, and then on south to the leaguer area just south of Aunay. As they passed through the town they were greeted by the shocking sight of its almost total destruction – only the church spire and a few shattered houses remained.

By this time it appeared that the American breakthrough in the west had been a success and the Germans were now on the run. Indeed, at Falaise, 25 miles away to the south-east, two German armies were already in danger of encirclement. The British were attacking south, and the Desert Rats were told to bypass Mont Pinçon to the east, clearing the heavily-wooded upland ridges as they went. The 1/7th Battalion attacked at night, supported by a series of concentrated artillery barrages and cries of 'wakey-wakey' from the advancing troops, who had to engage in man-to-man fighting with butt and bayonet before the area was cleared. The 1/5th Battalion then combed the forested slopes lower down.

On 8 August 1/6th was on the move again, this time in the lead, up the heavily wooded northern slopes of Mont Pinçon (which by this time had been captured), but the road up was in full view of the enemy and under constant shelling. The surrounding villages and orchards teemed with German snipers, and the whole area was heavily mined. Working their way around the eastern side of the hill, the Battalion lost seven men killed before nightfall, and their CO and another officer and thirty-four other ranks were wounded.

At midday on 9 August the Battalion was directed to continue attacking eastwards, and Leslie's A Company took the lead, using '*bocage* drill' in which two troops of tanks and infantry worked in close cooperation, the infantry scouting both sides of the hedgerows in each field before the tanks sought to blast their way through the heavy earth banks. It was grim, painstaking work, requiring both patience and determination, as the Germans had proved themselves adept at using the field landscape to their advantage. The advance was slow and difficult, but the nearby village of La Fresnée was eventually taken, with twenty-five prisoners captured.

The Desert Rats were now withdrawn from the fighting, and the three battalions of the Queen's Brigade moved to an area called Noir Nuit, under a ridge running south-east from Aunay, for five days rest and relaxation.

In the meantime, an increasingly unbalanced Hitler had decided to launch a major counter-attack in the west around Mortain, Operation Lüttich. The aim was to break through to the coast, cut off the supply lines to the American advance and then attack from the rear. This was contrary to the advice that he had been receiving from his generals, to fall back to the Seine in the face of the growing threat of an Allied breakout from Normandy. An advance westwards at this stage risked further massive air attacks on depleted German forces, and the serious possibility that they would find themselves encircled by the Allies. The counter-attack commenced on 7 August but, after some initial early gains, soon ground to a halt in the face of determined American resistance and Allied dominance of the skies above. Frenzied demands from Hitler for further attacks did nothing to halt an overwhelming defeat.

The German forces had no option but to fall back, the threat of encirclement now a serious reality, as the German army in the west found itself caught in a huge sack thirty miles long and eight miles across. As yet, though, the neck of the sack, running from just south of Falaise to Argentan a few miles away, was still open. Then, on 8 August, Montgomery launched Operation Totalise, ordering Canadian troops to take the lead in breaking through the German defences south of Caen and make all speed down to Falaise to close off the neck.

But the going was tough for the Canadians, against skilful and dogged German defensive skirmishing, particularly from the fanatical Hitlerjugend (Hitler Youth), many of whom fought to the death rather than surrender. Falaise itself, birthplace of William the Conqueror, was reduced to a shambles. It was not until 21 August that the neck of the sack into which the Germans had driven themselves was finally closed, by which time a substantial proportion (20,000 soldiers by some estimates) of the enemy army had escaped. Nevertheless, the destruction of those who failed to get away, whether by air attack, bombardment or in fighting on the ground, was on an epic scale.

It was hardly possible to move without stepping on some piece of dead flesh, human or animal. Some 10,000 bodies were counted on the battlefield, another 50,000 were taken prisoner, and thousands of vehicles, tanks, horses and artillery pieces were destroyed or converted to Allied use. The 77-day battle for Normandy was over, at an estimated cost of 220,000 casualties for the Allies, including 37,000 soldiers and 16,000 airmen killed. German losses during Operation Overlord are put at somewhere between 400,000 and 500,000, including over 200,000 killed or wounded and another 200,000 taken prisoner. Around 15,000 French civilians lost their lives, with many more injured. Dozens of French towns and villages were almost completely destroyed.

But now the Allies were ready to break out, and head east towards the Seine – and Germany itself.

Chapter 22

The Breakout

The Queen's Brigade, along with the rest of the Desert Rats, were still resting at Noir Nuit, where there was a chance to visit the mobile bath and laundry unit, to have a spell in a special rest camp on the beach or to see an ENSA show with George Formby. The Queen's Regimental History summed it up – 'the weather was gloriously fine and the rest was most enjoyable.'

Lieutenant General Horrocks, newly-appointed commander of XXX Army Corps, gave a lecture to the officers about the general situation. He was impatient with the slow, slogging progress in Normandy, was determined to get the men moving again and promised to have them in Brussels within four days. The effect of his bravado and bluster on morale, after the weeks of struggling in the *bocage*, was electrifying.

At midnight on 16 August, with Horrocks' words still ringing in their ears, the order came through for the three Queen's Battalions to be ready to move at an hour's notice. In the early morning they set off through Aunay, heading north-east to the western outskirts of Caen, then south-east again parallel with the Caen–Falaise road to Poussy-la-Campagne, where they paused for the night.

It was a 'long slow dusty journey', in the words of the Regimental History, through villages devastated by earlier fighting. The roads and fields were littered with burnt-out vehicles and tanks, dead cattle and blackened and unburied corpses. Houses, whole streets, were in ruins, forests a mess of fallen leaves and blackened stumps. A haze of smoke and the stench of death hung like a pall over the pretty orchards and cornfields of Normandy.

By 2200 hrs the Queens had their orders for the following day – 'drive hard east for Lisieux and the Seine', along the centre line of the proposed breakout advance. The Brigade was now leading the Desert Rats, with two battalions forward, 1/7th to the south and Leslie's Battalion, the 1/6th, to the north, and aiming for Lisieux itself.

Progress was again painfully slow, even though the terrain was easier and more open, with straighter roads and fewer hills. The retreating enemy, mostly SS and Panzer divisions, turned frequently to fight small, fierce rearguard actions with tanks, mortars and 88mms. On resuming the retreat, they left in their wake roadblocks and minefields to impede their pursuers. There were four rivers to reconnoitre and cross before Lisieux, and the Germans defended all of them, before blowing the bridges, laying another minefield and then setting off again on their flight – only to repeat the process a few miles further on.

At a mid-morning halt they were told that, because of the unexpected strength of German resistance, the direct advance on Lisieux had been cancelled, and the Division was now to move due east on Livarot. On they went in thick dust, over the bridge in the pretty riverside town of Saint Pierre-sur-Dives, the land rising 800ft now to a series of wooded plateaux separated by deep valleys. By nightfall the 1/6th had fought its way another four miles to the east, after hold-ups to cope with an outbreak of small arms fire from the rear and pockets of well dug-in enemy infantry which often had to be winkled out in hand-to-hand fighting. Surrendering German soldiers were sent rearwards under escort. This was intense, nerve-wringing fighting, made worse perhaps by a sense that victory was in sight – so why get killed now?

Overnight patrols established that there was still some enemy movement in Sainte-Marguerite-de-Viette, a mile or two down the road, so the next morning, Leslie led A Company forward to attack and take the high ground to the north of the village. By midday, having met little opposition, he reported the objective clear.

Moving cautiously forwards again, they were strafed by a Spitfire, leaving two dead and three wounded. Such tragic accidents were not uncommon in Normandy, despite the fact that all tanks and half-tracks were clearly marked with a white star of Bethlehem, and yellow smoke canisters were fired whenever an Allied air attack was in progress. Perhaps accidents were inevitable, with Allied forces moving forward so quickly, hard on the heels of the retreating Germans. Nevertheless, the effect on the men was dispiriting to say the least.

In the afternoon eight more prisoners were rounded up, and a carrier, recceing the road east beyond the village, was knocked out by an anti-tank gun and all but one of its occupants was killed. At 1700 hrs, having progressed only a mile or two all day, they pulled back to Sainte Marguerite for the night, enduring in the process two further strafings by the RAF and the USAAF (who had been given the wrong river as the bomb line), as well as a bazooka attack by a concealed German infantryman, who managed to escape into the darkness.

Another nervous night passed, with patrols spotting German soldiers laying mines along the Livarot Road ahead. In the morning, Leslie was again asked to take his Company forwards to clear the road, but after a slow and cautious advance they came under attack from three snipers in a building 200yds ahead of them. The snipers ran for it as soon as they were engaged, and the Company then set about establishing a firm base for the rest of the Battalion, while the tanks dealt with a self-propelled gun, probably a Howitzer, that had started taking pot shots at them. Meanwhile, their sister battalion, the 1/7th, was hit by three Tiger tanks and lost a dozen men wounded or taken prisoner.

Later that afternoon, having received information from a villager that the Hitlerjugend had carried out a massacre at a nearby farm, Leslie's Company found the bodies of six women lying in a house in Sainte Marguerite. They had been killed as a petty act of revenge for having given milk to some passing Canadian scouts, milk which they had earlier refused to the Germans.

The Company pulled back again to Sainte Marguerite for the night, with the Brigade's other two battalions, after another difficult and frustrating day. But they got little or no sleep.

Enemy planes, fifteen in all, bombed their positions, and this was swiftly followed by a night-time infantry attack, which was repulsed. At 0730 hrs the next morning, 20 August, the 1/6th Battalion led the main advance down the Livarot road, reaching the bridge across the River Vie in Livarot at noon. They met little opposition, as the enemy had pulled back overnight, blowing the bridge and leaving only a few stragglers and some abandoned tanks west of the river. The sappers quickly went to work so that the Battalion could pass through the town and take up defensive positions on the far side of the river, east of Livarot. There were more casualties in A Company, this time from an enemy mortar attack. By now, Leslie's command was down to about twenty men.

Livarot was the first undamaged town liberated by the Desert Rats, and the Battalion was greeted by cheering locals, tricolour flags, bottles of wine and hugs and kisses from the girls. But there was no time to relax as they set up camp again for the night, a mile or so east of the town, on the road from Livarot to Orbec. Members of the French Resistance appeared, with useful information about enemy dispositions and accompanied by a number of Allied airmen who had been hiding in the area awaiting the breakout. That night, as a reminder, if one was needed, that they should expect the unexpected, a massive storm crashed around them and lashing rain drenched them in their tents.

As they prepared a damp breakfast the next day, 21 August, a German Spandau heavy duty machine gun suddenly opened fire on Leslie's men. A few minutes later, soldiers from the fanatical 12th SS Panzer Hitlerjugend Division, some of them reeling drunk, waving swords and bayonets, charged forwards from the edge of the forest in a suicidal attack on the Company. A young and inexperienced Second Lieutenant called Cousins from the 11th Hussars, on patrol nearby, saw what was happening. His radio was out of action, so he raced across the fields in his Dingo scout car, through several hedges and under fire from machine guns less than 50yds away, and organized his Troop to help fight off the attack. Having done that, and with only one gear still working, Cousins led his men from the front, his machine gun spitting at the enemy.

A German Mark IV Panzer tank opened fire from the cover of the forest and, on its fourth attempt, destroyed the Company's 6-pounder before it had fired a shot. Leslie tried desperately to get his 17-pounder anti-tank gun trained on the tank, but the towing tractor was missing and the crew was unable to lug the gun around on ground softened by the previous night's rain. The tank then crashed out of the forest and stormed down the road towards them, whilst the Hitlerjugend charged forwards, shouting and screaming, and quickly overran Leslie's left flank.

Leslie immediately reorganized the men to the right of his Company HQ, which was in a house beside the road, whilst Cousins, the rest of his Patrol having withdrawn, continued to fire on the advancing Germans from his Dingo. As soon as his men were in place, Leslie ordered Cousins to bale out, but the Second Lieutenant was not giving up and withdrew just a few yards behind the Company's headquarters, to try and get his radio going so he could summon further assistance.

Meanwhile, advancing menacingly down the road, the tank took aim and opened fire on the Company HQ. Leslie was hit in the leg by flying shrapnel, as were his second in command and several other men. Before anyone had time to react, twenty of the Hitlerjugend charged down the road again with bayonets fixed and cut off the forward platoon. In the fierce hand-to-hand fighting that followed there were several further casualties, and Leslie feared that his position would be overrun.

In the meantime, however, Cousins had got his radio working and was able to call in assistance from the Mortar Platoon, which wiped out the Hitlerjugend. At the same time, the 5th Royal Inniskilling Dragoon Guards reduced the tank to a smouldering wreck. Cousins, his ammunition exhausted, then set off on his own in his damaged Dingo across country back to Livarot.

Leslie was taken off to the Field Hospital, together with his second in command, but according to David Coles, the A Company Sergeant Major:

> He begged not to be sent back [home]. Against the rules, the Medical Officer allowed him to travel in the Field Ambulance for two days, but on the second night he was back. His leg being dressed daily by our Medical Orderly. A very good commanding officer, fair to his men . . . a father any son would be proud of.

*

I drove out of Livarot on the road to Orbec on a hot sunny day in April 2018. Along the road, fields of yellow rape alternated with lush green pasture and ancient orchards. Suddenly, there on the right, was a tall, rather substantial red brick farmhouse – Leslie's Company HQ and the scene of the Panzer attack and Cousins' dramatic rescue. On a rise up ahead was the forest where the young German soldiers had been hiding, and over the road were the fields across which Cousins had charged.

In his letter recommending Cousins for the Military Cross, written two days after the action, Leslie described Cousins' bravery in some detail (whilst entirely omitting to mention either his own role, or the fact that he had been wounded), saying that 'if he [Cousins] had not stayed, the [Hitlerjugend] would most certainly have overrun us . . . This Officer's splendid example and disregard of personal risk had a great effect on my men.'

A few weeks later, in October, Cousins led his Troop across a canal bridge in Holland, under orders to reconnoitre the road and crossroads beyond, which was overlooked by a spinney. If the Germans had guns inside the spinney, the road would be impassable. The only way to find out was to drive along the road, which he did, at a fast dash. No shots were fired as they covered the first mile, but as soon as they came out into the open, a bazooka and a self-propelled gun opened fire. The lead vehicle was hit, and Cousins' vehicle, desperately trying to reverse, caught a wheel on the edge of a ditch and rolled backwards into the hedge. The driver died at the wheel, and Cousins and his other crewman scrambled out and started to run for some trees across the field. They were caught in a hail of machine gun fire half way across, and both dropped dead in their tracks. Cousins' gallant and effective leadership of the Troop was recognized with a posthumous Military Cross.

*

On 22 August, Leslie's Battalion was relieved by a Canadian unit; but after a day's pause, but they were soon on the move again, preparing for an attack on high ground to the east of Lisieux, 15 miles north. By the time they got there, however, the enemy had withdrawn in a hurry, so they paused for the night. The 1/5th lost a company commander and his second in command, and the Carrier Platoon commander was blinded when a tank drove over a mine.

The following day, they continued eastwards to the River Risle, where the Germans had established yet another line of defence. Undaunted, the Battalion managed to find an unguarded crossing over a shaky wooden bridge a little further north, and then continued up the valley of the tranquil River Risle to Bourneville, picking up many German stragglers on the way, including a complete heavy mortar platoon. They arrived on 27 August, 1/6th Battalion forming a firm base round an important crossroads three miles to the south of Bourneville, near Les Marettes.

On 28 August, having received a report from French civilians that there were more than a hundred Germans, three anti-tank guns and some horse-drawn transport nearby, 1/6th Battalion was sent off to clear the whole area, returning by noon with twenty prisoners. That afternoon, in steady rain, they were sent back across the Risle to Saint-Pierre-des-Ifs to join the rest of the Queen's Brigade for a short rest and a chance to maintain vehicles – they were just 10 miles from the Seine, and had a long journey ahead of them . . .

Chapter 23

The Great Swan

The Allies were now established on the banks of the Seine – nine days earlier than Montgomery had predicted in his final pre-D Day briefing – and the battle for Normandy was over. They had landed more than two million men in northern France, of whom nearly 40,000 had died and over 180,000 were wounded or missing. German losses have been calculated at around 290,000 killed or wounded, with a further 210,000 captured.

The defeat in Normandy was a massive, near-fatal blow to Germany, which had been unprepared for the invasion itself, successfully deceived

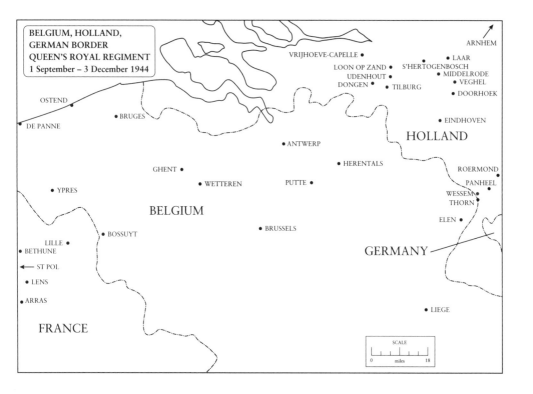

as to its location, comprehensively defeated in the air, inadequately supplied thanks to the disruptive bombing of key infrastructure and poorly led from the top.

The race for Europe was now on. As the German armies retreated back across the Seine – a move which several of his generals had been urging on Hitler for some time – the Allies embarked on what some described as 'the Great Swan' across huge tracts of France, Belgium and Holland, heading for the German border and beyond.

Monty was all for advancing hard and fast northwards to Antwerp, followed by a massive forensic thrust towards the Rhine and Germany's industrial heartland, the Ruhr. Eisenhower, the Supreme Allied Commander, however, favoured a broader advance on all fronts – Monty in the north, and the Americans under Bradley in the south.

The stage was set for the final battles – and the debacle of Arnhem.

Back at Saint-Pierre-des-Ifs, the Desert Rats had had just a day to recover, in the pouring rain, from their hard slog through northern France. By 30 August they were on the move again, heading east for the Seine. At Le Neubourg, Brigade Commander Pepper gathered his officers together. He told them that they were to form part of Monty's great thrust northwards and that they had been 'awarded the plum target of Ghent'.

Delaforce comments in *Churchill's Desert Rats in North-West Europe*:

> It seemed quite unbelievable that the stench and brutality of the bocage, the death traps of the little winding country lanes, and the river valleys were now to be left behind . . . The prospect of cantering through northern France, Belgium and Holland, with perhaps diminishing resistance, fewer 88mms, fewer Nebelwerfers and probably very few tanks was almost appealing.

Two other armoured divisions, the Guards and the 11th, were already over the Seine and on their way, meeting little resistance. The 7th Armoured Division was behind them on the northern flank and, as the Queen's Regimental History comments, 'was likely to have a more difficult task as its route lay directly across the rear of the still existent German Fifteenth Army, [which was] holding the Channel ports' and the launching sites for the V-1 flying bombs, which were causing havoc in London and the Home Counties. Whilst it was the role of the Canadians to mop up in these areas, their progress was likely to be slow, thereby exposing the 7th Armoured Division's flank. They would also be overtaking the remains of the German

Seventh Army, which had been badly mauled at Falaise and was now relying on horse-drawn transport, but was still expected to provide stiff opposition to their progress eastwards.

On 31 August the Desert Rats pulled out of Le Neubourg and crossed the Seine at Muids, following the line of the river round to the pretty village of Les Andelys, with its Crusader castle overlooking the river. They received a riotous reception from the locals, who pelted their trucks with flowers and fruit, plied them with wine and covered them in lipstick and French flags.

That day, the Queens travelled more than forty miles in a steady downpour, through Gournay-en-Bray to Grémévillers, passing through gentle farming land and pretty villages, without a sight of the enemy. Had it not been for some exasperating delays caused by traffic jams, particularly at river crossings and crossroads, they might have gone even further. The tanks were in the lead, with large 40-gallon petrol tanks strapped to their engine covers – fuel being now a major preoccupation as they travelled faster and further from the beachhead. For the Queens, 31 August was to be the only day when they could truly be said to have been 'swanning along' with any kind of enjoyment.

The following day brought another milestone – the crossing of the Somme via a bridge at Hangest, 10 miles north-west of Amiens, the only bridge in the area that had not been blown up. Unfortunately, the bridge quickly collapsed under the weight of armour, and there was another long delay while the Royal Engineers were summoned to fling a bailey bridge across the river at Picquigny, 5 miles further south. The engineers came under stiff small arms fire from the opposite bank, however, and the 1/5th Battalion was sent to support them, accompanied by a crashing concentration of artillery fire which sent the enemy streaming back over the open downland across the river. There, as the Regimental History reports, they 'offered a splendid target'.

One company was sent across a small footbridge to deter the Germans from returning, and the whole Battalion crossed via the repaired bridge at Hangest later that night and camped out, in pouring rain yet again, on a pitch-black moonless night, on a bombed out V-1 flying bomb site. Meanwhile, the other two battalions had found a shaky narrow bridge (later condemned as unsafe) by a lock in a field on the outskirts of Amiens, and hunkered down in the rain just north of the town for what was left of the night.

Next morning, 1/6th Battalion started following their tanks up the road north-east, but soon ran into mortar and machine gun fire, which they swiftly dealt with. A few miles further on, they met and engaged further pockets of enemy resistance, before being ordered to disengage and continue to Frévent, 20 miles north. In just a few hours they had taken 400 prisoners, knocked out four 105mm guns and smashed up a flying bomb site.

They reached Frévent at dusk and took up positions around it, with their headquarters at the railway station, where they captured some more German prisoners. It had been a tough day, mainly due to the fact that the Division was now threatening the line of retreat of the German Fifteenth Army, which had therefore established a defensive line with garrisons of 200 or more men and a few guns at nearby St Pol. That night, two officers of the 1/7th Battalion were found to have disappeared, minus their kit, after two shots were heard, and in the early morning an 'energetic patrol with tanks' was wiped out by the Germans, with eight men killed, wounded or missing.

An attack on St Pol was ordered, with artillery support, to try and remove this obstacle to the advance, but the attack was held up on the western outskirts by fierce defence from a well-concealed enemy, so the order was given to disengage for the time being and proceed further south, where they leaguered for the night. Leslie and his men captured a handful of Germans attempting to hide in their area.

But there was no chance to rest. During the night, a crowd of excited local people appeared with news of a 2,000-strong German column approaching from Béthune (where Leslie had narrowly missed being blown up by a mine in training in 1940), a few miles to the north. Everyone was ordered to stand to and prepare for battle, but the enemy failed to materialize, and everyone was stood down at dawn. Then, while 1/7th Battalion returned to the attack on St Pol (incurring significant losses), the rest of the Division either moved around St Pol to the north, or (as in the case of 1/6th Battalion) headed directly north-east to the heavily industrialized coalmining area around Lens.

Throughout the morning there were constant reports of strong forces of the enemy along the La Bassée Canal, just north of Lens. The 1/5th Battalion was tasked with neutralizing this threat, which they did very successfully by attacking across the canal and establishing a bridgehead on the other side, whilst the remainder of the Division, including the 1/6th, moved fast north-east across the Belgian frontier to Bossuyt, twelve miles into Belgium, where they leaguered for the night – a distance for the day of over seventy miles, through a narrow corridor within which they were frequently under shell and rifle fire from both flanks.

When they were not nervously anticipating engagement or actually dodging bullets, they were, as Trooper Harrison from the Royal Tank Regiment noted, 'treated like Gods and were borne around the square amongst the multitudes shoulder high, being clawed down every few yards to be kissed and pummelled by young and old. I didn't mind the young much. Never been kissed so much in all my life . . . We got back to the tanks at 2.30 am as drunk as lords. C'est la guerre . . .'

For Leslie, it must have been a strange time, revisiting the area where he fought in 1940 as part of the British Expeditionary Force, before the retreat to Dunkirk. That first night, at Bossuyt, he was just two miles from the bridge over the River Scheldt at Escanaffles that he helped to blow up in 1940.

As in France, life had been hard in Belgium under German occupation, with the population suffering mass deportations and imprisonment, a huge drop in living standards, rationing, rampant inflation, tight censorship, repression, persecution and hostile propaganda. Two-thirds of the country's national income was taken to pay for the costs of the military occupation and Nazi operations elsewhere. The country's gold reserves were looted, as was private property. The many factories, ports and other strategic sites used by the Germans became targets for frequent Allied bombing raids, and there were thousands of civilian casualties.

The next day, the Battalion continued its advance on Ghent. 'The country was flat,' notes the Regimental History, 'with poplar-lined roads, rich farms and orchards and ugly little villages. To make up for the drabness of the houses, they were almost all bright with flags and everywhere there were cheering excited civilians. There was no doubt we were welcome.' But nothing was certain – some villages changed hands several times during this period, and many Belgians were shot by the Germans for hanging out their national flag.

It was hard going for the soldiers, too. When they stopped for the night, some kind of rough camp had to be set up; rations had to be issued and hot food prepared, if possible; wounds needed dressing; tanks had to be repaired and refuelled, re-armed and maintained (a vital task when proceeding long distances at speed over rough ground); weapons had to be cleaned; guards had to be mounted and patrols sent out; for the officers, there were reports to be written, maps to be studied and orders to be received, discussed, passed on and explained to the men. Checking and maintaining supplies was a constant headache, this far from the Mulberry Harbour at Arromanches, and they were short of everything. Then they were up at first light, at around 0430 hrs, after maybe three or four hours sleep.

The 1/6th stopped about ten miles from Ghent. At 1800 hrs Leslie and A Company were sent off to help hold a vital bridge over the River Scheldt at Wetteren, six miles south-east of the city, which an SS Company was attacking and trying to destroy. The bridge had been found in the raised position, so members of the Belgian Resistance had swum across the river, with covering fire, to lower it into the horizontal and allow The Skins (Royal Inniskilling Fusiliers) to cross and establish a bridgehead. That night, there was fierce fighting in the houses and gardens around the bridge, and twenty-two SS soldiers were killed and sixty taken prisoner.

The Carriers, meanwhile, moved straight into Ghent, where they reported that a large number of German soldiers were shooting up civilians and refusing to surrender. There were roadblocks and snipers, and occasional shelling. B Company, moving up the main road to the west, were stopped in their tracks by the sight of a German major swathed in a white sheet who said that he was willing to surrender if his general agreed. Major Rodney Goodridge (a lifelong friend of Leslie's), with another colleague, went to meet the general, Lieutenant General Wilhelm Daser, who commanded the 70th Infantry Division, a defensive division full of men invalided from the Russian front. Daser, however, concerned only about losing face, refused to deal with anyone of lower rank than another general.

Hours of negotiations followed, until eventually, around midnight, Brigadier Mackeson of the Royal Scots Greys was wheeled out, claiming to be 'almost a general'. According to Delaforce in *Churchill's Desert Rats in North-West Europe*, Daser then consented to appear, with his staff, 'immaculate in his uniform, great coat with red collar, boots and spurs'. Negotiations continued, but looked like foundering until it was made clear to Daser that any loss of life or damage caused by his obstinacy would be his responsibility alone, whereupon he returned to his headquarters and grudgingly ordered his forces to retreat to the north of the town. As the Regimental History records, 'The beautiful old city was therefore spared the damage and casualties inevitable in heavy street fighting.'

The next day, as reports came in that numbers of German soldiers had been seen leaving the city and crossing the Scheldt in barges, the Battalion's Pioneer Platoon was sent into the city to hold the main bridge over the river, expecting at every turn to be met with fierce resistance – but the Germans had fled to the outskirts, and the city was theirs. Soon the streets were filled with cheering civilians, and the soldiers found themselves carried shoulder-high through the crowds.

Outside the city, the picture was mixed. Eine, north-west of Ghent, was captured by the Queens on 6 September after heavy fighting, with more than a hundred Germans killed or wounded. The Belgian Resistance helped free British soldiers who had been captured. A day later, the village was retaken by the Germans, who promptly slaughtered sixty men, women and children, before it was again taken by the Queens.

On 7 September A Company was still guarding the bridges and canals south and east of the city. Here, too, they were constantly harassed by snipers. Many of the men were adopted by local families and invited into their homes for meals; this taste of ordinary family life was such a treat for the men that many of them even offered to help with the washing up.

They were soon on the move again, drafted into the city itself to help with the painstaking task of clearing the factory area to the north. The Germans were still indiscriminately shelling the city from guns mounted on trains. The 1/5th forced a small bridgehead across a canal, enabling the sappers to build a bridge which could be crossed by the tanks, for the purpose of blasting German strong points still holding out.

Then 1/6th took over the attack, maintaining covering fire whilst the sappers swam the canal and, using a rope, pulled the swing bridge into position on the east side of the Bassin de Commerce, enabling the tanks, followed by A Company, to cross and clear and occupy the houses on the far side. Leslie and his men had a terrible night of it, as fifth columnists directed constant heavy and accurate fire on to their positions. They were reinforced the following day, and attacks by rocket-firing Typhoons were also called in.

As it became clear that German resistance in the area was still strong, it was decided to hand the Ghent clearance operation over to the Polish Armoured Division and move the Desert Rats to Putte, further east and nearer to Brussels (which had been taken on 3 September) for a short rest. The pause was needed and well earned, and enjoyable, too, with trips into a relatively undamaged Brussels and a chance to eat in a smart restaurant and enjoy a show, for those who could afford it. There was a lecture by the Brigade Commander, and a lot of maintenance work on vehicles and equipment.

The pause also helped the supply situation, which was now critical. Although the great port of Antwerp had been liberated on 4 September, fuel and food were still short for Allied forces, because the Germans held all the Channel ports apart from those liberated on D-Day, and the German

Fifteenth Army had been left in control of the approaches to Antwerp from the North Sea down the River Scheldt. The result was that, for another two months, the issue of supply would remain a crucial one. Many units were living off captured German rations and whatever could be begged, borrowed or stolen from the local population, whilst fuel still had to be trucked from Arromanches, 340 miles away.

Chapter 24

Operation Market Garden

The plan for Monty's 'northern thrust' was an ambitious and daring one: a massive carpet of airborne troops, comprising three Allied airborne divisions, was to be dropped into Nazi-occupied Holland to capture and hold five major bridges over the Rhine near the towns of Eindhoven, Nijmegen and Arnhem. This would open up a route for the Second Army along Highway 69, from the Albert Canal near Antwerp to the German border, and on into Germany's industrial heartland, the Ruhr.

The successful implementation of this plan involved the largest airborne operation in history ('Market'), delivering over 34,000 men by glider or parachute, with their vehicles and artillery. They were expected to capture the bridges almost simultaneously and hold them for two days, whilst the Second Army fought their way along a single road 64 miles behind enemy lines to relieve them ('Garden'). Any significant delay by the Second Army in reaching the bridges, particularly the final one at Arnhem, would be fatal to the whole operation.

Lieutenant General 'Boy' Browning, deputy commander of the First Allied Airborne Army, in discussion with Montgomery, thought it might be possible to hold the vital final bridge at Arnhem for up to four days if the Army's thrust along the road was delayed, but he was concerned that it might be just too ambitious.

By the time the first planes took off for Holland, on 17 September, the Queen's Battalions' rest was over, and they had moved up to guard the Junction Canal, between the outskirts of Antwerp and Herentals. Each battalion was responsible for about five miles of canal, with companies about a mile back from the water and several miles apart. There was little concerted enemy activity, but the Queen's snipers had some successful shooting.

From their new positions they had a memorable, confidence-building view of the Market Garden airlift, as planes droned overhead for two days carrying troops and supplies.

But Monty's plan was already in trouble, partly due to faulty intelligence as to the strength of German forces in the area around the bridges, and partly because of overconfident planning and weak preparation. The initial airborne landings caught the Germans completely by surprise, as did a huge artillery bombardment from beyond the Belgian border, but on the first day the Allies were unable to capture three key bridges at Son (near Eindhoven), Nijmegen, and Arnhem itself (though the Paras did manage to grab an isolated toehold at the northern end of the bridge), and they never really recovered.

The fog which blanketed airfields all over East Anglia for several days thereafter delayed planned drops of reinforcements and supplies, and the intended lightning strike along Highway 69 from Holland (which later became known as 'Hell's Highway') was held up by the delay in taking the bridges, fierce German defence and counter-attacks, and the fact that the road itself was simply too narrow, and the countryside around too restricting, to allow blockages to be bypassed. Many paratroops landed straight into the arms and guns of the Germans.

By Tuesday, 19 September, Day Three of the Operation, Market Garden was already 36 hours behind schedule, the problems on the front line having been exacerbated by the almost total failure of radio communications and the fact that the commander of airborne forces on the ground, Major General Robert Urquhart, became cut off from his headquarters for several days and was therefore unable to direct his forces.

Meanwhile, the Desert Rats were moved northwards across the Junction Canal to support the flanks of the advance towards Arnhem; but the Germans were concentrating their forces nearer the bridges, and it was only the snipers who saw much action ('kills' of 23, 16 and 9 were claimed on consecutive days). Several prisoners were found hiding, or were captured in minor skirmishes; a large minefield was cleared; and a young woman, part of a family alleged to have been collaborating with the Germans, was handed over by one of the local resistance organizations to Leslie's Company, who passed her on to the Field Security Service attached to 7th Armoured Division.

The Germans fought fiercely to hold the bridges and, although Nijmegen was eventually taken on 20 September, all attempts to relieve the Paras holding out at Arnhem against a determined German onslaught, failed. On the next day, those Paras remaining at the bridge at Arnhem were forced to surrender, sending a final message to their headquarters, 'Out of ammunition. God save the King'. Meanwhile, the remainder of the First British Airborne

Division had been forced to withdraw to Oosterbeek, three miles west of Arnhem, and mount a desperate perimeter defence.

On Friday, 22 September, with bad weather still impeding supply drops, the Germans succeeded in blocking Hell's Highway, the main land corridor to the bridges, between Uden and Veghel, about twenty miles north of Eindhoven, not far from 's-Hertogenbosch. The blockage, along forty miles of exposed roadway, lasted twenty-four hours and was probably the final nail in the coffin of Operation Market Garden. The Guards eventually cleared it, racing back along the highway from Arnhem, but it was blocked again on 24 September, and this time it was the Desert Rats who were ordered to clear it.

But it was already too late. At a meeting in St Oedenrode, a few miles to the north of Eindhoven, on Sunday 24 September, the bitter but inevitable decision was taken to withdraw Allied airborne forces from Arnhem and to maintain the front line for Monty's northern thrust at Nijmegen instead. That night, they started to fall back, silently and under cover of darkness, and withdraw across the Rhine. Operation Market Garden was over, and the Desert Rats were going to be clearing the road not for an advance, but for a retreat.

At the tail end of a frustratingly long queue of military traffic moving along the corridor, the Queen's Battalions left the canal and crossed the Belgian/Dutch border, heading initially for an area of woods and fields to the south-west of Eindhoven. It was a wearisome and dangerous business, tanks on the road, infantry in the ditches and hedgerows alongside. The weather was abysmal, cold and wet. The road was poor, narrow and embanked along most of its length and extremely congested as a result. The country around was bleak, flat, wet and sandy heathland, interspersed with stretches of birch and pine forest, and cut by numerous deep dykes filled with brackish water which presented a serious problem for the tanks and made it almost impossible to branch out across country.

To add to their dismay, as they advanced slowly northwards, they encountered columns of their defeated comrades heading south, away from the fighting, their faces covered in the grime of battle, their eyes unseeing.

On 25 September the three Queen's Battalions deployed around the large industrial town of Eindhoven, home to the famous Philips radio factories. The 1/5th struggled along the crowded road to St Oedenrode, where the main road to Nijmegen was threatened by two or three battalions of enemy troops in the village of Schijndel. The 1/7th advanced, as fast as they could given the congestion, a couple of miles along the main road towards Veghel and Nijmegen, but were hampered by the presence of both German and American airborne troops, often indistinguishable one from another, and by confusion about whose troops were to attack which target. They ended up, at last light, guarding a series of tracks through the woods. Meanwhile, 1/6th moved up in reserve to cover the junction of the two roads up which its sister battalions were working.

That night and the next day, and the day after that, the men worked feverishly to keep the Germans at bay, and to clear roadblocks, minefields and debris, search buildings, deal with snipers and take prisoners. The roadblocks were every few hundred yards, protected by mines and booby-traps and covered by well-hidden enemy troops with machine guns and mortars. Each morning, as they tried to push forward to reach their mates, along the single roadway across flooded fields, there were more mines to clear, more artillery attacks to shelter from, their tanks constantly bogging down in the soft ground beside the road.

It was desperate work for the men, lying on their stomachs for hours on end, and painstakingly poking the ground ahead with their bayonets, always on the lookout for booby-trap trip wires, prodding at an angle of forty-five degrees to locate the mines without causing them to explode, then rendering them harmless by jamming nails into the plungers. It only took one man exploring a minefield dozens of yards wide to make a mistake . . .

Chapter 25

Holding the Line

The debacle at Arnhem resulted in the loss, by death or injury, of between 15,000 and 17,000 Allied troops, and signalled the end of a dream that the war might be over by Christmas 1944. Both sides would now have to dig in for a long winter campaign.

In this part of northern Europe the most important tasks were to ease the chronic supply situation by clearing German forces from the Scheldt estuary and opening up the port of Antwerp, thereby protecting the Allies' northern flank. The job of the three Queen's Battalions was to work as far as possible towards 's-Hertogenbosch, which was still in enemy hands.

On 28 September they moved up Hell's Highway to Dinther, on the main road from Veghel to 's-Hertogenbosch and just over the Zuid Willemsvaart canal. The extensive woodland along the canal hid many scattered groups of German soldiers, and 1/6th was given the job of clearing them out. During the day there was little sign of the enemy, except at Dinther, where the Germans held the lock gates, so the order was given to launch an attack on the woods across the canal that night, after the moon had set. By this time, however, the Germans had dug in along the line of the canal and rigged up searchlights; after several unsuccessful attempts to get across, the operation was abandoned at dawn.

After a short rest, Leslie led A Company out again, with a troop of tanks and a company from 1/5th Battalion, to try and find a way across. After a day of fighting they captured a bridge on the main road about a mile short of Middelrode. The next day, they attempted to push on north towards 's-Hertogenbosch. Despite heavy opposition, they managed to reach Laar and capture twenty-four prisoners, before Middelrode Bridge was subjected to a sustained shelling and mortar attack. This resulted in several casualties, and they were forced to draw back to a farm half a mile away to regroup. Later that night, as they were now out on a limb, they were ordered to withdraw still further to avoid the risk of being surrounded.

It was a stalemate. The Desert Rats held a fourteen-mile salient from Veghel to the River Maas, and the area to the east of 's-Hertogenbosch, and there they stayed for the next three weeks. It was the wettest winter in Holland since 1864, and the battlefield became a cold, muddy quagmire. Moving trucks and tanks and armoured vehicles around waterlogged fields was next to impossible, and the men suffered from a constant round of colds and flu. They lived the whole time in the open, sleeping semi-upright in whatever shelter they could dig for themselves; their food was dreadful; their clothes were wet and filthy. It was a miserable time. The countryside was monotonous, and the local people, though generous by nature, had suffered badly during the German occupation and had little to give. The only town within reach was Eindhoven, and that was already overcrowded and expensive. After the rolling thrills of the 'Great Swan', and the anticipation and then the crushing disappointment of the 'northern thrust' at Arnhem, the atmosphere that had descended upon the troops in northern Europe, as they contemplated the long winter ahead, was one of gloom and depression.

Brigadier Pepper left the Brigade, to run the Infantry Training School back in England. His farewell letter to Leslie read:

> My Dear Porky,
> It was grand having you in the Brigade, and I can assure you that your efforts have been appreciated by everybody. I will ring your family as soon as I get home, and say how fit you are and what a magnificent job you are doing. Very best of good fortune, and do write and let me have all the news, and I hope we shall soldier together again before very long.

For Leslie and his Company, the chief activity was patrolling. This was mostly done in order to gain a thorough knowledge of the ground and enemy positions, rather than to fight, but encounters with the enemy were inevitable and bruising, as grand strategy gave way to small-scale local manoeuvring. Booby traps were sprung, prisoners were taken and interrogated, grenades were tossed, snipers were observed and killed or were killed, mines exploded, positions were shelled and machine guns were fired.

A Company was as busy as any other, as recorded in the Battalion's War Diary:

> 2 October. The Company's standing patrol heard vehicle movements and a self-propelled gun firing. A hayrick was seen to burst into

flames, which spread to two houses and civilians were heard screaming

3 October. A Dutchman suspected of collaborating was brought in and interrogated

4 October night. A bridge was found to have been blown by the enemy, but the patrol crossed by the girders and continued for 200 yards without meeting any enemy

5 October night. A recce patrol at Middelrode found that the Germans were still holding the canal. A crossing was simulated, much noise was made, planks were pushed into the water and machine guns were fired – but there was no response

7 October. A patrol was fired on by Spandaus, and flares went up from Middelrode Bridge. The patrol moved north-west but was fired on again, so they lay up for two hours listening and heard noises and movement

8 October. An outpost reported enemy movement a few yards in front of their position. A fighting patrol of Pioneers went through A Company, met a similar enemy patrol and a fierce fight ensued in the course of which the patrol leader and three others were killed and four men were wounded

10 October. The Company sent a patrol forward with a troop of tanks and shot up a group of enemy. The Company had three casualties

13 October. Flying Bomb seen travelling east to west

16 October. A harassing operation was carried out by the Company, with artillery, mortar and machine gun fire brought down on an enemy area the other side of the canal. Two Spandaus returned fire.

The stalemate seemed to go on for ever.

During the day constant vigilance was required, even behind the front line, as men went about the grinding routine of maintaining and washing vehicles and equipment, stocking and re-stocking supplies, cleaning weapons, filling magazines, disposing of the dead and tending to the wounded. At night, they used the time of darkness to dig trenches, lay minefields, bring supplies up from the rear and recover the bodies of dead colleagues – or they were sent out on yet another nerve-wringing patrol.

The Queen's Regimental History claims that patrols were 'bold and effective', despite the presence of some energetic and enterprising German parachutists in the opposing line, and that the Brigade dominated no-man's-land. But men still died, and fear still dominated in this facsimile of the Somme.

On 18 October the stalemate was broken at last with the launch of Operation Alan, a push to extend the front a modest six miles, to a line between Tilburg and 's-Hertogenbosch. The three Queen's Battalions lined up, with the 1/5th set to capture the hamlet of Laar, and the 1/7th and 1/6th to their left and right respectively. The latter moved to a forward position that day, to allow companies from the other two battalions to receive two days intensive training in 'village fighting' and in the use of two Churchill Tanks converted into armoured flamethrowers called 'Crocodiles', which were to be allocated to them for the attack.

The Operation was launched at 0200 hrs on 22 October, with 'terrific concentrations of artillery fire' against the German guns, followed by an advance across no-man's-land rendered painfully slow by the extensive fields of anti-tank and 'Schu' mines, which the Germans had laid. These mines, which blew off a man's foot if trodden on, were made of wood to foil metal detectors. 1/7th took the centre of Middelrode by 1000 hrs, but the enemy was still holding out further north, in posts prepared after the most recent aerial photographs and linked together by an elaborate tunnel system, so the Brigade withdrew to allow for another good artillery stonking, and then 1/7th finished off the job at last light, suffering over forty casualties in the day.

Meanwhile, 1/5th had captured Laar by 1430 hrs and Doornhoek by 1700 hrs – thanks to the Crocodiles, with their capacity to throw a flame 120yds, destroying bunkers and trenches in an instant – and 1/6th had taken Deelsburg.

'The enemy crust was broken and there was little behind', notes the Regimental History, and by the end of 23 October this had proved to be the case. The 1/5th took Berlicum, and Leslie's A Company was able to work steadily forward on the right, mopping up parties of Germans and taking ninety-three prisoners in the day, with only three casualties. By 0930 hrs the following day A Company had reached its objective of the Kloosterhoek Sanatorium, just three miles east of 's-Hertogenbosch. The Regimental History records:

A thoroughly successful operation, owing mainly to the knowledge of the enemy positions and the ground, acquired by the often dangerous patrolling of the previous weeks, and partly to the excellent co-operation of all arms, worked out by years of experience.

With only a day's pause, to allow a bridge to be built across the canal at Dinther, the Desert Rats were ordered to clear the Tilburg area and cut off the enemy's line of retreat between Tilburg and the Maas, with the Brigade being allocated the objectives of Loon-op-Zand, Udenhout and Oisterwijk, ten miles west of 's-Hertogenbosch. This was Operation Don.

By the evening of 26 October the Brigade had moved across the soggy landscape to the south of 's-Hertogenbosch and had gathered at Esch, where the sappers had been busy once again, hastily constructing a bridge over the River Aa. By the time the 1/5th had travelled the eight miles to Udenhout the next day, it had already been captured by the tanks. The 1/6th, meanwhile, had bypassed Udenhout and taken up a defensive position south-east of Loon-op-Zand, where an attack by the Germans was imminently expected, since the village was a key point in a new front line which the Germans were trying to establish north of the Wilhelmina Canal.

Two days of fierce hand-to-hand fighting followed, as the 1/5th and 1/7th Battalions fought their way through thick woods teeming with German soldiers, clearing trenches with hand grenades and mopping up prisoners as they went. The 1/6th, meanwhile, ordered to protect the Brigade's long northern flank between Laar and Udenhout, became engaged in a brisk battle with fifty enemy in the village of Zankant, on the eastern edge of the flank, routing the Germans with the support of the Royal Tank Regiment.

By 30 October the Brigade had moved ten miles west to Reijen, skirmishing with scattered parties of German soldiers as they went, and enjoying a warm welcome from local people. They passed through Tilburg, which had been liberated a couple of days earlier by the 15th Scottish Division, in a surprise attack complete with kilted pipers and skirling pipes. They found the town almost undamaged ('a refreshing change from the Eindhoven area', as the Regimental History drily notes), and eventually took up their positions between Dongen and Reijen, with the 1/6th guarding the southern approach to one of the few bridges remaining intact across the Wilhelmina Canal, patrolling the roads and clearing mines.

The next five days were relatively restful, as the troops were living, for a change, in relatively comfortable billets in people's homes and enjoying a range of entertainments laid on in the hospitable town of Tilburg, still celebrating its liberation. The 1/6th was at Vrijhoeve Capelle, a mile or two back from the southern bank of the River Maas, to avoid being overlooked from the higher northern bank. They soon settled in to a familiar routine of patrols day and night, to make sure that the Germans didn't try to infiltrate back across the river. There was sporadic shelling from the north, but few casualties. It was still raining. On their first night, four of the new long-range V-2 rockets were seen flying west towards London.

But it wasn't long before they were on the move again, with A Company ending up at Vlijmen, just west of 's-Hertogenbosch, also now liberated. They captured a few snipers and picked up a few demoralized deserters, but otherwise there was little sign of enemy movement.

With the task of clearing Holland south of the Maas virtually over, the Desert Rats were now moved nearly sixty miles south and east to the German border, where preparations were in hand to clear the enemy from a 40-mile bridgehead west of the River Maas, south-east of Roermond. The first task for the Desert Rats was to hold the area near the junction of the Wessem Canal with the river, ready for a big attack on the German forces planned for 14/15 November.

The three Queen's battalions got into position on the Canal, with 1/6th forward of the other two at Thorn. From these positions they patrolled regularly to the river and the canal, alert to the possibility of infiltration from German-held Wessem, its approaches lit up by searchlights. Where the canal joined the river, at Panheel, was a large lock, held by the Germans, its gates still undamaged, and it was essential they remain so, as any sudden alteration in water levels would hamper the big attack further north across the Wessem canal, an operation which depended on pontoon bridges. 1/7th Battalion was given the task of taking the lock, supported by the rest of the Brigade.

On 14 November, and in pouring rain, all known enemy positions were drenched with covering fire; then, precisely at 1615 hrs, the covering fire paused and two platoons went in to the attack, which was met by heavy machine gun fire. One platoon was pinned down in a hail of bullets, and there were heavy casualties, including several officers. But a third platoon, held in reserve and commanded by an engineer called Wilkinson-Cox, who had never been in action before, launched a frontal assault, overran the enemy trenches and reached the canal bank, but 100yds left of the lock due to smoke from the original bombardment.

As Wilkinson-Cox wheeled his platoon right, he was supported by the tanks, and by a fourth platoon which had worked its way round behind the Germans and now attacked them from the rear. He reached the lock, secured the gates and dug in under considerable shell fire. Seeking now to retreat back across the lock gates, the Germans were caught in the crossfire from the attacking platoons and snipers from the canal bank.

'So ended a most successful little operation', as the Regimental History put it. But at a cost, with an officer and five men killed, and six officers and twenty-five men wounded.

The men were exhausted, but they settled grimly into the task of holding the ground they had gained, struggling to stay awake in their trenches amongst the mud and the filth, and under grey, leaden skies.

For two more weeks, after the successful conclusion of the big attack across the Canal, the Queen's Brigade remained in position around Wessem. The 1/6th took over the Panheel Lock immediately after 1/7th's attack and, on patrolling cautiously the next day, found Wessem unoccupied, the enemy having withdrawn during the night. Leslie sent fighting patrols across the lock to deal with enemy snipers and round up prisoners, and his Company's positions were regularly shelled or mortared. The weather was dreadful, and the country sodden. The river began to rise, positions were flooded and it soon became almost impossible to mount patrols.

Then, on 30 November, the Battalion moved a few miles downriver to Elen – and the Divisional Commander of the Desert Rats, Major General Lyne, called his officers together . . .

Chapter 26

Farewell

It must have been a stunning moment. Within sight of the German border, and with the end of the war clearly only a few months away, the 1/6th and 1/7th Battalions were to be disbanded, Lyne told them. They had suffered so many casualties that they were no longer considered to be a viable fighting force. Only 1/5th was to remain in Europe to represent the Queen's Regiment, marching into the devastated city of Hamburg on 3 May 1945.

The men of the other two battalions, many of whom had been fighting in Europe without a pause since D-Day, were to be reassigned, with those veterans who had already been serving for five years going home to train new front line troops, and the remainder transferring to 1/5th or to other infantry battalions in the fighting area.

Leslie said goodbye to his men and stood in silence with them at the farewell parade, as they remembered their many fallen comrades. On 3 December the Carrier platoon led the Battalion across the start line on its long journey back to its final billet at Ypres, prior to embarkation at Ostend for Folkestone – where Leslie had landed in June 1940, after the agony of Dunkirk. As they drove out of the temporary camp, to the right and left of the exit the guns of their artillery colleagues formed a triumphal arch as the cheers and applause rang out for the men whose fighting days were finally over.

*

My father had escaped with his life at last.

Whether, at the end, he felt frustrated not be 'in at the finish', or grateful to be relieved of a further slog through Germany, I have no idea. I aim to complete my journey following his footsteps in 2019, with my son Ed, so maybe that will yield further insights.

He was granted eighty-one days Army leave from 12 October 1945 and released from military duty with effect from 1 January 1946. He then went straight back home to Epsom and took over the family building business from my grandfather.

A year later, he went to look at a job for some new clients in Worcester Park and quickly fell in love with the daughter of the house, the dark-haired beauty Mary Rudman, a former WAAF (Women's Auxiliary Air Force) officer, and then cook to the actor Lawrence Olivier. They married in 1948 and lived, pretty much happily ever after, in Cheam, Surrey.

As I have noted several times in this book, my father rarely mentioned the war or his part in it. But up in the attic of our house, hidden away in a trunk, were a few papers, an ancient Army-issue camp bed, his silk escape map and some other mementoes of a period in his life that, looking back, I realize he must have locked away in his mind, too. I can remember poking about in the trunk as a little boy, but I never dared ask him what the papers were all about. They just looked 'private', and from a time long ago.

We had an old German helmet in the garden shed, too, I remember, but although I used to wear it sometimes, as I chased around the garden on my tricycle, I don't think I ever asked him about it. It was just 'there', a fact of our lives, a clue to a hidden past that we never acknowledged.

In the two years that it has taken to write this book, and the many years more to research it, I have often held in my hands those dusty paper memories that my father had in his battered old trunk. With his photograph, taken in Army uniform early in the war, looking down at me from the mantelpiece whilst I wrote, I have paused very often to look at him, and ask, 'Why didn't you say?'

Basically, I believe he didn't talk about it because he didn't want to. He had seen the horrors of war and experienced its costs, in friends and comrades lost and injured, and had no desire to relive those memories. Like so many of those who survived, he paid for his survival with a sense of guilt that others had been less lucky. He felt no desire to boast, because he knew that many others had done as much, or more. And he didn't tell us, because he didn't think we needed to know.

He simply got on with his life, a caring and loving husband and father, quietly and with great dignity, and little fuss.

As I look at his picture again now, I hope he won't mind that I have gone rummaging in his old trunk and brought all his memories and mementoes out into the daylight. In so doing, I have come to know and love him in a completely new way and, in the process, I have forged a deeper relationship with a father I realize I only half understood.

I feel so fortunate to have had that chance, to get to know my Dad – a man who truly was, in the words of his friend and fellow soldier Tom La Fontaine, 'a completely first class person'.

*

Bibliography

Published works (place of publication London unless otherwise stated)

Absalom, Roger, *A Strange Alliance – Aspects of Escape and Survival Italy 1935–45*, Leo S. Olschki, 1990

Alanbrooke, Field Marshal Lord, *War Diaries 1939–1945*, Weidenfeld & Nicholson, 2001

Allan, Stuart, *Commando Country*, Edinburgh, National Museums Scotland, 2007

Barrow, Lieutenant Colonel T. J., DSO and others, *The Story of the Bedfordshire and Hertfordshire Regiment, Vol II*, Regiment 1986

Beevor, Antony, *D-Day*, Penguin, 2014

Billany, Dan, and Dowie, David, *The Cage*, Longmans, 1949

Blake, Victoria, *Far Away*, Kibworth Beauchamp, Matador, 2015

Carver, Tom, *Where the Hell Have you Been?*, Short Books, 2009

Chasseaud, Peter, *Mapping the Second World War*, Glasgow, Collins, 2015

Clark, Lloyd, *Anzio – the Friction of War*, Headline, 2006

Dann, Len, *Laughing We Ran*, Lincoln, Tucann, 1995

Davies, Tony, *When the Moon Rises*, Leo Cooper, 1973

Davison, G. Norman, *In the Prison of his Days*, Leeds, Scratching Shed Publishing, 2009

de Burgh, Lucy, *My Italian Adventures*, Stroud, History Press, 2013

Delaforce, Patrick, *Churchill's Desert Rats in North-West Europe*, Barnsley, Pen & Sword, 2010

Duke, Vic, *Another Bloody Mountain*, Iron City Publications, 2011

Dunning, James, *It Had to be Tough – the Origins and Training of the Commandos in World War II*, Barnsley, Frontline Books, 2012

Dunning, James, *The Fighting Fourth – No 4 Commando at War 1940–45*, Stroud, Sutton Publishing, 2003

English, Ian, *Assisted Passage – Walking to Freedom Italy 1943*, Uckfield, Naval and Military Press

English, Ian, *Home by Christmas?*, Privately published, 2017

Erskine, Ralph, *The Bletchley Park Codebreakers*, Biteback Publishing, 2011

Field, Jacob, *D-Day in Numbers*, Michael O'Mara Books, 2014

Foot, M.R.D. and Langley J.M., *MI9 – Escape and Evasion 1939–45*, Book Club Associates, 1979

Foster, Major R.C.G., *History of the Queen's Royal Regiment, Vol VIII*, 1953

Gibbs, Denis, DSO, *Apennine Journey*, privately published

Gilbert, Martin, *Second World War*, Fontana, 1990

Gilbert, Michael, *Death in Captivity*, Looe, House of Stratus, 2011

Goodall, Scott, *The Freedom Trail*, Inchmere, 2005

Graham, Dominick, *The Escapes and Evasions of an Obstinate Bastard*, York, Wilton 65, 2000

Hargreaves, Richard, *The Germans in Normandy*, Barnsley, Pen & Sword, 2006

Hastings, Max, *All Hell Let Loose – the World at War 1939–45*, Harper Collins, 2011

Hastings, Max, *Armageddon – the Battle for Germany 1944–45*, Macmillan, 2005

Hastings, Max, *Overlord*, Pan, 1985

Hibbert, Christopher, *Mussolini – the Rise and Fall of Il Duce*, New York, St Martin's Griffin, 2008

Hodges, Andrew, *Alan Turing – the Enigma*, Vintage Books, 2014

Holland, James, *Italy's Sorrow*, Harper Press, 2009

Holland, James, *Together We Stand – North Africa 1942–3*, Harper Collins, 2006

Hood, Stuart, *Pebbles from my Skull*, Quartet Books, 1973

John, Evan, *Lofoten Letter*, William Heinemann, 1941

Jones, Donald, *Escape from Sulmona*, New York, Vantage Press, 1980

Killby, J. Keith, Cav. Uff, OBE, *In Combat Unarmed*, Padstow, TJ International, 2013

Kindersley, The Hon Philip, *For You the War is Over*, Tunbridge Wells, Midas Books, 1983

Lamb, Richard, *War in Italy 1943–45*, John Murray, 1993

Lett, Brian, *An Extraordinary Italian Imprisonment – The Brutal Truth of Campo 21*, Barnsley, Pen & Sword, 2014

Lett, Brian, *Italy's Outstanding Courage*, privately published, 2018

Lett, Gordon, *Rossano*, privately published, 2001

Lord, Walter, *The Miracle of Dunkirk*, Wordsworth Editions, 1998

Lovat, Lord, *March Past – A Memoir*, Weidenfeld and Nicholson, 1978

Mann, Ronald, *Moving the Mountain*, Aldersgate Productions, 1995

Mather, Carol, *When the Grass Stops Growing*, Barnsley, Leo Cooper, 1997

Medd, Peter, *The Long Walk Home*, John Lehmann, 1951

Medley, Robin, *Cap Badge*, Leo Cooper, 1995

Medley, Robin, *Five Days to Live – France 1939–40*, Abergavenny, Dover, 1992

Mikes, Dr G., *The Epic of Lofoten*, Hutchinson, 1941

Moorehead, Alan, *Eclipse*, New York, Harper & Row, 1968

Moorehead, Alan, *The Desert War*, Hamish Hamilton, 1944

Newby, Eric, *Love and War in the Apennines*, Pan Books, 1983

Noble, Ronnie, *Shoot First*, Harrap, 1955

Origo, Iris, *War in Val d'Orcia*, Allison & Busby, 2008

Reeves, Valerie, *Dan Billany – Hull's Lost Hero*, Kingston Press, 1999

Reid, Howard, *Dad's War*, Bantam, 2004

Robillard, Chris, *Barry to Bari*, Bovey Tracey, Devon Matters Publishing, 2015

Ross, Michael, *The British Partisan*, Barnsley, Pen &Sword, 2019

Ryan, Cornelius, *A Bridge Too Far*, Hodder and Stoughton, 2007

Sebag-Montefiore, Hugh, *Dunkirk – Fight to the Last Man*, Penguin Viking, 2006

Sebag-Montefiore, Hugh, *Enigma – the Battle for the Code*, Cassell Military Paperbacks, 2011

Shirer, William, *The Rise and Fall of the Third Reich*, Simon & Schuster, 1972

Taylor, AJP, *The Origins of the Second World War*, Penguin Books, 1975

Tudor, Malcolm, *Among the Italian Partisans*, Fonthill Media, 2016

Tudor, Malcolm, *Beyond the Wire*, Newtown, Emilia Publishing, 2009

Tudor, Malcolm, *British Prisoners of War in Italy – Paths to Freedom*, Newtown, Emilia Publishing, 2012

Tudor, Malcolm, *Escape from Italy 1943–45*, Newtown, Emilia Publishing, 2003

Tudor, Malcolm, *Prisoners and Partisans*, Newtown, Emilia Publishing, 2006

Unwin, Frank, MBE, *Escaping has Ceased to be a Sport*, Barnsley, Pen & Sword Military, 2018

Walker, Stephen, *Hide & Seek – the Irish Priest in the Vatican who Defied the Nazi Command*, Collins, 2012

Westhorp, Christopher, *The Commando Pocket Manual*, Conway, 2012

Williams, Andrew, *D-Day to Berlin*, Hodder and Stoughton, 2004

Wilson, Patrick, *Dunkirk – from Disaster to Deliverance*, Barnsley, Leo Cooper, 1999

Wingfield, Rex, *The Only Way Out*, Arrow Books, 1957

Other Sources

Wikipedia, various

War Diaries, National Archive, Kew – 2nd Battalion, The Bedfordshire and Hertfordshire Regiment; 4 Commando; 1/6th Battalion The Queen's Royal Regiment

Private accounts, diaries and interviews: Peter Watson; Dougie Turner; Mike Howard; Tom La Fontaine; Robin Medley; Guiseppe de Michelis and family; Angiolina Bragagni; Piero Tevini; Don Lee; Peter and Tony Elfer; Keith Killby; Charlie Gatenby and family; Mrs Barbara Dickinson; Gianni Colabianchi; former inmates of PG Campo 49 Fontanellato too numerous to mention; James Dunning; David Coles; the Monte San Martino Trust.

Index